Violating Peace

Violating Peace

Sex, Aid, and Peacekeeping

Jasmine-Kim Westendorf

Cornell University Press

Ithaca and London

First published 2020 by Cornell University Press

Printed in the United States of America

Library of Congress Cataloging-in-Publication Data

Names: Westendorf, Jasmine-Kim, author.
Title: Violating peace : sex, aid, and peacekeeping / Jasmine-Kim
    Westendorf.
Description: Ithaca [New York] : Cornell University Press, 2020. |
    Includes bibliographical references and index.
Identifiers: LCCN 2019028618 (print) | LCCN 2019028619 (ebook) |
    ISBN 9781501748059 (cloth) | ISBN 9781501748066 (epub) |
    ISBN 9781501748073 (pdf)
Subjects: LCSH: United Nations—Peacekeeping forces—Sexual behavior. |
    Peacekeeping forces—Sexual behavior. | Sex crimes—Political aspects. |
    Sex crimes—Prevention.
Classification: LCC JZ6374 .W45 2020 (print) | LCC JZ6374 (ebook) |
    DDC 364.15/3—dc23
LC record available at https://lccn.loc.gov/2019028618
LC ebook record available at https://lccn.loc.gov/2019028619

To all who have suffered at the hands of those sent to protect them

It's hard to be in the middle of a war and keep the moral values you brought with you. War changes people. And some peacekeepers don't have any moral values to start with.
—Bosnian respondent during interview

CONTENTS

ACKNOWLEDGMENTS

I could not have written this book without the support of many people and the generosity of those who shared their time, expertise, recollections, and feedback with me. I am deeply indebted to the many people who agreed to be interviewed as part of this project and without whom this book would never have been possible.

I am especially grateful to Louise Searle, formerly of the Humanitarian Advisory Group (HAG), who partnered with me on the project in its early stages, including by joining me on field research trips to Timor-Leste and Sarajevo and conducting the interviews in Geneva. HAG also supported the project in other critical ways: the excellent Josie Flint came with us to Timor-Leste to assist with interviews, and Kate Sutton facilitated a workshop with policymakers and relevant scholars in Canberra in 2016 to test my initial conclusions.

The field research for this book was funded by a grant from the La Trobe University Transforming Human Societies Research Focus Area. I am particularly grateful to Katie Holmes, who led the Research Focus

Area, for providing support and guidance throughout the project. My colleague and friend Bec Strating read and commented on early drafts as I wrote them and was an endless source of encouragement, inspiration, and solidarity. Jem Atahan read multiple drafts and helped me iron out my thoughts. Dennis Altman mulled over the complexities of it all and shared his insights with me over many coffees. Sara Davies, Jacqui True, Laura Shepherd, and Paul Kirby provided feedback on early parts of this research and encouragement to write this book. As always, I'm thankful to Nick Bisley, Robin Jeffrey, and Judith Brett for their academic mentorship and encouragement, in this and all of my other projects.

During the course of this project I was fortunate to have the support of a number of phenomenal interns and research assistants. My sincere thanks to Nina Roxburgh, Alejandra Pineda Sanabria, Emma Jidinger, Monica Keily, and Gavin Height: without you, this would have been a much harder road to tread, and I'm so grateful to have had you all as part of the research team at various points in this project's life.

I'm grateful to Roger Haydon at Cornell University Press for his enthusiasm about the book and incisive comments and prompts on the manuscript as it evolved, to Julia Cook for her exceptional copyediting, and to the production and design teams for polishing everything up. My thanks also go to Oxford University Press for allowing me to republish some of my early thoughts on the nature and history of sexual exploitation and abuse.

I'm thankful for the support of my parents and sisters, Egon, Conny, Teagan, and Simone. I'm fortunate to be surrounded by a community of friends and strong women who cheered me on and helped me debrief on the often challenging material I was grappling with, and I send special thanks to Emily, Ruby, Carly, Lesley, and Suzi. And I'm grateful every day for the love and support of my partner Jem, with whom everything is possible, and for my baby Billie Sparrow, whose kicks in utero reminded me that I was writing to a hard deadline and whose giggles, smiles, and tentative first steps made the revision process so much sweeter.

Abbreviations

CAR	Central African Republic
HIPPO Report	report of the High-Level Independent Panel on United Nations Peace Operations, entitled *Uniting Our Strengths for Peace: Politics, Partnership and People*
IDP	internally displaced persons
IFOR	Implementation Force (Bosnia and Herzegovina)
INTERFET	International Force in East Timor
IPTF	UN International Police Task Force
KFOR	Kosovo Force
MINUSCA	UN Multidimensional Integrated Stabilization Mission in the Central African Republic
MINUSMA	UN Multidimensional Integrated Stabilization Mission in Mali
MINUSTAH	UN Stabilization Mission In Haiti

MONUC	UN Observer Mission in the Democratic Republic of the Congo
NGO	nongovernmental organization
OHCHR	UN Office of the High Commissioner for Human Rights
OIOS	UN Office of Internal Oversight Services
Oxfam GB	Oxfam Great Britain
PKO	peacekeeping operation
PSEA	prevention of sexual exploitation and abuse
SEA	sexual exploitation and abuse
SFOR	Stabilisation Force in Bosnia and Herzegovina
TCC	troop and police-contributing countries
UN	United Nations
UNAIDS	Joint United Nations Programme on HIV/AIDS
UNAMET	UN Mission in East Timor
UNMIBH	UN Mission in Bosnia and Herzegovina
UNMISET	UN Mission of Support in East Timor
UNMIT	UN Integrated Mission in East Timor
UNPOL	UN Police
UNPROFOR	UN Protection Force (Croatia and Bosnia and Herzegovina)
UNTAC	UN Transitional Authority in Cambodia
UNTAET	UN Transitional Administration in East Timor
WPS	Women, Peace and Security

VIOLATING PEACE

INTRODUCTION

In 2015, revelations emerged that peacekeepers from France, Chad, and Equatorial Guinea had regularly raped homeless and starving boys aged eight to fifteen in refugee camps in the Central African Republic, and that a French military commander had tied up and undressed four girls and forced them to have sex with a dog, after which one of the girls died.[1] Although alarming, these revelations were not unprecedented: interveners in peace operations (including military, police, and civilian peacekeepers; aid workers, diplomats, private contractors, and others) have been implicated in the sexual exploitation and abuse of local women and children in nearly every United Nations (UN) peace operation since the end of the Cold War. These behaviors are diverse and have ranged from opportunistic sexual assault and rape to planned, sadistic sexual violence such as that described above; from networked exploitation such as sex trafficking and the production of pornography to transactional sex, which is often also referred to as "survival sex."[2] They involve varying levels of violence, coercion, and consent and are not all criminal despite being prohibited by UN and humanitarian codes of conduct.

Two years before the Central African Republic scandal broke in international media, a UN investigation into sexual exploitation and abuse in African peace operations had declared it to be "the most significant risk to UN peacekeeping missions, above and beyond other key risks including protection of civilians."[3] Conventional wisdom, as articulated by the UN and other global leaders, is that sexual exploitation and abuse by interveners in peace operations undermines the capacity and credibility of the international community, thereby undermining peace processes. The UN's former secretary-general Ban Ki-moon himself argued that "a single substantiated case of sexual exploitation and abuse involving UN personnel is one case too many," and his successor, Antonio Guterres, has made reforming the UN's policies on sexual exploitation and abuse a cornerstone of his tenure, arguing that preventing it is key to achieving the UN's broader security, humanitarian, and political goals.[4] Yet despite such high-level concern and despite over fifteen years of policy development designed to prevent sexual exploitation and abuse and hold perpetrators to account, both civilian and uniformed personnel associated with peace operations continue to perpetrate it, and the impacts of such behaviors remain poorly understood. It is important to note at the outset that not all peacekeepers or interveners associated with peace operations engage in such abuse and exploitation—in fact, the vast majority do not. However, the actions of the few who do have significant impacts on the work of the many who do not, as this book demonstrates, which is why this is such a critical issue to consider in relation to the challenges facing peace operations today.

This book is about how sexual exploitation and abuse in peace operations affects the peacekeeping and peacebuilding outcomes of those operations. It revolves around a number of key questions: what is sexual exploitation and abuse by interveners, and what factors contribute to its perpetration in peace operations? What impacts does sexual exploitation and abuse have on the outcomes of peacekeeping operations? Does it limit the capacity of the international community to achieve its goals related to security, stability, and peacebuilding, or its credibility in the eyes of local and global populations? In answering these questions, the book also addresses how sexual exploitation and abuse relates to other challenges facing UN peacekeeping and how policies can be improved to prevent such abuse and exploitation in the future. This book thereby contributes to ongoing scholarly and policy discussions about the challenges that undermine effective peacekeeping and peacebuilding in conflict-affected societies and how the international community can address these to better support the establishment of peace and security and the prevention of human rights violations.

Sexual exploitation and abuse in peace operations is a remarkably understudied issue, despite the increasing policy and media attention it has received in the last decade as public awareness of peacekeeper misconduct has grown and scandals have regularly made international headlines. The relatively small body of scholarly work on sexual exploitation and abuse is likely due in part to the difficulties of accessing data on its perpetration and the ways in which numerous stakeholders, including the UN and troop- and police-contributing countries (TCCs), have obscured information about its prevalence in peace operations and institutional responses, as multiple whistle-blower scandals have demonstrated.[5] Nevertheless, scholars have produced important works on sexual exploitation and abuse that tend to fall into a number of broad thematic areas. Perhaps the most established body of work has emerged from feminist scholarship on international relations, which has long been concerned with the gendered implications of military engagements and peacekeeping. Scholars working in this field developed accounts of masculinities, including military masculinities, which have been crucial to our understanding of the causes of sexual exploitation and abuse perpetrated particularly by military peacekeepers.[6] These accounts have foregrounded analyses of the gender dynamics, the differential power between peacekeepers and local communities, racism, and the legacies of colonialism as lenses through which to make sense of peacekeeper abuse. Building on these analyses, scholars have developed accounts of the ways in which the deployment of peacekeepers leads to the establishment of peacekeeping economies, which revolve around formal and informal economic activities that directly link the international presence to local individuals and would not occur to the same scale without the international presence.[7] Much of this work has focused on the gendered aspects of peacekeeping economies, which produce expansive and lasting transactional sex industries between international personnel and locals and are crucial to understanding peacekeeper engagement in sexually exploitative behaviors.[8] Taken together, these works provide an important conceptual and contextual framework for understanding why sexual exploitation and abuse has become so ubiquitous to peace operations.

Another branch of research grounded in feminist critique has developed around the question of the appropriate regulation of sexual interactions between peacekeepers and locals. Scholars have grappled with the issue of women's autonomy in consenting to engage in transactional or other sexual relationships with peacekeepers, questioning whether it is appropriate to ban such relationships and examining the alignment of the UN's zero tolerance policy on sexual exploitation and abuse with international human rights norms.[9] Others have applied feminist lenses to the challenges of prevention of sexual exploitation and abuse training (often called PSEA training) for military units deploying into peace operations and to the challenges of implementing new UN policies around the repatriation of peacekeeping contingents that perpetrate sexual exploitation and abuse.[10] Still others have linked gender equality in the organization of peace operations to what happens in those peace operations, including instances of sexual exploitation and harassment by peacekeepers as well as discrimination against women peacekeepers and their relegation to "safe" tasks and spaces within peacekeeping, with implications for whether peace operations can serve as vehicles for promoting gender equality.[11]

Scholarship has also developed in parallel to this work explicitly grounded in feminist analysis. For instance, some scholars have produced qualitative work primarily focused on documenting the scale of sexual exploitation and abuse by peacekeepers in specific peace operations, drawing on empirical field research and available UN data.[12] Others have investigated the impacts of institutionalized policy responses for reducing abuse.[13] Legal scholars have studied the inadequacies of current international legal frameworks for addressing sexual misconduct by peacekeepers and investigated potential legal reforms at the international level.[14] And a small body of literature has emerged attempting to identify risk factors for the perpetration of sexual abuse and exploitation in peace operations.[15] What emerges from these various bodies of work on peacekeeper sexual exploitation and abuse is a picture of the complexities of responding to and regulating such misconduct when the sexual interactions involved often occur with consent from both parties and the legal and practical challenges facing policy reform.

However, while this existing scholarship helps us understand why sexual exploitation and abuse occurs in peace operations and the challenges of regulating it in an imperfect international system, what is missing is an account of its impacts. How does the perpetration of sexual exploitation and abuse by those involved in peace operations affect the outcomes of those operations and the international community's capacity to achieve the goals that animate the international peacekeeping project? These goals revolve around establishing security, protecting vulnerable groups from violence, promoting human rights, and establishing the foundations for lasting peace through institutional development. Furthermore, the existing literature focuses primarily on sexual exploitation and abuse perpetrated by military peacekeepers rather than by the broader range of civilian and non-UN interveners associated with peace operations, thus painting only half the picture of why such behaviors have become so ubiquitous to peace operations, what impacts they have, and how policy responses might better address them. In fact, UN data shows that while military peacekeepers are more responsible overall for allegations of sexual exploitation and abuse, civilian peacekeepers are more responsible per capita for allegations.[16] This reflects the far greater numbers of military personnel deployed in a peace operation but raises an important question about how we can understand the perpetration of sexual exploitation and abuse by both UN and non-UN civilian interveners in contrast to that perpetrated by military interveners. Comprehensive data on the perpetration of abuse by non-UN civilian staff is not available, which is one of the reasons that this particular aspect of sexual misconduct in peace operations is so under-studied. And finally, the literature to date has not addressed the intersections between sexual exploitation and abuse and other peacekeeping challenges and the potential for integrated policy responses.

This book aims to fill these gaps. It provides the first comparative account of the impacts of sexual exploitation and abuse by international interveners in peace operations on peacekeeping and peacebuilding outcomes, with a particular view to investigating misconduct not just by military peacekeepers but also by civilian peacekeepers and non-UN civilian interveners. It shows how the impacts of such behaviors reach beyond individual mission outcomes, affecting the broader capacity of the UN and the international community to pursue peacebuilding and humanitarian goals globally and undermining global perceptions of the legitimacy of peacekeeping and the moral authority of the UN at a time when the organization already faces a legitimacy crisis. Going beyond the important impacts of sexual exploitation and abuse as a set of behaviors in the context of peace operations, this book addresses throughout the ways in which these behaviors and their impacts intersect with other significant peacekeeping challenges. These include the failures of peacekeepers to enact their protective mandates, the perpetration of nonsexual abuses against local populations, and the emergent fractures between the Global North and South over peacekeeping policies and the distribution of responsibility for enacting them. Finally, the book considers the shortcomings and potential future development of policies related to sexual exploitation and abuse, in light of its findings about the nature and impacts of such behaviors. In doing so, I draw on the existing scholarship and extend it in ways of relevance not only to scholarly debates but also to policymakers and practitioners grappling with the phenomenon of sexual exploitation and abuse in practice.

Why This Matters and the Argument in Brief

The nature and scale of sexual exploitation and abuse in peace operations is often poorly understood even in peacekeeping circles, largely due to the limited reporting and data collection on these issues and the fact that they are often dismissed as less important than other challenges facing peacekeeping. According to the UN, *sexual exploitation* is "any actual or attempted abuse of a position of vulnerability, differential power or trust, for sexual purposes, including, but not limited to, profiting monetarily, socially or politically from the sexual exploitation of another."[17] In contrast, *sexual abuse* is defined in the same policy as "the actual or threatened physical intrusion of a sexual nature, whether by force or under unequal or coercive conditions." Sexual exploitation and abuse first emerged as an issue in peace operations during the United Nations Transitional Authority in Cambodia (UNTAC) in 1993, where a massive increase in organized prostitution followed the arrival of peacekeepers in the country. Instances of sexual exploitation and abuse have since appeared in all peace operations deployed by the UN, although to varying levels. These behaviors have ranged from sex trafficking, rape, and murder to prostitution, the production of pornography, and transactional sex, with differing degrees of coercion and consent. They have targeted adults and children alike, as the next chapter will show in detail, and the primary victims are women and boys and girls under the age of eighteen. Furthermore, the perpetrators are not just soldiers deployed into peacekeeping operations; they include the full range of uniformed and civilian UN peacekeepers as well as private contractors, aid workers, and others associated with peace operations. All of these trends will be discussed in greater detail in subsequent chapters.

Policy responses to sexual exploitation and abuse to date have been largely reactive, and have reflected an individualized understanding of the issue, framing it in terms of acts of misconduct perpetrated by individuals and eschewing the broader factors at play. This approach focuses attention on training and punishment mechanisms at the expense of one that addresses structural factors such as gender, racism, power dynamics, and economic structures that create the contexts in which individuals perpetrate sexual exploitation and abuse.[18] As a result, policy in this area has focused almost exclusively on conduct and discipline frameworks and has been pursued in isolation from other relevant policy frameworks and academic discourses such as the Protection of Civilians and Child Protection frameworks that guide humanitarian action, the Women, Peace and Security agenda, and work on conflict-related sexual violence.

The individualized approach to sexual exploitation and abuse has also delinked it from discussions of peace process failure more broadly, which is paradoxical given the common refrain from diplomats and UN leaders that such abuse undermines the credibility and capacity of the international community in peace operations. This comprehension gap is perhaps understandable given that accounts of the impacts of intervener behaviors and cultures have only recently been integrated into mainstream scholarly discourse about peace process failure, spearheaded by Séverine Autesserre.[19] As I show in this book, sexual exploitation and abuse perpetrated by interveners is deeply linked to the broader cultures and structures within which those deployed into peace operations work and which shape their perceptions of and interactions with local communities. Moreover, the sexual behaviors of interveners—including both those behaviors prohibited under sexual exploitation and abuse policies and consensual relationships not defined as misconduct but characterized nonetheless by unequal power dynamics—intersect with other aspects of intervener cultures and behaviors to produce dynamics and outcomes that conflict with the goals of peace operations and fundamentally undermine peacebuilding outcomes. It is only by understanding sexual exploitation and abuse in the context of these broader cultures, structures, and pressures that the international community will be able to effectively address it.

Although some of the research noted above has demonstrated how sexual exploitation and abuse affects the perceived impartiality of peace operations and contributes to the long-term entrenchment of transactional sex economies, there is a major gap in our understanding of how the impacts of sexual exploitation and abuse operate, whether they are similar across peace operations where it has been perpetrated, and the extent to which their operational impacts contribute to the phenomenon of peace process failure.[20] Based on extensive field and scholarly research, I demonstrate in this book that the perpetration of sexual exploitation and abuse by international interveners affects the goals and outcomes of individual peace operations on three levels, all of which can undermine peacebuilding to varying extents. These are: (1) the individual, family, and community level, primarily through compounding human rights abuses and poverty in already vulnerable communities; (2) the structural level, by normalizing sexually exploitative and abusive behaviors and institutionalizing impunity for sexual exploitation and abuse in both host state security sectors and among intervener communities; and (3) the operational level, by diverting resources available for other vital human rights work towards sexual exploitation and abuse response, seeding mistrust of interveners amongst local communities, undermining a mission's impartiality in the eyes of local communities, and diminishing the confidence interveners themselves have in their organization and in the international peacekeeping and peacebuilding project.

Perhaps more important, this book shows that the implications of sexual exploitation and abuse for the operational capacity of the international community reach beyond individual missions by diminishing global perceptions of the legitimacy of peacekeeping and of the organizations involved in peace operations, particularly the UN and humanitarian organizations. Both the UN secretariat and the UN member states actively participate in processes of legitimation of the UN's work, processes that are critical to maintaining support for the organization but that are fundamentally challenged by revelations of cases of sexual exploitation and abuse in peace operations and the problems of accountability processes to date. Diminished perceptions of legitimacy for the UN and humanitarian organizations can result in staff attrition and decreased funding and can bolster the advocacy of those seeking to limit their country's participation in peacekeeping and peacebuilding internationally.

Furthermore, this book shows that sexual exploitation and abuse in peace operations is not a standalone issue but rather is deeply connected to the other causes of peacekeeping failures. This is something that policy responses do not adequately grasp and that existing scholarship has not explored in great depth. I demonstrate that to better address the broader challenges facing peacekeeping efforts, we must understand the intersections between the factors that give rise to sexual exploitation and abuse and those that lead to peacekeepers failing in their protection responsibilities. Cases that are illustrative in this regard include Srebrenica in 1995, when peacekeepers' refusal to allow Muslim Bosniaks to shelter in the UN base led to their capture and the eventual genocide of more than eight thousand men and boys by Serb militias, and the Terrain Hotel attack in Juba in 2016, when peacekeepers refused to respond when humanitarian personnel came under sustained attack from local militias. In both of these contexts, peacekeepers were also extensively involved in the sexual abuse and exploitation of local women and children. Considering sexual misconduct in the context of other nonsexual abuses against local populations, such as violence or corruption, is similarly useful for developing a sound understanding of the cultures that develop within peace operations and their implications for peace outcomes. In drawing these links, I contribute to the emerging work on intervener cultures and their implications for the success or failure of peace operations. My analysis also addresses the way sexual exploitation and abuse intersects with structural and geopolitical challenges facing the international peacekeeping project, including the growing rift between the Global North and South over a fair way to distribute the burden of peacekeeping and determine the policies by which it is governed and the often competing interests of the various actors involved in peace operations.

Understanding the patterns of sexual exploitation and abuse in peace operations, the factors that give rise to it, and its impacts on the capacity and credibility of the international community is crucial to developing effective prevention and response policies globally. This book shows that the perpetration of such abuses by international interveners undermines the operational capacity of the international community to effectively build peace after civil wars and sustainably alleviate human suffering in crises. Furthermore, sexual misconduct by interveners poses a significant risk to the perceived legitimacy of the multilateral peacekeeping project and the UN more generally, with ramifications for the nature and dynamics of the UN's future roles in peace processes. Effectively preventing and responding to such behaviors is crucial to global peace, order, and justice. This book identifies how policies might be improved in the future based on an account of why they have failed to date and examines the nature and impacts of the sexually exploitative and abusive behaviors they must respond to.

This analysis yields a number of important policy insights. First, it highlights the importance of reframing how policymakers understand "the problem" of sexual misconduct by interveners, with special attention to the complex set of factors that give rise to different patterns and experiences of sexual exploitation and abuse in different contexts. Second, it underscores the importance of those in leadership positions being committed to and held accountable for the implementation of sexual exploitation and abuse policy—at all levels of peace operations and the organizations associated with them. This necessitates ensuring that all mid- to high-level officials understand how sexual misconduct by their personnel undermines their and their organization's interests, by compromising their mission's values and goals, affecting operational capacity, and undermining local and international perceptions of the legitimacy of their work. Third, this book shows how sexual exploitation and abuse policy can be developed proactively in the future by integrating it more closely with other relevant policy frameworks, particularly those related to Women, Peace and Security and conflict-related sexual violence. Fourth, it provides a foundation for the development of more effective training by illustrating the importance of complementing rules-based training with ongoing opportunities for discussions and political education about not only what behaviors are prohibited but also why personnel have been deployed, how their everyday behaviors affect mission goals and outcomes, and to what end certain behaviors have been prohibited or discouraged. Last, the book illustrates how sexual exploitation and abuse is one critically important piece of the puzzle of peacekeeping failure and argues that addressing it in a holistic manner will be an important first step in also addressing the other intersecting challenges facing peacekeeping.

Approach and Scope

Policymakers have often framed the issue of sexual misconduct in peace operations as one of principles: when peacekeepers abuse local populations, they undermine the human rights principles and values that underpin their deployment.[21] Formal statements in response to cases of sexual misconduct have also sometimes suggested in passing that such behavior affects the capacity and credibility of peace operations. While the former claim is fairly self-evident, the latter is a more complex proposition, around which this book revolves. In it, I seek to develop a better understanding of how the cultures and behaviors of interveners—in particular, sexual exploitation and abuse—affect the dynamics between local populations and the international interveners sent in to protect them, and the implications of such behaviors for mission outcomes.

This book is based on a combination of scholarly research, analysis of primary documents and news reports, and extensive interview-based data collection. It engages with cases and examples from peace operations globally in the post–Cold War era and complements this broad survey of experiences and impacts of sexual misconduct with in-depth field research in Timor-Leste and Bosnia-Herzegovina (henceforth Bosnia), as well as with the humanitarian community based in Geneva and the UN and diplomatic community in New York. Around one hundred interviews were conducted in 2016 with individuals who had both professional expertise of relevance to this project and direct personal experience in peace operations either in the case study countries or globally.

Interviewees tended to fall into one of two broad groups, although there was often some overlap. The first group was individuals who had been professionally engaged with peace operations and issues of sexual abuse and exploitation (including prevention and accountability processes). This included individuals who worked with international organizations (such as the UN, the Organization for Security and Co-operation in Europe [OSCE], and the North Atlantic Treaty Organization [NATO]), international and local nongovernmental organizations (NGOs), civil society organizations, foreign military or police forces, private military and security contractors, national and local governments, the national security sector, and the diplomatic corps, including various influential missions to the UN. The second group was individuals or organizations from communities that were affected by sexual exploitation and abuse by interveners in Bosnia and Timor-Leste during the international intervention. This group had generally been involved in responding to instances or patterns of sexual misconduct, including providing support to victims and working with international organizations to try to prevent and ensure accountability for abuses perpetrated by their staff. Across both groups and all contexts, all those interviewed had been involved in the international intervention at either the local or the international level. They also had knowledge of the nature of responses to sexual exploitation and abuse by interveners and valuable insights based on professional experience of the impacts of such behaviors on the relationship between the international community and host community and on the long-term peacebuilding outcomes of the international intervention.

The information gathered during these interviews was analyzed in tandem with the relevant scholarly literature, news reports, and documents or reports produced by the UN, NGOs, and think tanks. By integrating anecdotal and qualitative evidence with scholarly and other sources in this way, I was able to identify patterns and themes as the various accounts intersected with and buttressed one another. This laid the foundations for a credible, multifaceted account of the nature and impacts of sexual exploitation and abuse in peace operations. Evidence gathered and analyzed in this way generates a robust and holistic narrative account of the phenomenon of sexual misconduct in peace operations that foregrounds the voices and experiences of those at the frontlines in peace operations and, by drawing on examples and expertise from many peace operations alongside the detailed case studies, leads to conclusions that are globally relevant. Moreover, the information gathered during qualitative interviews lends a richness and complexity to this book's conclusions that would not have been possible in the absence of access to the diverse range of experiences and perspectives canvassed during interviews. For instance, it reveals the divergence in the way local communities and the international community understand and speak about sexual misconduct in peace operations and the implications for policy response. So while senior UN and humanitarian staff often spoke about the issues in terms of values and erosion of legitimacy, local respondents in Bosnia and Timor-Leste emphasized the way that economic necessity and power disparity shaped the choices made by local women and children about engaging in transactional sex with interveners and how wartime experiences of sexual violence colored local communities' perceptions of these interactions. While international officials emphasized the need for better training and reporting mechanisms, local respondents spoke of the deep disrespect and betrayal they felt as a result of the behaviors of interveners. And while international staff discussed the difficult dynamics of addressing or regulating relationships between foreign staff and local people, Bosnian and Timorese respondents spoke about sexual misconduct in the context of racism and the lack of empathy they felt from those ostensibly sent to protect them, questioning the goals of peacekeeping and asking what harm their communities would have to endure in order to reap its benefits. One respondent in Bosnia questioned the intention underpinning peace operations, asking, "Peacekeeping for whom? For what peace? Save from whom? Liberate from whom?" Others in both Bosnia and Timor-Leste suggested that sexual exploitation and abuse were simply things that communities needed to endure in return for peacekeepers bringing an end to the wars they had suffered. Similarly, interviews with interveners who had very different roles and experiences in peace operations illuminated divergent perspectives on how well the international community handled allegations of sexual misconduct, how important instances of misconduct actually are, and how such behaviors affect the perceptions of interveners themselves about their colleagues, their mission, and the broader peacekeeping project.

Interviews are generally referenced in full in the text of the book, using the name, organizational affiliation, or professional background of the respondent as they requested. However in some cases, due to the sensitive nature of the material shared during interviews, efforts have been made to obscure the identity of the individual interviewed—in those cases, I have chosen sometimes to reference alternative sources such as reports or news articles that present similar information, or I have noted in the text that the individual divulging that information requested anonymity. Often, information being referenced is descriptive—of the types of sexual exploitation and abuse and its impacts witnessed by respondents in the course of their work, and of organizational responses the respondents were involved in—so where relevant I have referenced multiple respondents who shared the same information or referenced written sources alongside interviews. In some cases, it was not possible to cross-reference data with other sources. Where I found the information and source to be satisfactorily credible nonetheless, I have presented it as an anecdote rather than something for which undisputed evidence is available. Lastly, in some instances, when describing themes that arose from multiple interviews and that were not tied directly to professional experiences but were instead impressions of the issues at hand, I indicate the prevalence of such comments among respondents rather than identifying each individual who made them.

A related issue is how perpetrators of sexual exploitation and abuse are described, given the inconsistent availability of details of their countries of origin. Where information about the nationality of perpetrators is available, I have included those details, in part to show that interveners hailing from many different countries perpetrate such misconduct. However, the annual UN reports on sexual exploitation and abuse have only systematically included that information from 2016 onwards, and even so, there have been cases where it has been obscured, as I discuss in detail in chapter 4. The nationalities of perpetrators have also sometimes been revealed in NGO or media reports. However, in many cases that information is not readily available, or I have been unable to verify details about nationality that were provided to me in interviews, and so in those I have used more generic descriptors, including "peacekeepers," "aid workers," "UN police," and so on. Furthermore, in some parts of this text I discuss general trends in the engagement of interveners in sexual exploitation and abuse—for instance, in terms of patronizing brothels—and because full data on the nationalities of those involved is not available I have opted to also use generic descriptors.

Bosnia and Timor-Leste were chosen as in-depth case studies for this project because they represent very different experiences of sexual exploitation and abuse during peace operations and both provide a long enough time frame to investigate the long-term impacts of such misconduct on the peacebuilding outcomes of international engagement in the country. Bosnia is one of the first peace operations where extensive sexual exploitation by interveners was documented—the timelines associated with this will be discussed in chapter 1. Peacekeepers and other interveners deployed during the war and subsequently were implicated in transactional sex economies and the forced trafficking of women and girls from neighboring states to work in brothels frequented by both peacekeepers and local men.[22] By contrast, although interveners in Timor-Leste also engaged in sexual misconduct, it was more limited than in Bosnia, despite the similar scale and form of the international intervention. Furthermore, the forms such misconduct took were markedly different, as my interviews illuminated: although interveners were implicated in transactional sex economies, far more instances revolved around public sexual harassment and the breakdown or abandonment of consensual adult relationships between foreign men and Timorese women, which are not prohibited by UN policy but which often resulted in what have become known as "peace babies" and were seen as exploitative in retrospect. These two cases represent two very different community experiences of sexual exploitation and abuse by international interveners, and therefore provide a valuable opportunity to investigate and understand the differing patterns of such behaviors in different contexts (including the factors that contribute to perpetration or provide protection against it). They also thereby facilitate an investigation of the varying (although, as this research shows, remarkably similar) impacts such behaviors have on the relationship between the local community and the international community, on peacebuilding outcomes, and on the broader credibility of the international community both in the country at hand and globally. The findings from these case studies are then triangulated with the other forms of data collection and analysis described above in order to build a broader analysis of the issues at hand and policy implications.

One last point worth noting here is that the information available about sexual exploitation and abuse in peace operations points primarily to the perpetration of sexual abuse and exploitation by men against local women and children—both boys and girls—under the age of eighteen. There are no recorded cases in the UN database of sexual exploitation or abuse perpetrated by women peacekeepers against locals, and there are only a very small number of cases that have involved adult men as victims.[23] That said, the sexual exploitation and abuse of adolescent boys by male interveners may suggest that such abuse is also perpetrated against men over the age of eighteen but underreported as a result of stigma. As a result, this book focuses primarily on sexual exploitation and abuse as perpetrated by male interveners against local women and children, although other patterns of misconduct are discussed as available evidence allows.

There is a growing awareness globally of the failure of existing approaches to preventing abuse and exploitation by international interveners. There is also growing global concern to identify why peace processes often fail to establish lasting peace and how international approaches and behaviors undermine peacebuilding.[24] By drawing on extensive primary research with both interveners and the communities that received peacekeeping operations, this book contributes significantly to scholarly and policy discussions on both of these issues, demonstrating how the sexual misconduct of interveners has significant and widespread implications for the success of peace operations and how it can better be addressed in the future.

A Note on Terminology

Several terms used in this study require clarification, although, as Mats Berdal notes, "[a] degree of terminological inexactitude is unavoidable in dealing with this subject."[25] While these definitions may not be precise, they are dynamic enough to reflect the shifting nature of the processes and groups described. I use the term *peace process* to describe the complex, long, and dynamic endeavor by which a society moves out of violent conflict and towards peaceful modes of social organization and the contestation of power. Peace negotiations and agreements are central to peace processes, but they are just one part of a longer process that incorporates peacebuilding, peace consolidation, and, often, peacekeeping. *Peacebuilding* is the overarching frame used in this book to describe the processes by which political settlements are implemented and translated into meaningful political and social change in the aftermath of violent conflict or, in the case of Timor-Leste, occupation. This term is used interchangeably with *peace consolidation*. *Peacekeeping* is one important element of these processes around which much international intervention revolves but it is not the only element—broader political, social, economic, and security processes intersect with peacekeeping to make up the work that comes under the banner of peacebuilding. Consequently, peacebuilding outcomes are broader than just those associated with peacekeeping and encompass the political, social, economic, and security goals that drive international intervention in conflict-affected societies.

In line with this, I use the term *international intervention* to describe this broader project of the international community supporting the transition to peace, and the term *interveners* as an inclusive term that denotes civilian, military, police, and other security personnel associated with a peace operation, as well as aid workers, diplomats, private contractors, and other individuals associated with the international response to support the transition of civil-war affected states towards peace. In some cases, I use the term *intervener community* to refer to this broad group of interveners in a particular context. Finally, the term *international community* is understood to mean the broader group of international actors from which these interveners are drawn and who provide them with their mandate (both political and moral)—in particular, the key states, organizations, and actors involved in peace processes in civil war. In the context of this book, this international community often centers on a UN peace operation but operates more broadly and encompasses other organizations in the UN family: humanitarian and development NGOs, the diplomatic community, and private sector companies contracted to support the operation of a UN mission. Despite the obvious differences in scope, mission, and capacity of these actors and despite their various levels of engagement in different contexts, they are similar in that they are broadly engaged in the promotion of peace in conflict-affected states. They form the community of actors engaged as interveners in peace operations.

Organization of the Book

This book is broadly organized into three main parts: the background and context of sexual exploitation and abuse in peace operations, its impacts on peacebuilding outcomes and the capacity and credibility of the international community, and the challenges facing effective policy response.

Chapter 1 provides an overview of the history of sexual exploitation and abuse in peace operations globally, including the various forms it takes (only some of which are criminal) and the range of international interveners who perpetrate it. It presents an account of how and why these behaviors occur in peace operations by investigating the local, international, normative, systemic, and structural factors that give rise to them. It also addresses the connections between sexual misconduct by interveners, conflict-related sexual violence perpetrated during wars, and the sexual harassment and abuse that is perpetrated by interveners against their colleagues in peace operations.

Chapter 2 introduces the case studies that underpin the analysis of the long-term impacts of sexual exploitation and abuse. It develops a detailed account of the context, nature, and scale of sexual misconduct by interveners during peace operations in Bosnia and Timor-Leste based on extensive primary data. It demonstrates that the ways in which local communities experience such abuses is grounded in historical experience, cultural norms, and, in many ways, the particular forms of material deprivation and conflict-related sexual violence they experienced, with implications for what they consider to be inappropriate behavior by interveners.

Chapter 3 investigates the micro- and mission-level impacts of sexual exploitation and abuse perpetrated by interveners in peace operations on the international community's capacity to fulfill its goals related to security, stability, and peacebuilding in postconflict contexts. It examines the long-term impacts of such abuse on the relationship between the local community and the international community, the perceived outcomes of the peace operation, and the new structures of governance and security established during the peace operation.

Chapter 4 shifts focus to investigate the macro- and institutional-level impacts of sexual exploitation and abuse. It shows that sexual misconduct in individual missions has far-reaching impacts that reduce international capacities to engage effectively in peace operations and diminish the perceived legitimacy of the international community engaged in peace-keeping and peacebuilding, thereby undermining the international community's capacity to pursue the broader aspirational goals that animate peacekeeping. It tracks the international responses to the 2015 peace-keeper sexual abuse scandal in the Central African Republic and the 2018 Oxfam sexual exploitation scandal in Haiti to explore the global political implications of such scandals. It demonstrates how sexual exploitation and abuse undermines the capacity and perceived legitimacy of the international community in a number of mutually reinforcing ways, with serious implications for the future of peacekeeping and peacebuilding.

In developing a broad account of the nature, causes, and impacts of sexual exploitation and abuse by interveners, this book reveals the intersections between sexual misconduct and many of the other challenges facing UN peace operations today, including the failure of peacekeepers to fulfill protective mandates, the growing rift between the Global North and South over the distribution of the burden of peacekeeping, and the competing interests at play in peace operations, including between the UN and troop- and police-contributing countries. In chapter 5, I draw these issues together by considering how intervener cultures interact with the broad range of factors that challenge and undermine the effectiveness of peace operations, including by giving rise to the perpetration of sexual misconduct against local communities. In light of this, I discuss the key insights the book has revealed about the nature and impacts of sexual exploitation and abuse by interveners in peace operations and suggest how the international community might better address this phenomenon and its complex, interlinked implications in the future.

1

The History and Nature of Sexual Misconduct in Peace Operations

In early 2018, the global humanitarian community was rattled by international media reports of aid workers hiring prostitutes and hosting sex parties in Haiti during the emergency response to the 2010 earthquake. As the story unfolded, it became apparent that some of the staff involved had previously been implicated in similarly inappropriate sexual behaviors in previous humanitarian deployments, including in conflict contexts. Moreover, after their dismissal from Oxfam, a number of them found work in other organizations also working with vulnerable populations in emergency and conflict zones.[1]

At the time of the incidents in Haiti, the humanitarian response to the earthquake was inextricably linked to the ongoing UN Stabilization Mission In Haiti (MINUSTAH), which had been deployed since 2004 in response to violence and instability in the country. MINUSTAH consistently experienced some of the highest number of reports of sexual exploitation and abuse in UN peacekeeping, including reports of transactional sex, sex with minors, and rape.[2] MINUSTAH's mandate included the restoration of a secure and stable environment, the promotion of formal political processes, the strengthening of Haiti's governance institutions and rule of law, and the promotion and protection of human rights in the country.[3] After the 2010 earthquake, the peace operation was also tasked with assisting the Haitian authorities and the humanitarian community in a response for affected communities. As a result, the distinction between peacekeepers deployed under a UN mandate and humanitarians deployed in response to the natural disaster was blurred—they worked in the same context, they were drawn from similar organizations, they worked closely together to serve the same affected communities, and, perhaps most important, the dynamics of their relationships with local communities were similar. This close association reinforces the importance of studying not only sexual exploitation and abuse by peacekeepers but also the interlinked perpetration by the broader range of actors associated with a peace operation's presence in a country. It also raises questions about whether the nature of such abuses perpetrated by peacekeepers, particularly military and police peacekeepers, differs significantly from those perpetrated by civilian interveners—including civilian peacekeepers, aid workers, and diplomats. Private security contractors add a layer of complexity to this mix, sitting as they do between the uniformed and civilian sectors.

The Oxfam scandal raised another important issue, namely, which behaviors are considered to fall under the category of sexual exploitation and abuse and what role consent plays in determining this, particularly when adults are involved. The sexually inappropriate behaviors in this particular case included purchasing sex from adult women who were working as prostitutes. There was speculation that some of the women may have been underage; the Oxfam investigation was unable to substantiate that allegation, but noted that the possibility could not be completely ruled out.[4] Such transactional sex, even when it involves consenting adults, breaches the UN and humanitarian community's codes of conduct relating to sexual exploitation and abuse, but it is not necessarily criminal—that depends on the regulation of prostitution within the host state's legal frameworks.[5] This adds another level of conceptual and practical difficulties in understanding and responding to sexual exploitation and abuse: the behaviors the category encompasses are varied, only some are criminal, they involve radically different levels of consent, and it can be difficult to substantiate allegations because of the contexts into which peace operations are deployed.

This chapter revolves around these complexities, aiming to untangle the nature of sexual misconduct in peace operations, the ways in which different groups of interveners perpetrate it, and the factors that contribute to its perpetration in peace operations. I begin by briefly tracing the history of sexual exploitation and abuse in peace operations before delineating a typology of sorts that distinguishes between four main types of behavior that fall under the category of sexual exploitation and abuse. This is crucial to the study of how such behaviors affect the international community's capacity to achieve its peacebuilding goals and why policy responses have largely failed to date. I then discuss the causal and contextual factors that underpin the perpetration of sexual exploitation and abuse and consider the interconnections between the abuses by interveners, conflict-related sexual violence, and sexual harassment and abuse perpetrated within the international intervener community. Finally, I will look in greater detail at the issue of sexual misconduct by civilian interveners. To date, the majority of data and analysis has focused on uniformed peacekeepers, despite the fact that civilian peacekeepers are more responsible per capita for allegations of sexual exploitation and abuse in peace operations and despite growing awareness of the pervasiveness of sexual harassment and abuse within intervener communities. Understanding this particular element of the puzzle is critical to developing a comprehensive understanding of the nature, causes, and consequences of sexual exploitation and abuse in peace operations.

Sexual Exploitation and Abuse: A Brief History

Sexual exploitation and abuse first emerged as an issue in peace operations during the United Nations Transitional Authority in Cambodia (UNTAC) in 1993, when the number of prostitutes in the country grew from six thousand before the UN arrived to more than twenty-five thousand in 1993.[6] The widespread use of prostitutes by UN personnel involved violence and the sexual abuse of girls, with some women reporting that "UNTAC customers could be more cruel" than Cambodian customers at brothels.[7] In fact, a group of women working in brothels wrote to the UN complaining about this and requesting that the UN ask peacekeepers to behave less violently in the future. Although the exact scale of peacekeeper involvement in sexual exploitation and abuse in Cambodia is impossible to know, some data sheds light on its prevalence: a Joint United Nations Programme on HIV/AIDS (UNAIDS) survey found that 45 percent of Dutch navy and marines personnel deployed to UNTAC had sexual contact with sex workers or other members of the local population during their five-month deployment and did not use condoms consistently.[8] At the time, the UN response to the growing problem of peacekeeper participation in sexual exploitation and abuse was threefold: the head of mission, Yasushi Akashi, dismissed the significance of the issue, declaring that "boys will be boys"; mission leadership advised peacekeepers not to wear uniforms when visiting brothels nor to park UN vehicles directly outside; and an additional eight hundred thousand condoms were shipped to the country to prevent the spread of HIV/AIDS among UN personnel.[9]

In 1995, the issue of peacekeeper misconduct was again brought to international attention, this time in relation to Bosnia-Herzegovina, where evidence emerged first of the trafficking of women to work as sex slaves in brothels frequented by UN mission personnel, including peacekeepers and particularly American DynCorp private contractors working within the mission; and later, of the complicity of interveners in this trafficking, including the purchase of women and girls as young as twelve as sex slaves.[10] These behaviors came on the back of years of UN peacekeepers engaging in transactional sex with Bosnian women during the war.[11] Nevertheless, it was not until 1999 that the negative media and rising public attention prompted the UN Mission in Bosnia and Herzegovina (UNMIBH) and the Office of the High Commissioner for Human Rights (OHCHR) to pursue policy responses to address the problem—suggesting that the UN was reluctant to acknowledge and address the involvement of peacekeepers in trafficking.[12] Once underway, the UN response failed to provide adequate protection to victims and adopted a more limited definition of trafficking than that set out under international law, excluding women who were aware that they would work as prostitutes upon arrival in Bosnia and only including those who were not.[13] These women were therefore excluded from any protections or support services; in fact, the two gender advisors in UNMIBH and the International Police Task Force (IPTF) who made determinations of trafficking status until 2001 referred to these women as "migrant prostitutes" and suggested to Human Rights Watch that the UN had no responsibilities towards them.[14]

Shortly thereafter, attention turned to West Africa, where independent consultants raised the alarm that staff from the UN and from NGOs had been abusing and exploiting local women and girls in refugee camps in Guinea, Liberia, and Sierra Leone. A subsequent UN Office of Internal Oversight Services (OIOS) investigation in 2001 verified that sexual misconduct among aid workers was prevalent, documenting, for instance, the sexual relationship between a UN civilian staff member and a seventeen-year-old refugee in exchange for school fees, the violent rape of girls by NGO staff in refugee camps, the rape of boys by UN peacekeepers in Sierra Leone, the exchange of sex for food provided by NGO staff, and the refusal of international staff to take responsibility for children they had fathered with local women and girls.[15] In his statement releasing the report, Secretary-General Kofi Annan declared that

> sexual exploitation and abuse by humanitarian staff cannot be tolerated. It violates everything the UN stands for. Men, women and children displaced by conflict or other disasters are among the most vulnerable people on earth. They look to the UN and its humanitarian partners for shelter and protection. Anyone employed by or affiliated with the UN who breaks that sacred trust must be held accountable and, when the circumstances so warrant, prosecuted.[16]

In response, the general assembly adopted a resolution "*expressing its grave concern* at incidents of sexual exploitation and abuse against vulnerable populations" and directing the secretary-general to extend remedial and preventive measures to all peace and humanitarian operations, to ensure that reporting and investigative procedures are in place in all such operations, and to maintain data on sexual exploitation and abuse. It "encouraged" all UN bodies and NGOs to do the same.[17] The secretary-general consequently issued the 2003 bulletin, which outlined a zero tolerance policy on sexual exploitation and abuse for all UN staff and the duties of mission leadership in holding perpetrators accountable, including through referring cases to national authorities for criminal prosecution. This is also known as the zero tolerance bulletin or policy, and it promulgated six specific standards:

(a) Sexual exploitation and sexual abuse constitute acts of serious misconduct and are therefore grounds for disciplinary measures, including summary dismissal;

(b) Sexual activity with children (persons under the age of 18) is prohibited regardless of the age of majority or age of consent locally. Mistaken belief in the age of a child is not a defence;

(c) Exchange of money, employment, goods or services for sex, including sexual favours or other forms of humiliating, degrading or exploitative behaviour, is prohibited. This includes any exchange of assistance that is due to beneficiaries of assistance;

(d) Sexual relationships between United Nations staff and beneficiaries of assistance, since they are based on inherently unequal power dynamics, undermine the credibility and integrity of the work of the United Nations and are strongly discouraged;

(e) Where a United Nations staff member develops concerns or suspicions regarding sexual exploitation or sexual abuse by a fellow worker, whether in the same agency or not and whether or not within the United Nations system, he or she must report such concerns via established reporting mechanisms;

(f) United Nations staff are obliged to create and maintain an environment that prevents sexual exploitation and sexual abuse. Managers at all levels have a particular responsibility to support and develop systems that maintain this environment.[18]

It also mandated that all non-UN entities or individuals working in cooperation with the UN accept and implement those standards of behavior as a condition of their cooperative arrangement. The zero tolerance policy has been a cornerstone of sexual exploitation and assault policy ever since, albeit hotly contested on the basis of its treatment of consent between adults (all transactional sex is prohibited, regardless of whether it involves consenting adults) and its implications for understanding the agency of local women involved (all sexual relationships between peacekeepers and locals are strongly discouraged—but not prohibited—because of the unequal power dynamics, even if they are not sexually abusive or exploitative).[19] These tensions have significant implications for the implementation of the policy on the ground in peace operations and for its credibility among intervener communities, which will be revisited in chapter 6. During interviews, some respondents argued that the incoherence and inexactitude of the policy with regards to consensual adult relationships results in some staff treating the rest of the policy as equally flawed.

These early examples reveal some key characteristics of sexual exploitation and abuse in peace operations: the pervasiveness of such behaviors and the prevalence of abuse against children; the variety of behaviors involved, only some of which are criminal; the involvement of both uniformed and civilian UN peacekeepers as well as private contractors, aid workers, and others associated with peace operations; and the failure of policy responses to prevent sexual misconduct despite significant efforts. These themes will recur throughout this book.

A Typology of Bad Behavior

The data available on sexual exploitation and abuse perpetrated by interveners suggests that the range of misconduct is diverse, encompassing opportunistic sexual abuse, transactional sex, networked sexual exploitation, and extremely violent or sadistic attacks. It also suggests that acts of abuse and exploitation are driven by a range of different motivating and permissive factors. As a result, it is useful to analyze sexual exploitation and abuse in terms of the way individual cases involve cash and other material resources, the extent to which they have been planned or involve a number of perpetrators, and whether they are linked to larger criminal networks. It is also useful to understand those actions that are criminal in contrast to those that are not. By distinguishing the different types of behaviors that the general category encompasses, it is possible to better understand the form and function of specific instances of sexual exploitation and abuse and identify those factors that either cause such actions or create the context in which they occur.

As Kate Grady's study of UN data collection on allegations of sexual misconduct demonstrated, the UN has abandoned and developed new taxonomies of sexual exploitation and abuse on an annual basis, which has made tracking trends or using the data for analysis virtually impossible.[20] This highlights the need for robust categories that are broad enough to be useful in understanding the nature and dynamics of the abuses that occurred. Understanding the different forms sexual exploitation and abuse takes and the factors and motivators that give rise to them is crucial to understanding the varying impacts it has on peacebuilding outcomes. It is also essential to understanding why policy responses to date have failed to effectively prevent such behaviors or hold perpetrators accountable. Those policies have tended to characterize sexual exploitation and abuse as one form of misconduct perpetrated on an individual basis, rather than a very diverse set of behaviors reflecting myriad causal and contextual factors, only some of which are addressed by the conduct and discipline approach to prevention and accountability mechanisms.[21]

A typology of this sort inevitably raises questions about the prevalence of the different types of behavior identified. Unfortunately, however, the quantitative data on sexual exploitation and abuse in peace operations is not sufficiently robust to support credible claims of the prevalence of the specific behaviors I delineate. Quantitative data on sexual misconduct in peace operations is primarily available through the UN's Conduct and Discipline Unit—it is included in the annual reports of the secretary-general on Special Measures on Protection from Sexual Exploitation and Abuse and it is the basis for most quantitative studies of such abuse.[22] The UN data relates only to allegations against UN staff and personnel in UN peace operations and, as Grady's close analysis of UN data collection and reporting trends over time shows, is unreliable due to poor data management, potential false allegations, and a likely underreporting.[23] The lack of uniformly robust reporting mechanisms for misconduct in peace operations globally also affects the data collected: an expert from the Inter-Agency Standing Committee for the Prevention of SEA Taskforce reported that a pilot project in multiple countries found that the lack of trust in reporting mechanisms leads to far fewer allegations of sexual exploitation and abuse; when trust in these mechanism was built, the number of sexual misconduct cases reported increased significantly.[24] These factors are compounded by the way the data is presented in the UN database and annual reports, with multiple victims grouped under a single allegation and no disaggregation of the specific forms of abuse experienced by each. Moreover, as discussed later in this chapter, the way specific allegations are coded in the UN database as particular forms of misconduct is highly variable, which is in part due to the complexity and intersection of various forms of sexual abuse and sexual exploitation and the difficulties involved in investigating allegations of misconduct. In addition, there is evidence that not all allegations and cases of sexual misconduct by peacekeepers appear in the official reports, as the Code Blue Campaign at AIDS-Free World has documented.[25] Ragnhild Nordås and Siri Rustad's Sexual Exploitation and Abuse by Peacekeepers dataset includes valuable data on a number of non-UN peace operations also active between 1999 and 2010, but the time-limited nature of the dataset and the fact that it relies heavily on the UN data means it is also unable to generate robust conclusions regarding prevalence of different forms of sexual misconduct that I discuss in this chapter.[26] As a result of these limitations, it is impossible to rank the types of behavior by prevalence, but it is possible to indicate general patterns of perpetration, based on a combination of the qualitative and quantitative data available. Furthermore, the limitations of the quantitative data highlight the value of developing a robust qualitative account of the nature and patterns of sexual exploitation and abuse perpetrated in peace operations.

Opportunistic Sexual Abuse

Soldiers have a long history of perpetrating sexual and gender-based violence in both conflict and post-conflict situations, and rape and sexual violence have taken place on a mass scale in many conflicts into which peace operations have been deployed, including Sierra Leone, Sudan, the Democratic Republic of Congo, Bosnia-Herzegovina, Timor-Leste, and Liberia.[27] While some conflict-related sexual violence may be used strategically in aid of military objectives—often characterized as "a weapon of war"— it may also be perpetrated opportunistically for private reasons, or as a "practice of war," one which Elisabeth Wood argues "is not ordered (even implicitly) or institutionalized, but is tolerated for a variety of reasons."[28] Given the many reasons rape occurs during war, it is perhaps not surprising that soldiers also perpetrate such violence during peace operations.

Sexual abuse, according to the UN, includes sexual assault, rape, and other intrusions of a sexual nature, and it is perpetrated both by individuals and groups.[29] Nordås and Rustad found reports of rape in eleven of the thirty-six peace operations they investigated (although specific data was not available in nearly half of the peace operations, so this figure is likely higher).[30] In 2017, the UN's Conduct and Discipline Unit recorded twenty allegations of sexual abuse, defined as "any sexual relations with a minor and any non-consensual sexual relations with an adult," by military, police, and civilian peacekeepers across ten peacekeeping operations.[31] This accounted for one third of all sexual exploitation and abuse allegations recorded, a steep decrease from 2017 when sexual abuse accounted for half of all allegations. Fourteen of the allegations were categorized as rape, nine of which involved children, and some involved more than one victim—one allegation related to acts involving fifty-two victims, although fifty victims were subject to sexual exploitation and two to sexual abuse.[32] In addition, the secretary-general's annual report on sexual exploitation and abuse noted thirty-four allegations of sexual abuse perpetrated by implementing partners of the UN, which included abuse against twenty girls, three boys, nine women, and two men. These statistics suggest the relative prevalence of rape as a form of sexual misconduct in peace operations, although it is unlikely that these statistics accurately reflect the true scale of this form of behavior given the paucity of quantitative data available, as noted above.

Putting aside questions of prevalence, many non-UN investigations have documented the perpetration of what appears to be opportunistic rape by interveners. For instance, in 2015, Human Rights Watch documented a number of rapes in the Central African Republic: two young women, aged eighteen and fourteen respectively, recounted being dragged into the bush and gang-raped by armed peacekeepers from the UN Multidimensional Integrated Stabilization Mission in the Central African Republic (MINUSCA) peacekeepers near their base—the former had been seeking food or money from the peacekeepers and was threatened with death if she resisted, while the latter was simply walking by.[33] Another fourteen-year-old girl raped by a Burundian peacekeeper in the Central African Republic, who gave birth to a son as a result, recounted to the *Washington Post*, "Sometimes when I'm alone with my baby, I think about killing him. He reminds me of the man who raped me."[34] Similar accounts have emerged in other countries. In Haiti, a girl told the *BBC* that a Brazilian peacekeeper raped her when she was fourteen years old: "He held me down by the arms and held both my wrists, twisting them back and we struggled together. And then he raped me." Her mother told the reporter, "When I found her I didn't recognise my own child. . . She had the face of a dead person."[35] South African peacekeepers serving in the UN Observer Mission in the Democratic Republic of the Congo (MONUC) have been convicted of the rape and murder of children, while in Sierra Leone, Ukrainian peacekeepers gang-raped a local woman, and a Guinean peacekeeper raped a twelve-year-old.[36]

As I have noted, sexual abuse by peacekeepers often occurs in a context where sexual violence has long been a norm: contemporary civil wars are often (but not always) characterized by the extensive use of sexual- and gender-based violence by fighting groups that rests on deep-rooted social constructs of masculinity, constructs that can produce such violence even outside of war.[37] Moreover, a recent survey of civil wars from 1989 to 2009 found that peace operations were more likely to be deployed into conflicts that had experienced high levels of sexual violence than into those that did not.[38] Further, military peacekeepers are, first and foremost, soldiers, and anecdotal reports of peacekeeper rape seem to revolve primarily around military peacekeepers rather than civilian peacekeepers or aid workers. This trend is borne out in the detailed discussions of sexual exploitation and abuse in Timor-Leste and Bosnia in the next chapter. Extensive research has demonstrated that the deliberate militarization of masculinity within armies as a training mechanism produces sexually violent behaviors, which goes some way to explaining this form of violence.[39] In some cases, there are also parallels between the normalization of sexual violence in peacekeepers' home countries and their perpetration of sexual abuse when on deployment with a UN mission. For example, UN statistics from 2016 show that uniformed peacekeeping personnel from the Democratic Republic of Congo and South Africa are responsible for the highest number of allegations of sexual misconduct. Sexual and gender-based violence is endemic in both countries, suggesting a culture of violence against women that would shape the behaviors of individual men in the military, including on peacekeeping deployments.[40] In this vein, Sabrina Karim and Kyle Beardsley's recent study suggested that higher proportions of peacekeeping troops contributed from countries with relatively strong records of gender equality correlates with a lower incidence of sexual exploitation, abuse, and harassment reported in those peace operations.[41]

The main factor that distinguishes this form of sexual misconduct from those discussed below is that it is opportunistic insofar as it is for the private purposes of the rapist (or rapists) and it does not include the level of preplanning or coordination that is characteristic of the other three types of behavior described below.

Planned, Sadistic Abuse

The second type of sexual misconduct apparent in the available data is related and similarly criminal, but distinct in that it is characterized not by its opportunistic nature but by the perpetration of rape in a planned, sadistic form. In 2015, an internal UN report was leaked after suppression by the UN hierarchy, documenting extensive and horrific instances of sexual abuse perpetrated against children in the Central African Republic by peacekeeping soldiers.[42] The report documented the regular oral and anal rape of homeless and starving boys aged eight to fifteen by twenty-six peacekeepers from France, Chad, and Equatorial Guinea, noting that some of the children fled the relative safety of the refugee camp they were in after the attacks. In early 2016, more than 108 additional cases were investigated, including the sexual abuse of ninety-eight girls by international peacekeepers who had all returned to their home countries by the time interviews with victims occurred.[43] The report documented allegations that in 2014 a French military commander from the Sangaris force (a non-UN French military intervention in Central African Republic that operated under a UN mandate) had tied up and undressed four girls and forced them to have sex with a dog. One of the children consequently died, and another reported that she was ostracized by her community and called "the Sangaris' dog" after the rape.[44]

These cases are emblematic of this particular planned and sadistic form of sexual abuse and are clearly distinct from the other forms of misconduct I discuss in this chapter. These abuses are not perpetrated in pursuit of financial benefit, as are the production of pornography or involvement in sex trafficking. Nor are they transactional or opportunistic. They appear to be perpetrated for the sadistic pleasure of the perpetrators and involve both planning and coordination. These incidences are less common than the other forms of misconduct discussed, but they are not isolated. For instance, in 1993, Canadian peacekeepers in Somalia beat, raped, and tortured to death a Somali teenage boy whom they caught attempting to steal food and water that they had left out as bait for petty thieves.[45] And in 2005, a French logistics employee in the Democratic Republic of Congo "was found with hundreds of videotapes that showed him torturing and sexually abusing naked girls."[46] The use of torture and sex slavery in Bosnia, which will be discussed in the next chapter, is a further example of this type of sexual abuse.

This form of abuse has parallels with other torture perpetrated by peacekeepers—for instance, in early 2016, evidence was found that peacekeepers from the Republic of the Congo serving in Central African Republic had tortured to death two anti-balaka leaders, beat to death two civilians, and murdered twelve others, including women and children.[47] It also has parallels with the sexual torture perpetrated by American soldiers against Iraqi prisoners at Abu Ghraib.[48] This suggests that this sadistic abuse does not just operate in the sexual sphere, but is facilitated by similar factors that give rise to military misconduct and torture more broadly.

Transactional Sex

According to the Zeid Report, commissioned by the UN to provide a comprehensive report on peacekeeper sexual exploitation and abuse, the vast majority of allegations investigated by the UN relate to transactional sex, or "survival sex," including "the exchange of sex for money (on average $1–3 per encounter), for food (for immediate consumption or barter later) or for jobs (especially affecting daily workers)."[49] The zero tolerance bulletin explicitly prohibits any "exchange of money, employment, goods, or services for sex," but this form of behavior is not necessarily criminal in the same way that the two discussed above are—whether it is criminal or not depends on the nature of the transaction and the host state's laws on prostitution and age of consent (if they exist).[50] The fundamental point of distinction between transactional sex and other forms of sexual misconduct is that transactional sex "involves a level of agency and negotiation" even though it is negotiated in the context of often extreme deprivation, desperation, and insecurity.[51] (In the Central African Republic, for instance, most reported cases of sexual exploitation by peacekeepers occurred at the peak of the conflict.[52]) In 2003, civilians from Bunia in eastern Democratic Republic of Congo were displaced and took refuge in and around UN headquarters and camps where an extensive survival sex economy sprung up. The *Independent* reported the story of thirteen year-old Faela, who became pregnant after repeated wartime rapes by soldiers and whose father refused to support her because of the shame of her being an unmarried mother. In the internally displaced persons camp, she and her baby faced starvation and so every night she, along with other girls in the same situation, climbed through the fence into the compound where Uruguayan and Moroccan soldiers were based.

> "If I go and see the [MONUC] soldiers at night and sleep with them, then they sometimes give me food, maybe a banana or a cake," she says, looking down at her son. "I have to do it with them because there is nobody to care, nobody else to protect Joseph except me. He is all I have and I must look after him." . . . "Going over to the camp is OK because the soldiers are kind to me and don't point their guns like the other soldiers did," Faela says.[53]

A *Washington Post* investigation in Bunia documented similar stories, with one fourteen-year-old, known locally as "the one-dollar UN girl" because of the price she charges for sex with peacekeepers, telling reporters, "I'm sad about it. But I needed the dollars. I can't go farm because of the militias. Who will feed me? . . . But at least they paid us. I was worthless anyhow. My honour was lost [due to wartime rape]."[54]

This is not an uncommon story in post-conflict situations, where the intersection of wartime sexual violence, strong cultural norms around "shame," material deprivation, and the presence of international interveners creates the conditions for survival sex economies to emerge and flourish. In Haiti, minors reported being offered food and small amounts of cash in exchange for sex.[55] In Guinea and Liberia, male humanitarian staff withheld services or essential commodities including food and oil, tent materials, medicine, ration cards, loans, and education or training courses until they received sex.[56] In Timor-Leste, locals, especially children, were "offered money and other material benefits in exchange for sex more or less at random," and t-shirts were sold with the logo "Feel Safe Tonight: Sleep with a Peacekeeper," explicitly referencing the irony of those sent to protect the population exploiting them.[57] It is unclear who designed and sold the t-shirts, which were accompanied by a cartoon image of a burly, threatening, and highly sexualized masculine bulldog wearing a peacekeeper's beret. In Côte D'Ivoire, peacekeepers enlisted the assistance of local boys to procure girls for sex, offering them money, clothes, and souvenirs and impressing on them the need for secrecy to avoid the peacekeepers being punished and their line of supplies being cut off.[58] And research in West Africa has suggested that some parents saw their children's participation in transactional sex as essential to their family's survival and therefore either encouraged or tacitly accepted it as a necessary harm.[59]

Interestingly, some peacekeepers have made similar arguments, positing that their sexual "transactions" were acceptable because the "donated" food, resources, or money made the women involved more secure— essentially suggesting that exploitation can be benevolent in the context of peacekeeping economies.[60] It is important to recognize that it is not only peacekeepers and aid workers that participate in these transactional sex economies. Save the Children found that a diverse range of adult men between thirty to sixty years old were involved in sexual exploitation in Liberia; some were from the communities in the camp, but many were from outside, either visiting or working in or near the refugee camps where the exploitation occurred. These included "sugar daddies" who provided cash or other support to young women and girls in exchange for a regular sexual relationship, businessmen, video club operators, "big men" in the camps who held significant power or authority, government workers and officials, police officers, excombatants, soldiers from the Liberian army, and teachers in the community.[61] It is also worth noting that prostitution by soldiers—or military prostitution—is also a well-documented phenomenon in nonpeacekeeping contexts.[62] However, soldiers' engagement in transactional sex during peace operations carries with it particular implications, given the protective mandate under which peacekeepers are deployed and the higher expectations of the behavioral standards of peacekeepers.[63] This issue will be revisited in subsequent chapters, but it is within the context of these broader conflict and postconflict economies that transactional sex involving interveners must be understood and addressed.

While both adults and children engage in transactional sex and UN policies do not distinguish between the two (although interviews with UN staff suggested that the practical implementation of policies does, and it is primarily concerned with transactional sex involving children, which is supposed to be recorded as sexual abuse), the implications of transactional sex with children and adults differ significantly, and the majority of transactional sex reported in the literature relates to children. In fact, a former MONUC employee told Sarah Spencer that "the Belgians [in MONUC] won't touch anything over fourteen, and peacekeepers interviewed by Paul Higate suggested a fetishization of sex with children, with some arguing that soldiers "want to see what [sex with young girls] is like . . . to see if it is different" and others claiming that "having sex with [young girls] was 'respectful' of local culture" where age-of-consent norms are different.[64] That said, extensive transactional sex economies with adults do emerge in peace operation contexts, as the cases of Timor-Leste and Bosnia discussed in chapter 2 illustrate. Multiple respondents interviewed for this book lamented that when on deployment they had often been reluctant to raise such behavior with their superiors because they weren't sure of the nature of the relationships in question or their transactional elements. Such relationships may involve various forms of compensation for sex—whether material goods such as food or money or, sometimes, forms of support that might also come as part of longer-term relationships such as accommodation, meals at restaurants, or school fees—and various levels of coercion, including withholding of aid or other humanitarian support. These forms of transactional sex between adults are perhaps less visible in the literature on and reports of transactional sex because of the less straightforward nature of exploitation given the involvement of consenting adults.

Transactional sex entails varying levels of consent, which is particularly tricky to determine when it involves children or adolescents. The Zeid Report notes that some girls interviewed described "rape disguised as prostitution" whereby the perpetrator "pays" the victim afterwards in order to suggest a legitimate consensual transaction. This has very different implications in terms of consent and agency and it demonstrates significant overlap with opportunistic sexual abuse discussed above. A case of the rape of a young boy in Côte d'Ivoire suggests something similar: the young returnee boy alleged that he was lured away from where he was fishing with friends by a uniformed peacekeeper whom he knew and trusted from previous encounters. The man raped the boy and gave him money to keep him quiet.[65] There are also questions about how consent is determined by investigators: one child who reported being raped by a Burundian peacekeeper in the Central African Republic had her case recorded as transactional sex rather than assault.[66] In addition to issues of consent, there is evidence that this sort of sexual exploitation and abuse creates a situation of dependency whereby those who were abused seek out further transactional encounters. A fourteen year-old boy in South Sudan recounted in 2007 that after being raped by a uniformed peacekeeper, he now returns regularly to the same spot in the hope he will be picked up by other peacekeepers and paid for his services. He told reporters, "I know it is a terrible thing to do but I see the UN cars around late at night by the drinking places and I sit there in the hope of being picked up. If I get 1000 SD ($3USD) a day then that is a good day."[67] Reports have found that children are often cheated out of promised payments even where they have agreed to transactional sex.[68]

On the other end of the spectrum, transactional relationships between consenting adults are murkier, particularly those that have some transactional elements but are also characterized by ongoing romantic or sexual relationships. The zero tolerance bulletin identifies "inherently unequal power dynamics" in relationships between UN staff and beneficiaries of assistance and "strongly [discourages]" them because they "undermine the credibility and integrity of the work of the UN" but it does not prohibit them.[69] This stance has been strongly criticized for disregarding the capacity of locals, particularly women, to freely consent to such relationships, which may or may not involve transactions.[70] Further, who counts as a beneficiary is unclear: while one senior official in the UN's Conduct and Discipline Unit argued that for peacekeepers, the whole population in the country into which they have been deployed qualify as beneficiaries because of the broad protection mandate of peacekeepers, others interviewed did not seem to share this broad definition.[71] As the experiences in Timor-Leste and Bosnia will show in the next chapter, the reality in peace operations is that these ambiguous relationships are relatively common and pose challenges to the development of appropriate responses by international organizations, to the international community's capacity to achieve its goals, and to its perceived credibility within host communities.

Putting aside questions of the appropriate regulation of transactional and other relationships between consenting adults, it is clear that transactional sex economies arise in situations of poverty and insecurity, where wars have contributed to the dissolution of the social, familial, and economic structures that might provide protection from exploitation, especially for children. Jane Holl Lute, as the assistant UN secretary-general for peacekeeping operations, said that her "operating presumption is that this is either an ongoing or potential problem in every single one of our missions."[72] Because the economic push factors for survival sex are high in many peace operations, some interveners have interpreted transactional sex and the associated relationships as being driven by local women, who "enthusiastically" compete to attract peacekeepers.[73] However, it is evident that the underlying structural conditions of poverty and the unequal power dynamics between interveners and locals creates a permissive environment in which transactional sex economies can thrive. As Sarah Spencer argues, in the context of the distorted power dynamics present in conflict, the expression of agency involved in exchanging sex for material goods or protection masks the fact that "these exploitative circumstances do not involve real choices" and it can cause harm for the locals involved.[74] Regardless, despite being prohibited by the zero tolerance bulletin, not all transactional sex is criminal; it is only criminal when it involves children or when it involves prostitution in jurisdictions where national laws prohibit it.

Networked Abuse and Exploitation

One of the most alarming revelations that emerged from the international interventions in the former Yugoslavia in the 1990s was the involvement of peacekeepers and associated personnel in the sex trafficking of women from neighboring countries into Kosovo and Bosnia. Just as the arrival of peacekeepers in Cambodia vastly increased the demand for sex "services," so too did the arrival of the international intervention in Bosnia and Kosovo drive a rapid expansion of the sex industry. International personnel, particularly soldiers from the Stabilisation Force in Bosnia and Herzegovina (SFOR), accounted for an estimated 70 percent of the profits made from prostitution in Bosnia and an estimated 30 to 50 percent of the clients in brothels, and it is estimated that the vast majority of women working in brothels patronized by interveners were trafficked.[75] International personnel—particularly American DynCorp private contractors deployed as the US contribution to the UN peace operation's police component, but also other military and police peacekeepers—were implicated in the use of prostitutes, in trafficking women to work in brothels, in purchasing women and girls as sex slaves, and, in some cases, in purchasing illegal weapons from brothel owners and covering up illegal activities.[76]

There is even evidence that UN peacekeepers patronized brothels being operated out of Serb-run concentration camps outside Sarajevo during the war.[77] Officials have testified that there was no "legitimate" sex industry separate from trafficking and forced prostitution, and that that fact was "not acknowledged or [was] disregarded by many UN peacekeepers who involved themselves with prostitution in Bosnia. Others knowingly become deeply involved in the sex slave trade in partnership with organized crime."[78] Similar accounts of trafficking and sex slavery emerged in relation to Kosovo Force (KFOR) personnel, and in both Kosovo and Bosnia, evidence suggests that neither sex trafficking nor forced prostitution was an issue before the arrival of international interveners.[79] It is important to note that research has shown that peacekeeping economies like this tend to outlast peacekeeping operations, "shaping gendered economic and social power relations in the long term" and embedding sex work and trafficking in the postwar economy.[80] The primary research conducted in Timor-Leste and Bosnia, discussed in the following chapters, will illuminate this particular point further.

The connection with criminal networks makes this form of sexual misconduct distinct from transactional sex. Interveners not only interact with middlemen or criminal networks to access the women (as distinct from the more direct negotiations that characterize transactional sex) but may also be engaged in profit-making themselves through their interaction with these networks. For instance, Italian peacekeepers allegedly ran child prostitution rings from their barracks in Sarajevo, while Ukrainian peacekeepers supplemented their small income by smuggling alcohol, contraband, and women and setting up a brothel that was largely patronized by other peacekeepers.[81] In Eritrea, a peacekeeper from the UN Mission in Ethiopia and Eritrea was found guilty of producing pornographic movies with a local woman, and in Somalia Belgian soldiers allegedly bought a teenage girl as a birthday present for a paratrooper and forced her to perform a sexualized show and have sex with two soldiers.[82] In Timor-Leste, the increased demand for sex services after the arrival of the UN Transitional Administration in East Timor (UNTAET) led to the emergence of an internationalized sex industry, with women being trafficked from Thailand, China, and other regional states.[83] This suggests that even where interveners themselves are not involved in trafficking, they may be implicated in networked sexual abuse and exploitation by virtue of patronizing brothels that "own" trafficked women.

The close links between this form of sexual misconduct by interveners and global criminal networks as well as the extensive coordination involved in these trades distinguishes this type of behavior from the others discussed. The centrality of profit-making, either by interveners or the networks they become entangled with, and the planned nature of this form of misconduct is crucial to understanding why it has been so prevalent in international interventions and what factors create the permissive environments in which it has flourished.

Why Do Different Forms of Sexual Misconduct Emerge?

This analysis of the forms that sexual exploitation and abuse take in peace operations demonstrates that incidences of misconduct are distinguishable on the basis of the extent to which they were perpetrated opportunistically, there was a level of negotiation or transaction involved, they were connected to profit-oriented criminal networks, or they were sadistic and planned. What is also clear from this discussion is that while there is great variation between these four general forms of misconduct, there are some areas of overlap—such as the blurry line between transactional sex and opportunistic rape, which is complicated even further by often opaque and inconsistent investigative and recording processes. However, paradoxically, it also suggests that the differences between these behaviors are perhaps greater than the overarching descriptor sexual exploitation and abuse suggests: while they are all united by the sexual nature of the behaviors involved, the behaviors are only loosely related in practice—rape is a world away from negotiated, consensual transactional sex, even in a context of unequal power dynamics, and sex trafficking for personal profit is markedly different from sadistic sexual torture.

In the following chapters, one of the questions I will consider is whether these different forms of sexual misconduct have had different impacts on peacebuilding outcomes, and on the international community's capacity and credibility in peace operations. For now, however, it is important to consider what factors give rise to these various forms of sexually exploitative and abusive behaviors.

A range of contextual factors is often mobilized in order to rationalize the perpetration of sexual exploitation and abuse by interveners in peace operations. For instance, officials and policymakers point variously to the difficult deployment conditions for peacekeepers, the lack of recreational facilities, inadequate rest and recuperation provisions, and sometimes simply the assertion that "boys will be boys" and that soldiers deployed into such difficult conditions need to destress somehow, echoing Akashi's statements in Cambodia.[84] The corollary of this is that sometimes standing orders relating to fraternization, alcohol consumption, and curfews—or, more recently, increasing the proportion of women deployed to peace operations—are presented as ways to limit sexual exploitation and abuse.[85] Nordås and Rustad's analysis of thirty-six peace operations between 1999 and 2010 identified a range of other contextual factors that increase the likelihood of sexual exploitation and abuse by peacekeepers.[86] These include a history of high levels of conflict-related sexual violence, lower economic development (which increases the push factors for transactional sex), and the deployment of peace operations into contexts with lower levels of battle-related deaths (possibly because peacekeepers deployed into such contexts have greater interaction with local populations than those deployed into contexts with higher levels of battle-related deaths, which are normally subject to stricter security arrangements). Moreover, they found that misconduct was more likely to occur in larger operations, possibly because of the challenges such operations face with regard to monitoring and controlling soldiers. This finding is echoed by Stephen Moncrief's analysis of sexual exploitation and assault allegations from 2007 to 2014, which suggested that disciplinary breakdowns at the peacekeeping mission's lower levels of command are associated with higher levels of sexual misconduct.[87] Keith Allred has linked the perpetration of sexual misconduct to the perception among peacekeepers that they have immunity from prosecution, which derives from the jurisdictional arrangements between TCCs, the UN, and the host country.[88]

My analysis above reiterates the relevance of many of these contextual factors, showing that the presence of large displaced civilian populations, a context of conflict-related sexual violence, the separation of families, and the breakdown of normal social safety nets may increase vulnerability to sexual exploitation and abuse. It also highlights the roles played by peacekeeping economies that are based on material inequality between interveners and locals and the particular vulnerabilities women and children face in such contexts. The presence of existing criminal networks may also contribute. However, these contextual factors alone cannot explain the pervasiveness and patterns of sexual misconduct by interveners in peace operations.

The sexual nature of the behaviors that the category "sexual exploitation and abuse" encompasses, along with the fact that they are perpetrated predominantly, if not exclusively, by men, suggests that they are underpinned by constructs of gender that make the sexual abuse and exploitation of locals an important element of the performance of masculinity among male interveners in peace operations. By understanding sexual violence as an act related to social power and by locating gender practices as embedded within "a historically located hierarchical system of differentiation which privileges those defined as masculine at the expense of those defined as feminine," we can see that sexual exploitation and abuse as a practice is irrevocably tied up with gendered power dynamics and performances of masculinity.[89] This view is bolstered by accounts by peacekeepers themselves: peacekeepers have told researchers that they need to prove they are not homosexual by "going out and getting a woman," that disciplining soldiers for sexual harassment "[limits] the military's capacity to produce effective soldiers," and that they need to "satisfy" their sex drives as a fundamental component of their masculinity.[90] Moreover, it may be that the traditionally civilian tasks that soldiers are now being asked to perform in contemporary multidimensional peace operations—in contrast to the combat roles they are conditioned for—contribute to undermining their sense of identity as soldiers and give rise to behaviors including the sexual exploitation and abuse of the local population or the harassment or abuse of other members or units of the UN mission.[91] In this vein, Karim and Beardsley have argued that the militarization processes inherent to peace operations produce gender power imbalances, which in turn manifest as acts of sexual exploitation, abuse, and harassment.[92] Scholars have also demonstrated how the production of hegemonic masculinities more generally in contemporary society embeds the dominant position of men over women, thereby facilitating sexual violence even outside of militarized contexts—for instance, as perpetrated by aid workers in the cases discussed above.[93] However, as Paul Kirby has shown, understanding gender orders and structures such as masculinity or patriarchy as being causally responsible for the perpetration of sexual misconduct may inadvertently mask both the individual and collective moral responsibility for it: individual men make choices about their sexual behaviors, and groups can act as bystanders, facilitators, and beneficiaries of those behaviors.[94] It is therefore necessary to go beyond a gender analysis to understand the broader range of factors that can help explain the phenomenon of sexual exploitation and abuse in peace operations.

Marsha Henry's analysis of peacekeeper misconduct highlights the range of explanations that have been marshaled to explain conflict-related sexual violence and military prostitution in feminist scholarship: military cultures, the politics of race in civilian-military relations, the role of international relations and international governments in perpetuating systems of military prostitution, the economies shaped by military presence, and the intersection of interests between international and local actors in the control of women's sexuality and bodies.[95] Most of these were also apparent in the analysis above of the different types of sexual misconduct in peace operations, which demonstrated that permissive factors are distinguishable in each of the types of behavior examined. Opportunistic sexual assault is facilitated by the intersection of military cultures, gendered norms of sexual behavior, and the unregulated situations into which peacekeepers are deployed. Transactional sex economies develop in the context of deprivation, poverty, and material inequality between interveners and locals, where survival sex is seen by civilians as a way to secure basic needs. Networked abuse and exploitation occurs in an unregulated profit-seeking context where criminal trafficking or prostitution networks exist and can prosper by co-opting interveners in their operations—and is backstopped by the long and institutionalized history of military prostitution. As Cynthia Enloe has argued, "There is nothing inherent in international peacekeeping operations that makes soldiers immune to the sort of sexism that has fuelled military prostitution in wartime and peacetime."[96] And the sadistic, planned instances of sexual abuse appear driven by opportunism, the perversions of individuals working in unregulated environments, and the shadows of colonial violence. In her analysis of this last form of sexual abuse as perpetrated by Canadian peacekeepers in Somalia, Sherene Razack argued that the racialized and sexualized violence bore the hallmarks of a colonial encounter, and in a later study she found such violence to be ubiquitous to peace operations "from Somalia to Bosnia" and posits it as the product of latent coloniality in the peacekeeping project.[97] Henry has similarly shown that the "racial features and colonial power relations of the peacekeeping encounter" are crucial to understanding sexual exploitation an abuse by peacekeepers more broadly, particularly in relation to transactional sex or networked exploitation.[98] The relevance of coloniality is underlined by the explanation given by the French MONUC civilian peacekeeper who admitted to having sex with twenty-four underage girls in 2004—he said, "Over there, the colonial spirit persists. The white man gets what he wants."[99]

By moving beyond a gender analysis, we can see that a range of local, international, normative, and systemic factors intersect with gender orders and structures to create the conditions under which sexual misconduct is perpetrated in a number of distinguishable forms. This indicates that particular contexts do not directly cause particular types of misconduct, but rather the conditions for all four types of sexual exploitation and abuse coexist in most peacekeeping (and humanitarian emergency) contexts: it is the way the local, international, normative, and systemic factors interact with one another and with peacekeeping operations that gives rise to the quite distinct forms misconduct takes and the varying levels of perpetration in particular contexts. Understanding these intersections and interactions is crucial to developing robust policy responses that are responsive to the various forms of sexual misconduct, and, more important for this book, to understanding the impacts such behavior has on peacebuilding outcomes.

Intersecting Issues: Sexual Exploitation and Abuse, Conflict-Related Sexual Violence, and Sexual Harassment and Abuse

One of the most striking things that this analysis of the nature and causes of sexual exploitation and abuse by interveners illuminates is the parallels and interconnections between sexual misconduct and conflict-related sexual violence, and between sexual misconduct and harassment and abuse within the intervener community. Unpacking these connections helps us understand more about the role contextual factors play in amplifying vulnerability to sexual exploitation and abuse as well as the ways different actors (i.e., military and civilian) perpetrate it in different ways, with different permissive or causal factors at work. This in turn provides a more robust foundation from which to investigate first the impacts of sexual misconduct on peacebuilding outcomes, and second the ways in which policy responses might better address the issue.

Conflict-Related Sexual Violence

Conflict-related sexual violence, according to the UN, encompasses any act of "rape, sexual slavery, forced prostitution, forced pregnancy, enforced sterilization and other forms of sexual violence of comparable gravity perpetrated against women, men, girls or boys that is linked, directly or indirectly (temporally, geographically or causally) to a conflict."[100] In practice, this means that perpetrators tend to be affiliated with an armed group or entity that is party to the conflict, that the victims tend to be an actual or perceived member of a persecuted minority or opposing group, and that the act of conflict-related sexual violence takes place either in a conflict context or in an conflict-adjacent context such as a displacement camp. It also encompasses human trafficking for sexual exploitation committed in situations of conflict. Crucially, although the majority of victims of conflict-related sexual violence are women and girls, there is a growing awareness of the scale of such violence against men and boys in conflicts as well.[101]

As discussed earlier in this chapter, acts of sexual violence by soldiers may be perpetrated strategically, as weapons of war, but they may also be perpetrated opportunistically or as practices of war that are tolerated—or sometimes even encouraged—by political or military leadership for a variety of reasons. The discussion above about opportunistic sexual abuse by interveners demonstrates that there are clear similarities between conflict-related sexual violence and some forms of sexual exploitation and abuse; the primary difference is that conflict-related sexual violence is perpetrated as part of a conflict, whereas sexual exploitation and abuse is perpetrated by interveners as part of a peace process, albeit one that occurs in the context of violent conflicts where conflict-related sexual violence is often common. In fact, some have suggested that sexual exploitation and abuse should be seen as a form of conflict-related sexual violence and addressed within the same conceptual and policy frameworks.[102] There are, however, risks in subsuming sexual exploitation and abuse responses under conflict-related sexual violence frameworks and policies. First, in order to develop effective policy responses, our understanding of these connected but different forms of violence must be robust and dynamic. Lumping peacekeepers and aid workers who engage in sexual exploitation and abuse into the same category as soldiers or rebels who engage in sexual violence is problematic as it papers over (a) the very real differences in the nature of the actors involved (those whose mandate is warmaking and those whose mandate is peacemaking), (b) the somewhat different factors that contribute to perpetration, and (c) the policy responses required. Second, victims' accounts suggest that the violence carries with it different meanings when perpetrated by those who have been sent to protect. One victim's advocate in Timor-Leste, when describing the differences between the well documented conflict-related sexual violence perpetrated by Indonesian soldiers during the twenty-four-year occupation of Timor-Leste and the (admittedly rare) cases of rape by peacekeepers, told me, "We knew the Indonesian soldiers hated us, we didn't think that the peacekeepers did too."[103] While it is important not to collapse sexual exploitation and abuse under the umbrella of conflict-related sexual violence, I think that there are some very important intersections between the two that help explain the way the latter creates and consolidates the factors of vulnerability, as well as the permissive causal factors, that contribute to the perpetration of sexual misconduct by interveners in peace operations.

Earlier in this chapter, the story of thirteen-year old Faela in the Democratic Republic of Congo showed how the prior experience of conflict-related sexual violence could lead to displacement, isolation from family networks, and pregnancy, which make young women particularly vulnerable to sexual exploitation and abuse when interveners arrive as part of a peace operation. Rape and other forms of sexual assault—whether opportunistic or preplanned—have received perhaps the greatest amount of attention in the literature on conflict-related sexual violence, likely due to the high prevalence of this form of sexual violence. In many cases, they have similar impacts to those described by Faela: a global overview of conflict-related sexual violence between 1987 and 2007 found that sexual violence has serious socioeconomic implications for survivors, as a result of stigmatization by and marginalization in their communities.[104] The report found that this could lead to poverty, unemployment, and social exclusion, all of which make survivors particularly vulnerable to sexual exploitation and human trafficking more broadly. Furthermore, it found that conflict-related sexual violence is one of the factors that can exacerbate the prevalence of violence within families, including sexual violence, which may also fracture community and family ties and lead to stigmatization and victims leaving their families. There are also structural implications that may increase vulnerability to sexual exploitation and abuse by interveners: impunity for conflict-related sexual violence can consolidate a tolerance of such acts against women and children, which can be a further permissive factor for such misconduct by interveners.[105] A number of the victims whose voices were included earlier in this chapter suggested that once they "lost" their "honor" as a result of conflict-related sexual violence, they sought out transactional sex with interveners as a way to address their poverty because they had nothing left to lose. All of these socioeconomic and structural implications are, of course, in addition to the often grave and long-term consequences conflict-related sexual violence can have for victims' physical and psychological health.

What this shows is the importance of understanding the broader factors and processes that create the conditions under which certain individuals or groups are particularly vulnerable to sexual abuse or exploitation by interveners when a peace operation is deployed. These will be crucial both to understanding whether the impacts of sexual exploitation and abuse by interveners compounds the personal, social, and structural impacts of previous abuses and violations and to the development of effective prevention mechanisms based on the particular vulnerabilities at play in specific contexts.

Sexual Harassment and Abuse within the Humanitarian Sector

The second issue that intersects with sexual exploitation and abuse by interveners and that can help shed light on the factors contributing to its perpetration is sexual harassment and abuse within the intervener community. Despite the commonly held assumption that sexual misconduct is perpetrated primarily by military peacekeepers, the evidence available shows that while military peacekeepers are more responsible overall for allegations of misconduct, civilian peacekeepers are more responsible per capita for allegations.[106] This reflects the far greater numbers of military personnel deployed in a peace operation, but it also raises an important question about how we can understand the perpetration of sexual exploitation and abuse by civilian interveners in contrast to that perpetrated by military interveners. Comprehensive data on the perpetration of sexual misconduct by non-UN civilian staff is not available, which is one of the reasons that this particular aspect of the phenomenon is so under-studied.

However, sexual harassment and abuse by civilian interveners against their colleagues in the humanitarian community has been subject to some investigation and can help shed light on sexual misconduct perpetrated in parallel by the same group of interveners against local communities. A number of surveys have been conducted on the experiences of aid workers in relation to sexual harassment and assault.[107] These, along with growing media attention to stories of abuse against humanitarians, has meant that some victim testimony is available on the nature and perpetration of sexual harassment and abuse by interveners against their colleagues and the factors that underpin such behaviors. My analysis here will look at these issues in turn before reflecting on the broader implications of this particular set of sexually inappropriate behaviors for our understanding of sexual misconduct by civilian interveners in peace operations. It is worth noting that, while there are some accounts of abuse by uniformed peacekeepers against their civilian and military counterparts, the bulk of information available on this issue relates to abuse and harassment perpetrated by civilian peacekeepers and other civilian interveners against their civilian colleagues. This does not necessarily reflect prevalence but rather the constraints of collecting more comprehensive data on this phenomenon. Furthermore, while female humanitarians have faced sexual harassment and assault at the hands of local men not associated with peace operations or humanitarian organizations, this falls outside the purview of this book as it does not relate to sexual exploitation and abuse by interveners but rather speaks to the prevalence of sexual violence globally in general and the particular vulnerabilities facing women working in conflict contexts.[108]

In July 2015, the *Guardian* published a short article by Megan Nobert, who recounted that while working for a humanitarian organization in South Sudan she was drugged and raped by a fellow member of the humanitarian community, who was working for a subcontractor employed by a UN agency.[109] The response to Nobert's assault was poor, due to a range of factors including the inadequacy of legal or administrative frameworks to address assault by an employee of a UN subcontractor, the absence of a useful local accountability framework, inadequate response processes by her employer, and what seemed to be the unwillingness of the UN's Office of Internal Oversight to investigate the case before significant media pressure developed.[110] As a result, Nobert set up the NGO Report the Abuse, to collect accounts of sexual violence against humanitarians and promote the development of better policies and mechanisms to address such violence within organizations and at the global level. Around the same time, the Humanitarian Women's Network and the Feinstein International Centre were investigating the same issues, conducting broad surveys of women's experiences of sexual harassment and abuse while on deployment in peace operations. More recently, the UN secretary-general commissioned a survey on sexual harassment within the UN, which was conducted by Deloitte and released in early 2019. The testimonies and data collected, along with the ad hoc media reporting on sexual harassment and abuse experienced by humanitarians, illuminate a few key themes that are of use in our understanding of sexual misconduct by civilian interveners against local populations, given that they relate to the same broad group of perpetrators.

The first trend that emerges is the pervasiveness of sexual harassment and, to a slightly lesser extent, sexual aggression and assault against female humanitarians by other interveners while on mission. It is worth noting that the behaviors reported fall under these more limited categories rather than the broader set of categories described above in relation to sexual exploitation and abuse. I have not come across cases of sexual exploitation or transactional sex in the evidence available; this may reflect gaps in the data, but I suspect it reflects the different circumstances and vulnerabilities that expatriate female humanitarians face, in comparison with those faced by local women and children, or even their national staff counterparts. Moreover, sexual harassment falls outside the boundaries of what is considered sexual exploitation and abuse in the zero-tolerance policy, and in most organizations is dealt with under a completely separate policy framework, although, as chapter 2 will show, some host communities see it as part and parcel of sexual exploitation and abuse.

Since Nobert's story of her rape broke in international media, it has become clear that, although horrifying, her experience was not unique. Other female aid workers have since recounted similar stories, including being drugged or plied with alcohol and then raped by their boss or colleagues; being forced to perform oral sex on colleagues; being raped by a colleague while on the way to the latrine when on assignment in a community; fighting off colleagues attempting to assault them at parties, hotels, or in their shared homes; being so scared of colleagues that they slept with a cricket bat for safety; having male colleagues from other organizations enter their tent while they slept and rape them; and being fired after reporting being raped by colleagues.[111] In addition to these accounts of sexual assault, myriad accounts of sexual harassment were documented, including women being promised jobs in return for sex, being groped or touched inappropriately both at work and in social contexts by colleagues, or experiencing verbal sexual harassment.[112] In all of these anecdotes, women reported experiencing this behavior primarily from male colleagues in their organization but also from men working with other civilian agencies and organizations in their country of deployment—in only a few cases did women specify that the man involved was a local staff member; in most cases they referred to international staff. So, anecdotally, it appears that many humanitarian women experience sexual harassment and assault at the hands of fellow international interveners, but what information do we have about the prevalence of these behaviors within intervener communities?

The Humanitarian Women's Network surveyed of over one thousand women working in the humanitarian field, covering respondents from seventy organizations across the NGO, UN, and private sectors.[113] The survey found that over two thirds of women had experienced some form of sexual harassment, and that of these, over half reported that it came from a male supervisor. Furthermore, around half had experienced sexual aggression and/or assault, with 4 percent reporting they had been raped.[114] Respondents reported that male colleagues committed all of these acts, and one third of women reported that the perpetrator was a male supervisor, highlighting the relevance of power in our understanding of sexually inappropriate behaviors. It is important to note that although international and national staff were equally represented in respondents reporting rape, national staff reported more cases of multiple experiences of rape than their international counterparts.[115] The vast majority of cases reported across all categories took place in missions in sub-Saharan Africa. The scale of sexual harassment and abuse suggested by the

Humanitarian Women's Network survey is broadly corroborated by the survey conducted by Report the Abuse with over 1400 respondents, 96 percent of whom were international humanitarian staff. Of those respondents, nearly three quarters had experienced sexual violence, nearly 90 percent knew a colleague who had experienced such violence, and the vast majority knew and worked with their attacker.[116] The 2019 Deloitte study of individuals working in the UN system and related entities globally found somewhat different results, which is understandable given the different nature of the survey—unlike the other surveys discussed, the 2019 survey included both men and women and included only those within the UN system. There were 30,364 respondents, which represented 17 percent of all relevant personnel, and there was an almost equal representation of men and women. Nearly 39 percent of respondents had experienced some form of sexual harassment while working with the UN. Women were 1.7 times more likely to report experiencing sexual harassment, while transgender, binary gender non-conforming, and those who identified as "other" were 2.1 times more likely to report sexual harassment. Although this survey finds a lower rate of experiences of harassment among women than previous studies that included respondents from both the UN and other organizations, that rate was nonetheless high, at approximately 42 percent of respondents.[117]

These statistics are helpful, although their opt-in nature and methodological limitations mean that they cannot be generalized to aid workers who did not respond to the surveys. Nevertheless, they do suggest, in conjunction with media reports on this issue, that sexual harassment and abuse by male humanitarian workers against their female colleagues is a pervasive issue in the context of peace operations. This has severe consequences not only for the women directly involved but also for the humanitarian community as a result of women opting to leave this field of work to avoid future harassment and abuse.[118] Furthermore, this data demonstrates that sexually abusive behaviors are not solely the purview of soldiers deployed into peace operations; rather, they are perpetrated extensively also by international humanitarian staff against their colleagues, both international and national. It is unsurprising, then, that the UN data mentioned earlier shows that civilian personnel in peace operations are also responsible for high rates of sexual exploitation and abuse against local communities.

The second trend that emerges from the data available on sexual harassment and abuse within intervener communities is that systems for responding to these behaviors are inadequate. This data helps shed light on why so little information is available about the perpetration of sexual exploitation and abuse by civilian personnel, why many civilian humanitarians may decide not to report suspected sexual misconduct by colleagues against local populations, and why individuals with long histories of inappropriate sexual behaviors may continue to work in the sector without being held accountable for their actions.

Of the women who responded to the Humanitarian Women's Network survey, 69 percent did not report the harassment, aggression, or assault they experienced at the hands of colleagues for a range of reasons that includes concern about professional consequences, the feeling that it was not "serious" or "violent" enough to report, a lack of trust in the system and those in positions to respond, and the paucity of reporting mechanisms and appropriate evidentiary standards, as well as shame, fear of reprisals by their aggressor, or the instruction not to report because of cultural considerations.[119] Report the Abuse, the Feinstein International Centre, and Deloitte found similar reasons for low reporting rates—the latter also found that a sexist or misogynistic work setting, patterns of victim-blaming, and failures to take allegations seriously contribute to low reporting rates and that victims often only choose to report harassment and abuse if they are confident that accountability mechanisms are trustworthy and proper medical and psychological care will be provided.[120] It is not a great leap to assume that similar factors prevent the reporting of abuse perpetrated by civilian interveners against local individuals.

Perhaps most surprisingly, when Report the Abuse conducted a review of the policies of ninety-two UN agencies, INGOs, and governmental bodies, it found that only 16 percent of them had any strategy, policy, or procedures to respond to sexual violence against their employees; this underscores why so many victims opt out of formal reporting processes.[121] Furthermore, of those who did formally report abuse and harassment, most were unsatisfied with the responses: in nearly half of the cases, nothing happened; in only 10 percent of cases were women given social support or referred for psychological support; and in 22 percent of cases women reported suffering negative professional consequences themselves as a consequence of reporting.[122] These issues that discourage reporting suggest that there is an underlying problem with the way organizations understand the nature and impact of sexual harassment and abuse on their employees. In fact, existing prevention strategies, including training and security advice, largely place the onus on women themselves for minimizing the risks they may face while on deployment, despite the fact that the causes of such abuse and harassment have little to do with the choices women themselves make.[123] The cultural and organizational factors that result in organizations responding to sexually abusive and inappropriate behaviors by staff against colleagues in this way likely function in similar ways to prevent the establishment and maintenance of robust prevention and accountability mechanisms for sexual exploitation and abuse by interveners against local communities.

This foreshadows the final trend that emerges from the data and literature on sexual harassment within intervener communities, which relates to the contextual factors that create environments in which such behaviors flourish and are perpetrated also against local communities. These do, in many ways, mirror the factors discussed above in relation to sexual exploitation and abuse by interveners, suggesting that these behaviors are two sides of the same coin. In their anonymous account of sexual abuse and harassment, three women aid workers argued that

> What makes female humanitarians particularly vulnerable to abuse is the fact that we work, socialise, and live with our co-workers; we live in volatile environments where laws and rules are broken regularly, and expatriates can often act with impunity. We're far removed from normal society, and some men seem to be emboldened to behave in ways they never would at home. In many places where we work, legal justice and accountability rarely occur because the structures simply do not exist.[124]

The authors also highlight that factors like isolation, lack of communication, cultural clashes, long work hours, and alcohol and drugs contribute to creating an environment where harassment and abuse happens. Dyan Mazurana and Phoebe Donnelly confirmed these suggestions in their extensive qualitative research on the issue, identifying three key environmental factors.[125] First, they found that sexism, machismo, and male domination in the humanitarian sector, which fosters a "boys will be boys" culture, is critical to creating environments in which sexual harassment and abuse of colleagues is so pervasive. Second, the broader environment into which humanitarian operations are deployed—in which there is often a breakdown of law and order and a prevalence of sexual assaults against women more broadly—contributes to these behaviors. And lastly, the high rates of alcohol and drug consumption and associated party culture, which are often used as stress-relief mechanisms for aid workers, create contexts in which women are particularly vulnerable to abuse and harassment.

These three trends are illuminating not only in relation to sexual harassment and abuse within the intervener community but also in terms of understanding sexual misconduct perpetrated by male civilian interveners against local communities. First, the cultures that facilitate such pervasive sexual harassment within organizations will not stop at the boundaries of those organizations, and it is conceivable that perpetrators are likely to also treat local women in similar ways. Interviews in Timor-Leste suggested this was the case and that there was a widespread culture of street harassment of local women in particular, by both military and civilian interveners, as will be discussed in the next chapter. Second, many women who recounted their experiences in the studies discussed above mentioned a culture of transactional sex, in particular commercial sex, with locals as part of their accounts of sexual harassment and abuse by male colleagues. Third, if reporting and accountability mechanisms are so poor in relation to abuse and harassment within organizations and given the structural and cultural factors noted above that further undermine responses, it is unsurprising that the very same organizations have trouble ensuring accountability for sexual misconduct perpetrated by their staff against locals. And finally, what this analysis shows is that the broader normative, cultural, and gendered factors that can explain sexual exploitation and abuse by military interveners are relevant also to understanding the factors that give rise to sexual misconduct by civilian interveners, both against local populations and against the people with whom they work—or, in other words, against their fellow interveners.

What is particularly useful about this information—despite the fact that it is limited—is that it is the first step in filling in a major gap in our understanding of sexual exploitation and abuse in peace operations. Significant scholarly and policy attention has been devoted to understanding why soldiers perpetrate sexual violence. This has produced valuable theoretical and conceptual frames through which we can make sense of sexual misconduct by military personnel in peace operations—for instance, by understanding the pressures and incentives created by militarized masculinities and the legacy of military prostitution. We do not, however, have a well-developed conceptual framework for understanding sexual misconduct perpetrated by civilian personnel, and this is partly because the data on sexual exploitation and abuse in peace operations is patchy and difficult to disaggregate, especially when considering nonpeacekeeping civilian personnel, such as those working in humanitarian organizations or as diplomats in the host state. Although it is beyond the purview of this book to develop such a conceptual framework in relation to sexual misconduct by civilian interveners, the analysis above makes some important first steps by drawing the links and identifying parallels between these different forms of sexually inappropriate and abusive behaviors and by indicating some of the permissive and/or causal factors that give rise to them. Being aware of the fact that civilian interveners are at least equally implicated in sexual exploitation and abuse in peace operations is critical to setting up adequate prevention and accountability mechanisms and to understanding the implications of misconduct by this group of interveners on peacebuilding outcomes, which is considered in the next chapter.

This chapter has shown that sexual exploitation and abuse encompasses a broad set of behaviors that are perpetrated by the range of interveners associated with peace operations. Understanding the variety of forms the category encompasses, the intersections between this category and other forms of sexual violence and abuse, and the contextual, normative, and systemic factors that give rise to them is crucial to understanding also the impacts such behaviors have on the individuals involved, the peace operations in question, and the broader capacity and credibility of the international community in peace operations. It is also critical to understanding the ways in which sexual misconduct overlaps and intersects with other peacekeeping challenges, how it can better be addressed, and why policy responses have not resulted in robust prevention and accountability mechanisms. The rest of this book is devoted to answering these questions.

2

SEXUAL EXPLOITATION AND ABUSE IN BOSNIA AND TIMOR-LESTE

The ways in which interveners in the peace operations in Bosnia and Timor-Leste engaged in sexually abusive and exploitative behaviors are illustrative of the forms of sexual misconduct and their complexities discussed in the last chapter. This chapter introduces the two case studies that underpin the analysis that animates the remainder of this book—an analysis of the long-term impacts of sexual exploitation and abuse. It develops a detailed account of the context, nature, and scale of sexual misconduct during peace operations in Bosnia and Timor-Leste, drawing extensively on primary research in the two countries. The behaviors spanned all four types of misconduct and were perpetrated by a variety of uniformed and civilian interveners, including peacekeepers and non-UN personnel associated with the international community's presence in each country. They confirm many of the trends identified in chapter 1 about patterns of perpetration and contributing factors. However, this analysis also demonstrates that the ways in which local communities experience sexual exploitation and abuse is grounded in historical experience, cultural norms, and, in many ways, the particular forms of material deprivation and conflict-related sexual violence experienced, with significant variation between what was considered inappropriate behavior in the two countries. In fact, in some cases, what members of these communities considered the most harmful forms of sexually inappropriate behaviors did not fall under the international community's definition of sexual exploitation and abuse as laid out in the zero-tolerance bulletin. Specifically, these were consensual sexual relationships between interveners and locals that resulted in children who were subsequently abandoned by their foreign fathers. As I have noted, such relationships are strongly discouraged under UN policy because of the "inherently unequal power dynamics" on which they are based, but they are not prohibited.[1]

These cases provide a valuable foundation for an investigation of the impacts of sexual misconduct on mission outcomes for a number of reasons. First, the experiences and scale of sexual exploitation and abuse in each country were quite distinct, despite similarities in mission size and objectives and the fact that both countries experienced high levels of conflict-related sexual violence prior to the deployment of international forces. Additionally, local perceptions of which sexual behaviors were inappropriate diverged significantly. These differences provide a valuable opportunity to investigate the differing patterns of misconduct in different contexts and the varying impacts it has both on mission outcomes and on the relationship between local communities and the international interveners deployed to protect and assist them during the transition from conflict to peace. The following sections will unpack the different experiences and types of sexual exploitation and abuse in each country, beginning with the peace operations in Bosnia before turning to the experiences in Timor-Leste.

Sexual Misconduct during Peace Operations in Bosnia

The peace operation in Bosnia gave rise to one of the earliest sexual misconduct scandals in UN peacekeeping, with revelations emerging in the late 1990s about the direct and indirect involvement of UN police in the trafficking of women to work as sex slaves in brothels frequented by both peacekeepers and local men. However, sexual exploitation and abuse by interveners in Bosnia began in earlier international deployments to the conflict zone.

International forces were first deployed into the former Yugoslavia in 1992 in order to help foster the conditions of peace and security required for a peace settlement, including through protecting civilians in the UN Protected Areas across the country, through securing the airport and facilitating humanitarian assistance to Sarajevo during the siege of the city, through monitoring a no-fly zone and demilitarization in certain zones, and through supporting the implementation of ceasefires as they were negotiated.[2] The UN Protection Force (UNPROFOR) included military, police, and civilian elements, numbering over 40,000 in total by 1995 (38,599 military personnel, 803 civilian police, 2017 international civilian staff and 2615 local civilian staff).[3] UNPROFOR was replaced in 1995 by the NATO-led multinational Implementation Force (IFOR), which was responsible for all military aspects of the implementation of the Dayton Agreement that bought an end to the violence in Bosnia in 1995.[4] A year later, IFOR was replaced by the multinational Stabilization Force (SFOR), which continued IFOR's work but with a much reduced personnel size.[5] IFOR/SFOR worked in concert with the UN International Police Task Force (IPTF) and the UN civilian office, which were brought together under the umbrella of the UN Mission in Bosnia and Herzegovina (UNMIBH).[6] A crucial element of the IPTF's makeup was that the American contribution was comprised of police recruited and employed by the private security company DynCorp International, which secured the contract to deploy police to the IPTF on behalf of the US, as the lack of a federal police force meant the US did not have the structures to deploy American police itself. All other contingents were deployed directly by the states that contributed them, as is the norm in peace operations.

Although the majority of accounts of sexual misconduct relate to the post-Dayton period, there are accounts of UNPROFOR peacekeepers engaging in sexually exploitative and abusive behaviors. For instance, there are reports, including by the UN, of some peacekeepers frequenting brothels that were being operated out of Serb-run concentration camps outside of Sarajevo.[7] A senior government official with a legal background and experience addressing war crimes similarly recounted that in one area under Serb control, Bosnian women and girls were raped and forced to provide sexual services to international forces—some of whom provided testimony about this but were not prosecuted.[8] This highlights the interconnection between conflict-related sexual violence and sexual abuse by interveners in the Bosnian context. There are also accounts of peacekeepers engaging in transactional sex with local women, particularly in the UN protected areas or on UN bases.[9] A key factor fueling this was the extreme deprivation faced by local families during the war, which drove women to offer sex for food, water, and other essentials to provide for their families. One interviewee who lived in Sarajevo during the siege and worked extensively with the international community both during and after the war recounted the pain of working in the office of an international NGO where there were boxes of tinned food under her desk, even though locals could not access enough food to feed their families. After she finally stole some canned fish to feed her family, she was confronted the next morning by her boss and the organization's security advisor, accused of thieving, and warned not to do it again or she would lose her job. "The peacekeepers had everything, and we had nothing," she said. "We were starving; we had no food. I would have done anything for food."[10]

This sentiment was echoed by two local researchers who had investigated local narratives of war, which included many accounts of transactional sex with peacekeepers that were never shared with younger generations because of the shame involved.[11] One of the researchers recalled her own experiences during and after the war, when she would run with other children to UN peacekeepers and ask for candy ("gummi, gummi?"); the peacekeepers would respond asking the children to bring their mothers ("mummy, mummy?"), implying that the children should bring their mothers for sex. In addition to sexual exploitation, peacekeepers were involved in a variety of other illegal activities, including the smuggling of humans, goods, alcohol, and drugs.[12]

These patterns of transactional sex continued in the postwar period with the successive peacekeeping deployments and the influx of other interveners into Bosnia, at a time when Bosnians remained very poor and therefore vulnerable to such exploitation.[13] Some interviewees suggested that such behaviors should not necessarily be seen as inappropriate because they were generally accepted as a necessary strategy of survival by local communities and likely "saved many lives" by providing desperate families with food and other essentials and by building connections between locals and the international forces.[14] Nevertheless, while transactional sex was apparently quite common and fairly widely accepted as a survival mechanism, there was and remains a strong culture of silence and shame around it, which prevented women from speaking about their experiences. To illustrate this, one interviewee recounted a joke often told during the Sarajevo siege:

> There was a common joke at the time, where a kid asks, "Daddy, what is de facto and what is de jure?" And the dad says, "if a UN soldier asks for your mum to sleep with him for 100DM, she will do it. And then if he asks also for your sister to sleep with him for 100DM, she will do it too. De jure, we have 200DM. De facto, we have two whores in the house." Compared to all the other stuff going on in the city, this didn't seem too bad.[15]

I will return to these cultures of silence around sexual exploitation and abuse and their implications shortly.

In the aftermath of the war, the nature of sexual misconduct by international interveners shifted from primarily an engagement in transactional sex economies, with some notable exceptions as described above, to human trafficking, forced prostitution, and slavery. The involvement of American DynCorp contractors deployed to the IPTF was revealed through the work of IPTF whistleblowers Kathryn Bolkovac and Ben Johnston, and by Madeline Rees, who at the time was head of the Office of the High Commissioner for Human Rights in Bosnia. The news of the involvement of DynCorp personnel in sexual exploitation and abuse soon led to a broader awareness of such behaviors by other IPTF personnel. Women and girls were trafficked from neighboring states to work as sex slaves in brothels patronized by both peacekeeping personnel and local men—experts estimate that at least 70 percent of brothel profits came from foreign men, even though they made up only 30 percent of customers.[16] In addition, some DynCorp IPTF personnel became involved in the trafficking networks and in protecting those who ran them.[17] The trafficked women and girls were often starved, beaten, tortured, and kept in horrific living conditions. When IPTF raids against brothels were conducted, some victims recognized IPTF officers involved in the raids as their clients and abusers, and in some cases, evidence collected against men who ran trafficking and forced prostitution networks included detailed documentation of IPTF personnel who regularly attended their brothels.[18] Human Rights Watch also documented the involvement of peacekeepers deployed in later missions, particularly DynCorp contractors to SFOR, in trafficking.[19]

The networked exploitation of women and children by interveners also included buying and selling them as slaves. According to Liliana Sorrentino, an independent expert on human rights, migration, and modern-day slavery, some were held in domestic servitude after being bought at the Arizona Market in Brčko, a town in the north of the country on the Croatian border, while others were held in sexual slavery.[20] Ben Johnston, one of the original whistleblowers on IPTF involvement in sexual exploitation and abuse, made his initial reports after hearing his American DynCorp colleagues boasting about buying and selling women and girls for sex, bragging about the ages and talents of their "slaves," and extolling the benefits of having a sex slave at home.[21] Human Rights Watch has also extensively documented this phenomenon: numerous interveners, including IPTF and SFOR personnel and contractors, were found to have purchased women and girls (and their passports) from brothel owners or other traffickers and forced them to live as sex slaves in their private residences; some also purchased illegal weapons and at least one was involved in making a pornographic film while raping a woman.[22] The Human Rights Watch Report documented that perpetrators included men deployed to the international mission from Spain, France, Britain, Mexico, Fiji, Pakistan, Russia, and Argentina.

These behaviors appear to have been fairly normalized and included the active sharing of purchased women among work units and even with superiors—this included, for example, Pakistani IPTF monitors purchasing women and then providing them to the "chief" of the Pakistani contingent, who served also as chief of the IPTF internal investigations unit.[23] The UN, according to Human Rights Watch, subsequently transferred the official out of the investigations unit.

It is also important to note the prevalence of another sexual exploitation and abuse–adjacent form of behavior that was prevalent in Bosnia in the aftermath of the war, namely, consensual relationships between adults (primarily local women and expatriate men), which have been discouraged, but not prohibited, by sexual misconduct policies since 2003 because of the unequal power dynamics involved. As discussed in the previous chapter, these relationships fall into a murky middle ground because of the presence of both consensual and transactional aspects. In Bosnia, research has shown how these relationships were shaped by a combination of factors, including both genuine romantic interest and the desire of some women involved to secure a better future for themselves or their families.[24]

While it is clear from these accounts that sexual exploitation and abuse was prevalent in Bosnia during international interventions during and after the war, it is impossible to identify the scale of such abuse and exploitation due to a variety of factors, including the lack of reporting and transparency. UN policies on sexual exploitation and abuse at the time were only nascent, having been put in place partway through the international engagement. Another factor is the pervasive culture of silence around the issue, which is strongly linked to the shame and stigma associated with conflict-related rape and sexual violence.[25] According to one local women's rights activist, after the war many people said that a true Bosniak (i.e. Bosnian Muslim) woman would rather kill herself than allow herself to be raped; this underlines how difficult it is for women to speak out about their experiences of wartime rape and how far the community has come in breaking the silence on wartime sexual violence.[26] Furthermore, Nela Porobic, a local researcher and activist of the Women's International League for Peace and Freedom in Bosnia, argued that the narrative of sexual exploitation and abuse by interveners in Bosnia against Bosnian women is an unwritten one. She suggested this is in large part because the Bosniak narrative of the Yugoslav war has come to focus heavily on their experiences of sexual violence at the hands of Serb soldiers, which necessitates a distinction between wartime sexual violence and what is seen as consensual transactional sex that happened with peacekeepers.[27]

This was not, however, the case in relation to women from neighboring states who were the victims of trafficking for and by international interveners. These women were often seen by native Bosnians as "consenting whores" who had chosen to be trafficked and therefore did not deserve sympathy or concern; in the view of many, the concerns of the trafficked women paled in comparison to the ongoing suffering of local Bosnians.[28] Others who worked in the trafficking response at the time had an alternative perspective: that "there is never any outrage in a post-war country. You've seen so much blood. We who survived the war are different to other humans."[29] Researchers also pointed out the hopelessness some locals felt in relation to the trafficking, particularly those within the women's networks who knew it was going on but felt there was nothing they could do because of the lack of reporting and accountability mechanisms in the international missions.[30] A number of factors contributed to this, including the involvement of senior IPTF officials in the abuse and exploitation of trafficked women, the fact that Bosnian police had no jurisdiction over peacekeeping personnel they found to be complicit in trafficking or sexual exploitation or abuse, and the direct involvement of some Bosnian police units in the networked exploitation of women and girls.[31] Although the UNMIBH repatriated eighteen international interveners on account of their involvement in sexual exploitation, not a single intervener was arrested and tried in Bosnia for these crimes (only a few local mafia members were tried), which compounded the sense that reporting was useless.[32] These various factors reinforced the culture of silence around sexual misconduct by interveners, and they provide some further context to the issues discussed in the previous chapter about the inadequacy of UN data in capturing rates of sexual exploitation and abuse.

Sexual Misconduct during Peace Operations in Timor-Leste

The experiences of intervener sexual exploitation and abuse during the peace operations in Timor-Leste differed substantially from those in Bosnia, despite the similarities in mission size and mandate and despite a similar personnel makeup of the deployment. This raises questions about the risk factors for sexual misconduct and picks up on issues discussed in the previous chapter. In contrast to the experiences in Bosnia, there was less transactional sex for food or other basic goods, but there were isolated cases of rape and significant engagement by peacekeepers in networked exploitation, including prostitution and the production of pornography. What was more prevalent, and what seemed to be of greater concern to the local community, were behaviors that do not satisfy the standards of sexual exploitation and abuse as set out in the zero-tolerance bulletin, namely street harassment and consensual relationships that broke down and resulted in women being abandoned with "peace babies" resulting from their relationships with peacekeepers.[33]

In 1999, the UN Mission in East Timor (UNAMET) organized and ran an independence referendum on the future relationship between Timor-Leste and Indonesia, which had annexed the region in 1975 after Portuguese colonial rule ended. The international community first deployed peacekeepers into Timor-Leste after an overwhelming vote in favor of independence from Indonesia was met with widespread violence, including sexual violence, perpetrated by Indonesian-backed militias who primarily targeted Timorese civilians. The crisis resulted in large-scale displacement and destruction across the territory and led to the Security Council adopting Resolution 1264, which expressed its concern "at reports indicating that systematic, widespread and flagrant violations of international humanitarian and human rights law have been committed in East Timor" and authorized the establishment of a multinational force in response.[34] The International Force in East Timor (INTERFET) was deployed four days later, led and largely staffed by the Australian Defence Force, although it included contributions from twenty-two other states. It numbered eleven thousand personnel at its peak and was mandated to restore peace and security in Timor-Leste, protect and support UNAMET in carrying out its work, and facilitate humanitarian assistance. INTERFET handed over military command and control responsibility five months later to the UN Transitional Administration in East Timor (UNTAET), which had been established by the Security Council in October 1999. It was mandated to administer the territory including through the provision of security and maintenance of law and order, exercise legislative and executive authority during the transitional period to independence, support capacity building for self-government, and coordinate humanitarian and development assistance.[35] UNTAET included an armed peacekeeping force equivalent in size to INTERFET, as well as a civilian police component of 1,640 personnel, plus military observers and a sizeable civilian component.[36] UNTAET operated until Timor-Leste became an independent state on May 20, 2002, having adopted a constitution and elected a president. It was succeeded by the UN Mission of Support in East Timor

(UNMISET), which was mandated to assist Timor-Leste in its transition to independence and full responsibility for all governance of the territory.

The UN peacekeeping presence in Timor-Leste was withdrawn in 2005 once this transition had occurred, but quickly redeployed a year later when conflict between elements of the military led to a coup attempt and the outbreak of widespread violence across the country. In response to the crisis, the Timorese government initially requested police and military assistance from Australia, New Zealand, Malaysia, and Portugal, and within a month requested a UN police force be established to maintain law and order while the national police force was restructured. The Security Council, on the recommendation of the secretary-general, subsequently authorized the establishment of the UN Integrated Mission in East Timor (UNMIT) in August 2006, mandating it to assist Timor-Leste in addressing the causes and consequences of the crisis.[37] UNMIT closed at the end of 2012, although UN agencies remain as part of a development support mission.

Accounts of sexual exploitation and abuse in Timor-Leste are noticeably absent from most literature and data on sexual misconduct in peace operations; that was one of the reasons for choosing the country as one of the in-depth case studies for this book. The low reported rates of sexual misconduct raise questions about whether it was actually more widespread than is commonly understood, what impacts it had nonetheless, and what explains the low rates. Of the accounts publicly acknowledged, perhaps the most well known relate to rapes perpetrated by some Jordanian peacekeepers in the early period of UNTAET's deployment. In fact, the battalion's first rape occurred en route to Timor-Leste, during a forty-five-minute stopover at Darwin Airport in Australia.[38] This was followed by a number of further rapes in Timor-Leste, including the rape of a woman working as a cleaner in a Dili hotel where they stayed, and that of at least four young children, boys and girls, in the enclave of Oecusse, some of whom were offered food and money in exchange for oral and anal intercourse.[39] The Jordanian peacekeepers involved reportedly also asked those children for women with whom they could have sex. Another two Jordanian peacekeepers were evacuated home with injured penises after raping goats.[40] Although no documentation confirms this, a number of Jordanian peacekeepers were court-martialed and executed upon their repatriation to Jordan as a result of this misconduct, according to interviews I conducted and similar accounts provided to Myrttinen and Koyama, including by a senior UN source.[41]

While opportunistic sexual abuse seems to have been relatively limited and perpetrated primarily by the Jordanian contingent—with the caveat, however, that cultures of silence around such violence are likely to have led to underreporting—networked abuse and exploitation was more prevalent during the interventions in Timor-Leste. Interveners in the country fueled the growth of the local sex industry, which involved not only local sex workers but also those who had been trafficked into the country from East and Southeast Asian states in order to service the growing sex industry.[42] Some of those trafficked to work in brothels frequented by UN and other international interveners were as young as twelve years old.[43] Pedophilia also operated more broadly. According to a major 2004 survey, over 75 percent of the male sex workers in Dili were under eighteen years of age with the average age of entry into sex work 14.5 years old; the rate was lower among the female Timorese sex workers surveyed, although over a third began sex work at age fourteen.[44] No foreign sex workers were found to be under eighteen years old. In addition, there was fairly public teenage prostitution in the streets in exchange for money or other goods, and minors not engaged in sex work were offered money or other goods in exchange for sex "more or less at random."[45] These networked forms of sexual abuse and exploitation were concentrated around Dili, but also occurred in regional areas; for example, the investigation into sexual misconduct by Jordanian peacekeepers in Oecusse found that the same contingent had regularly procured prostitutes from across the border in West Timor.[46] Some of these interactions also involved violence: a former UN national staff member recalled three to five cases of Timorese women who worked in prostitution being severely harmed by the Portuguese peacekeepers who purchased sex from them and seeking hospital treatment as a result, and the coordinator of the Scarlett-Timor sex worker collective similarly recounted issues of foreign men not paying sex workers, being violent towards them, and raping them.[47] Some of these transactional interactions resulted in the birth of children.

Furthermore, while some interveners simply patronized brothels, others were involved in networked exploitation more directly. Numerous local interviewees and international staff who worked in Timor-Leste during the interventions recalled that the Portuguese contingent deployed after the 2006 crisis was housed in the Dili 2001 Hotel, which doubled as a karaoke club and brothel. Similarly, multiple interviewees who had responded to sexual exploitation and abuse in their professional capacities recounted that interveners who had been housed on the "floating boat"—a hotel ship moored just off the Dili shoreline to accommodate the influx of UN and other NGO staff in 1999–2000—had regularly brought prostitutes over to the ship.[48] This included underage girls and some boys who they kept on board for two to three days, and the boat was also the site at which Timor's first local pornography film is rumored to have been produced.[49] Pornography, including child pornography, was also produced at other brothels frequented by interveners, and in some cases involved interveners themselves.[50]

There was one last form of sexual misconduct that was mentioned in passing in some interviews and reports about sexual violence in Timor-Leste, namely, the practice of "soft pillow," which is a customary practice of parents offering their daughters to sleep with visiting authorities or dignitaries. This practice stretches at least as far back as the Portuguese colonial occupation of the country, but has continued postindependence with the influx of international interveners: senior peacekeepers and international NGO staff have been implicated in the practice and it is likely that a broader range of interveners have also participated.[51]

In addition to these forms of intervener sexual misconduct, all of which are now prohibited under the zero-tolerance bulletin but which were not uniformly regulated pre-2003 during the initial deployments in Timor-Leste, other forms of sexual behavior by interveners occurred that were considered sexually abusive and exploitative by local Timorese and are therefore worth considering here. These are sexual harassment and consensual relationships that are viewed as exploitative in retrospect, in some cases because they produced peace babies.

There are numerous accounts of peacekeepers sexually harassing local women and children in both public and private spaces. For instance, a group of Japanese peacekeepers are reported to have repeatedly harassed adolescents at an orphanage in Oecusse—after several incidents the unit was reportedly confined to its barracks to prevent further misbehavior—and a West Timorese journalist alleged sexual harassment by the Pakistani UNPOL contingent.[52] Multiple interviewees mentioned how prevalent street harassment by peacekeepers was, noting that it was particularly

frightening for women and girls because peacekeepers used their own lan-
guages so the women could not understand what they were saying, and
that some peacekeepers taught local boys what their words meant so that
they could harass women and girls in the same way.

However, this and all of the other forms of sexual exploitation and
abuse discussed above were eclipsed in interviews by discussions of peace
babies and associated relationships between local women and foreign men
that were consensual but became viewed as exploitative when they broke
down or when the men left to return home after their deployment. (Angkis
Leonora, coordinator of the sex worker collective Scarlett-Timor, reported
that at least as many babies had been born to sex workers to foreign
fathers, but these did not seem to be referred to as peace babies in the
same way—perhaps due to the additional stigma associated with prostitution.[53]) When asked about their knowledge of sexual misconduct by interveners in Timor-Leste, nearly all of the individuals interviewed mentioned
peace babies before any other forms of misconduct and all shared stories
of individual women they knew of who had had relationships with foreign men associated with the international presence. These relationships
seemed to fall into two main categories: those where the women involved
were hired by men to work as housekeepers, and a sexual relationship was
then developed; and those that did not involve an employment relationship. Interviewees suggested that a key problem with such relationships
was that the men involved made promises about marriage and long-term
relationships but in some cases had families in their home countries and in
many cases had no genuine intention to stay in Timor-Leste beyond their
deployment. One local civil society leader who had been at the forefront
of responding to the needs of women in such situations recalled that it was
not uncommon for the women involved to be underage, between fifteen
and seventeen years old.[54] Others who worked in the women's rights sector confirmed that young women were often sought after by peacekeepers for such relationships; in fact, some reported being asked by foreign
colleagues to help find them a "temporary wife" for the duration of their
deployment.[55] It is worth noting that the fact that the women involved
were underage classifies this as sexual abuse under the UN standards now
in existence, although the confusion over reporting mechanisms and deep
reluctance of women to report to the UN means that few cases were referred to UN authorities.[56] That many of these cases occurred before the

zero-tolerance policy and associated mechanisms was in place complicated the response, as officials relied on women to make complaints in order for the cases to be investigated formally even if they knew informally of some of these behaviors.

Furthermore, even in contexts of long-term relationships, some interviewees emphasized the presence of transactional elements—such as money or housing being provided for the women or a foreign partner being seen as a passport out of poverty. One national UN staff member who worked in the Conduct and Discipline Unit argued that even if the men involved professed their love for the women, the fact that they knew the women they were in a relationship with required the money they gave means that "the perpetrators knew it was exploitation, even if the victims didn't."[57] Furthermore, in at least one documented case, the capacity of the woman involved to consent to the relationship is in question: a Portuguese peacekeeper stationed in a small regional town fathered a child with a deaf and mute Timorese woman, and subsequently refused to support the child.[58] This is not to suggest that *all* relationships between foreign staff and local women were exploitative but rather to highlight the murkiness in making sense of these consensual relationships that are understood by many in the local community to have exploitative elements because of the huge disparity in the material wealth of the individuals involved, particularly in retrospect if children are left behind for the women to raise alone.

It is interesting to note that much of the international media attention and UN reporting on sexual misconduct also focuses heavily on the relationships that produced peace babies, even though at least some of these relationships do not fall under the now-prohibited behaviors.[59] It is also worth noting that there are some accounts of national staff also taking "temporary wives" when stationed away from their own families, and these elicited similar reactions from local communities in terms of the unacceptability and shame involved in such behavior.[60]

A related but distinct form of behavior that some interviewees raised was marriage to local women for property and market access reasons, because local law restricts property and business ownership to Timorese citizens.[61] This seems to have been more prevalent within the private sector and business community associated with the international presence in Timor-Leste, rather than peacekeepers or NGO staff. One director of a local NGO that has been heavily involved in advocating for women's rights and protection, including from sexual exploitation and abuse, argued that despite having raising this issue multiple times with officials, the government has shown no interest in addressing it.[62]

Reporting rates for sexual misconduct and public discourse around all behaviors considered sexually inappropriate, exploitative, and abusive in Timor-Leste have been low, for very similar reasons to those that perpetuated the cultures of silence on sexual exploitation and abuse in Bosnia. Most interviewees noted that one of the challenges regarding addressing such misconduct was that many of the women and children affected were reluctant to report their experiences because of the shame and stigma associated with extramarital sexual interactions and with sexual violence more broadly. The shadows of shame associated with occupation-era sexual violence by Indonesian soldiers were also mentioned in this context, as was the overlap in behaviors: Indonesian soldiers were extensively involved in similar forms of sexual abuse and exploitation, particularly rape and networked exploitation, and also left children behind to be raised by their Timorese mothers.[63] A national UN staff member who worked in the human rights section of UNPOL suggested that the historical experiences of abuse also prevented reporting because people did not trust authorities and were therefore reluctant to report directly to the UN or police.[64] Others suggested that while some of this mistrust of the authorities has shifted with time, local communities continue to feel that there has been a lack of transparency about the investigations and outcomes in cases that have been referred to the UN, which has further discouraged victims or their families from reporting sexual exploitation and abuse to the UN or other authorities.[65] There was also recognition from some interviewees that women may not have reported because they had consented and enjoyed the sexual interactions, even if others considered them exploitative or inappropriate. These cultures of silence are bolstered by the gendered behavioral expectations in Timor-Leste, one element of which is the presumption that women who experience sexual violence are at fault because they should have been at home, and another being the high rates of violence against women and abuse of children in the country.[66]

This overview of the nature and scale of sexual exploitation and abuse by interveners in Bosnia and Timor-Leste during the international interventions suggests a number of themes that are worth noting before proceeding to the analysis of the long-term impacts of such misconduct on local communities and mission-level outcomes. First, these accounts reinforce the arguments made in the previous chapter that sexual misconduct takes a number of distinct but interconnected forms and that it is analytically useful to disaggregate them in order to properly understand the nature of sexually exploitative and abusive behaviors in peace operations, the factors the give rise to them, and their varying impacts. Furthermore, it highlights the blurred boundaries of what is considered sexual exploitation and abuse, with a somewhat greater tolerance for transactional sex in Bosnia and a reluctance of many to consider it sexual exploitation and, by contrast, a broader conceptualization of the behaviors constituting exploitation in Timor-Leste. This shows that the way local communities experience sexual exploitation and abuse by interveners is highly grounded in historical experience, cultural norms, and, in many ways, the particular forms of material deprivation and conflict-related sexual violence experienced—for instance, in Bosnia, the nature of wartime sexual violence meant that sexual misconduct by interveners was considered a far lesser evil, particularly consensual forms like transactional sex between adults. Second, these cases highlight that even though the statistics available may suggest that sexual misconduct is higher in some contexts than others, in-depth research can reveal the true prevalence of behaviors that constitute sexual exploitation and abuse, either as prohibited by UN policy or in the eyes of local communities. In both cases, the strong cultures of silence, produced by a combination of gendered, social, and historical factors, led to underreporting, which skews the available data.

These cases also reinforce some of the trends around the prevalence of different forms of sexual exploitation and abuse suggested by the analysis in the previous chapter. Transactional sex appears to be, by far, the most common form of sexual misconduct by interveners, and networked exploitation and abuse appears to be ubiquitous to peace operations, although with varying levels of intervener involvement in the organization of the networks. Rape and planned, sadistic abuse appear to be less common, although underreporting, stigma, and cultures of silence may mean that anecdotal reports of these are less openly shared than the other forms of sexual exploitation and abuse. Lastly, the differences between the experiences of sexual misconduct in Bosnia and

Timor-Leste highlight the ways in which the myriad local, historic, international, normative, and systemic factors interact and operate differently in each particular context to give rise to different patterns of sexual exploitation and abuse by interveners.

So, what impacts did these varying forms and of sexual misconduct in Bosnia and Timor-Leste have on peacebuilding outcomes? It is to this question that the next chapter turns.

3

Making Matters Worse

The Long-Term Impacts of Sexual Exploitation and Abuse

In 2012, UN Secretary-General Ban Ki-moon commissioned a team of three experts to investigate and evaluate the risks to effectively implementing the 2003 zero-tolerance bulletin and the associated UN policies on prevention of sexual exploitation and abuse. The team was tasked with investigating four major peacekeeping operations that had consistently experienced the highest sexual misconduct allegation rates: the UN Organization Stabilization Mission in the Democratic Republic of the Congo, the UN Stabilization Mission in Haiti, the UN Mission in Liberia and the UN Mission in South Sudan. Together, these four missions accounted for 85 percent of all sexual exploitation and abuse allegations reported by the UN. The expert team submitted their report to the secretary-general in November 2013, but the report, which was very critical of the responses by the UN secretariat and troop-contributing countries to sexual misconduct in peace operations, was never officially released; the NGO AIDS-Free World published a leaked copy in 2013.

The report opened with the assertion that sexual exploitation and abuse has been judged the "most significant risk to UN peacekeeping missions, above and beyond other key risks including the protection of civilians."[1] Less than two years later, a similar review commissioned to investigate sexual misconduct by international peacekeeping forces in the Central African Republic made similar claims, arguing that sexual exploitation and abuse by peacekeepers (and the poor institutional responses to it) "[taints] the important and valuable work of peacekeepers as a whole, . . . seriously threatens the relationship of trust between civilian populations, troop-contributing countries, the UN and the international community, and undermines the sustainability of peacekeeping missions in the longer term."[2] However, despite these claims, neither the UN report nor academic scholarship has investigated *how* sexual exploitation and abuse undermines peacekeeping missions and the sustainability of their goals and achievements. This chapter sets out to fill that gap in relation to the micro- and mission-level impacts of such behaviors by interveners in peace operations.

According to the UN Peacekeeping website, peacekeeping has five key goals: to protect civilians from armed conflict (with a particular focus on child protection and conflict-related sexual violence); to prevent conflicts in order to reduce human suffering, build stable and prosperous societies, and enable people to reach their full potential; to strengthen rule of law and security institutions at national and local levels, in order to support the establishment of sustainable peace; to protect and promote human rights; and to empower women to participate in peace processes and advocate for women's inclusion in political and electoral systems.[3] These goals are broadly applicable to all peace operations mandated by the UN and regional organizations and are reflected in most mission mandates. So how do sexually exploitative and abusive behaviors by interveners in peace operations affect the achievement of these broad goals in host countries? This chapter builds on the detailed analysis of such behaviors in Bosnia and Timor-Leste in the previous chapter in order to answer this question. I also draw on interviews conducted within intervener communities, in particular the humanitarian community in Geneva and the UN and related organizations and missions in New York. I triangulate this primary data with accounts of the impacts of sexual misconduct that have been published in the media and with broader academic scholarship.

The research I conducted suggests that these impacts operate on three levels, each of which is discussed in successive sections in this chapter: the individual and community level, the structural level, and the operational level. In each of these sections, I identify parallels with the experiences of sexual misconduct in other peace operations, thereby grounding conclusions about its impacts so that they are relevant beyond this book's two central case studies. In doing so, I consider the ways in which these impacts undermine the achievement of core peacekeeping goals, which revolve around establishing security, promoting human rights, protecting civilians, and supporting conflict-affected states and societies to transition to lasting peace. The impacts on the international community's credibility and capacity at the international level will be discussed in the next chapter.

Compounding Poverty and Human Rights Abuses: Individual- and Community-Level Impacts of Sexual Misconduct

It is perhaps obvious, after reading the accounts of sexual misconduct by interveners in Bosnia and Timor-Leste in the previous chapter, that such behaviors have significant impacts on the individuals, families, and communities involved. It is clear that some of the sexually exploitative and abusive behaviors directly violate the human rights of victims involved, but it may be less clear the ways in which these behaviors undermine the stated goals and values of peacekeeping operations. The protection of human rights is one of the central tenets of the UN. Indeed, the Charter of the United Nations begins with the assertion that

> We the peoples of the United Nations determined
>   to save succeeding generations from the scourge of war, which twice in
> our lifetime has brought untold sorrow to mankind, and
>   to reaffirm faith in fundamental human rights, in the dignity and worth
> of the human person, in the equal rights of men and women and of nations
> large and small . . .[4]

UN peacekeeping has become one of the primary ways by which the international community pursues these goals, and there is a general conviction among UN policymakers that effective peacekeeping and the establishment of sustainable peace requires a strong grounding in norms of human rights and democracy.[5] In other words, human rights is taken to be one of the pillars on which stable peace can be built, and without which states and societies risk a return to war. By contrast, human rights violations are seen to be one of the underlying causes of violent conflict that threatens international peace and security, and a key reason for deploying peacekeepers is to prevent and address such violations. While scholars have challenged the liberal peacekeeping paradigm that sees "universal values" such as democracy and human rights as central to the lasting resolution of civil wars, this has not shifted the centrality of the commitment at the UN that the protection and strengthening of human rights is crucial to effective international support for states transitioning from war to peace.[6] This conviction was affirmed, for instance, in the 2000 Report of the Panel on UN Peace Operations (the Brahimi Report), the 2004 report by the High-Level Panel on Threats, Challenges and Change, entitled A More Secure World: Our Shared Responsibility, and the 2015 report by the High-Level Independent Panel on United Nations Peace Operations, entitled Uniting Our Strengths for Peace: Politics, Partnership and People (the HIPPO Report).[7] Ultimately, the fact that some peacekeepers are directly involved in compounding poverty and perpetrating human rights violations against the very communities they have been sent to protect from such violations is at odds with the stated values and goals that underpin UN peacekeeping. So how did sexual exploitation and sexual abuse in Bosnia and Timor-Leste undermine the international community's goals and values at the individual and community level, and what impacts did it have on peacebuilding outcomes?

A key theme emerging from interviews was the significant way in which sexual misconduct by interveners affects the women and children directly involved, by compounding their experiences of human rights violations in contexts where the prevalence of human rights violations are a key reason peace operations have been deployed and where recourse through legal or police channels is unavailable.[8] Many of the accounts detailed above involved the sexual exploitation or abuse of young women and children, particularly in Timor-Leste—and this is in line with the high rates of such abuse against children reported in other peacekeeping contexts and discussed in the previous chapter. Children face particular difficulties in reporting abuse by interveners, and the targeting of children by perpetrators exploits these particular vulnerabilities.

In the case of the slave trade at the Arizona market in northern Bosnia, international involvement in these human rights violations was paradoxical. The international community helped set up the market next to a US peacekeeper base, in order to foster connection and harmony between Bosniaks, Serbs, and Croats after the intercommunal violence of the war, in the belief that economic interdependence would prevent further violence and human rights violations.[9] However, the market quickly became a thriving black market where women and girls were sold at open auctions and where drugs and weapons were sold alongside bootleg media and secondhand goods.[10] The international community largely turned a blind eye to this, even while peacekeepers actively participated in the trade and trafficking of women through the market, because of a strong commitment to the peacebuilding benefits of economic integration. It was thereby complicit in the human rights violations that occurred at the market, violating mission goals related to the protection of civilians and the promotion of human rights in the postwar state and society.

There were also direct health impacts of sexual exploitation and abuse of relevance to human rights. The director of a Timorese NGO that works on issues of security and violence reported that he was aware of a number of cases of women contracting HIV as a result of sexual interactions with interveners.[11] The coordinator of the Timorese sex worker collective also raised this issue, recounting that peacekeepers often demanded no protection during sex, sometimes appealing to the high rates they were paying to justify this.[12] Contracting sexually transmitted infections from interveners further compounded the vulnerabilities of the women, men, and children involved, with significant human rights implications. Reports of increased HIV and other sexually transmitted infections and diseases among both local populations and UN peacekeepers as a result of sexual exploitation and abuse have also been documented elsewhere.[13]

Furthermore, in cases of women engaging in prostitution with interveners, the police response to such exploitation often puts them at risk of greater human rights violations. For instance, when police began targeting illegal brothels in Timor-Leste, the women found working in them were often held in arbitrary detention and prosecuted for visa violations, despite objections from the UN's human rights unit.[14] Similarly, in Bosnia, women arrested during IPTF and national police raids on brothels—the majority of whom were trafficking victims—often faced further human rights violations. They were interviewed by some of the same IPTF staff by whom they had been abused while working in forced prostitution, denied the rights and protections trafficking victims are entitled to under international law, prosecuted for visa-related crimes, prostitution, or crimes against public morality, and sometimes deported out of the country.[15] As a result of these responses, many of the women were put at risk of further exploitation: the director of one anti-trafficking NGO in Bosnia who had also worked in the International Organisation for Migration's counter-trafficking programs recounted that many of the women arrested would opt to return to the bars they were arrested in rather than report truthfully to IPTF investigators about having been trafficked for sex because they were fearful of the consequences they would face. [16] She also recalled that in some cases, women were returned to their "owners" by police themselves, or were deported out of the country and thereby put at immediate risk of being trafficked again by the same networks that originally exploited them. One of the factors that contributed to this poor response was the general perception, by both police and the local community, that trafficked women were "consenting whores" and therefore did not deserve a human rights–based response—which is at odds with UN goals about embedding a culture of human rights in postwar states and societies.[17] The 2018 Oxfam scandal about aid workers buying sex in Haiti further highlights the ways in which sexual exploitation and abuse by interveners, and institutional responses to it, might compound the risk to the women involved, particularly in contexts where prostitution is illegal, as it is in Haiti: the demands that abounded in the scandal's aftermath for national authorities to be alerted to cases of foreigners engaging with prostitutes ignore the ways that this can put women at greater risk—not only of prosecution but also of further exploitation and abuse by police.

In addition to directly compounding the human rights violations of the victims involved, sexual abuse and exploitation by interveners also produced strong social stigmatization of victims and sometimes, by extension, their families, which further exacerbated their vulnerabilities. For instance, in Timor-Leste, girls who had engaged in transactional sex with interveners often found it hard to return to school to finish their education, with lasting impacts on their economic prospects and those of their families and communities.[18] Some were pushed out of their communities and ended up working in the sex industry in Dili in order to support themselves and sometimes their children.[19] Furthermore, as will be discussed shortly, once vulnerable women became involved in prostitution as a way to support themselves in the context of poverty, it was difficult for them to get out of it, even when they wanted to.[20] Although these particular impacts were not as pronounced in Bosnia, probably because of the different forms sexual exploitation and abuse took there, there were some parallels. One interviewee, a lawyer who had worked extensively on human rights, rule of law, and refugee return, recounted that some children left behind by peacekeepers in the country were put up for adoption by their mothers, just as many children born of wartime rape were adopted out.[21] Others noted that women who had been in relationships with peacekeepers also sometimes experienced long-term stigma and were judged as opportunists who had acted immorally—although it is important to note that this was in relation to postwar relationships, rather than transactional sex during and immediately after the war.[22] Similarly, many interviewees in Timor-Leste pointed to the traditional expectations of relationships to suggest that women who had experienced abuse or exploitation by interveners or been involved in consensual relationships with them had limited opportunities for relationships or marriage in the future because of stigma. Where "peace babies" were left behind, a number of interviewees mentioned that this produced additional stress within families and communities, not only because of the shame associated with unmarried mothers but also because families were now left with an extra mouth to feed in an already impoverished situation, which in some cases resulted in intrafamilial and intracommunity conflict.

In some contexts, this stigma and its impacts can be transgenerational, with children born of sexual exploitation and abuse also marginalized by their family and community and faced with further discriminations. In Timor-Leste, peace babies cannot inherit land because it is passed down through the father's bloodline; they may not be able to secure birth certificates because of the absence of a father's name, which affects their schooling prospects; they are more likely to experience racism if they look markedly different from other Timorese children; and they may have difficulty marrying because of the stigma they carry with them.[23]

This analysis has illustrated how the sexual misconduct by interveners in Bosnia and Timor-Leste was at odds with the values and goals that animated the UN peace operations deployed. Indeed, such human rights violations conflict with the United Nations' raison d'être, namely to "reaffirm faith in fundamental human rights, in the dignity and worth of the human person." The implications of this are felt not only by victims themselves, but their families and communities, with long-term and intergenerational impacts. Furthermore, when the UN fails to ensure that its responses to intervener misconduct are grounded in a human rights based approach and fails to hold perpetrators accountable, this undermines the credibility of its claims that the UN is committed to respecting human rights and that respect for human rights is critically important to effective peacebuilding. This will be discussed further in the next section.

Embedding Cultures and Economies of Sexual Exploitation and Abuse: The Structural Impacts of Sexual Misconduct

In addition to the impacts at the individual and community level, sexual exploitation and abuse by interveners has significant structural impacts on the cultures, economies, and institutions of host societies. These impacts directly undermine the international community's goals related to strengthening rule of law and embedding cultures of human rights at local and national levels, which are seen as crucial to the establishment of sustainable peace. As Jeremy Farrall has demonstrated, the UN Security Council has shown an increasing interest in rule of law since 1992 and uses the term variously to refer to the reestablishment of law and order institutions after civil wars, ending impunity for crimes, the protection and promotion of human rights, and principled governance more broadly, which includes efforts to eradicate corruption.[24] Rule of law has become a common feature of peacekeeping mandates and doctrine as a result. The Brahimi Report emphasized the importance of a whole-of-mission approach to upholding and strengthening rule of law and respect for human rights as a cornerstone of effective peacekeeping.[25] The HIPPO Report went a step further, arguing that security sector reform is crucial to effective peacekeeping, given the sector's potential to disrupt peace, and that this should include a significant change in policing approaches to support police development and reform that integrates human rights and rule of law capacities.[26] In fact, it argued that past peacekeeping operations that focused on rule of law capacity development without due attention to human rights were unable to achieve the institutional reform necessary for the establishment of stable peace, and that "peace operations should work to ensure that the rule of law operates in a manner that protects human rights," including by addressing impunity.[27] Missions in both Bosnia and Timor-Leste were given rule of law mandates, but the perpetration of sexual exploitation and abuse by interveners associated with those missions introduced cultural, economic, and structural consequences that fundamentally undermined the capacity to achieve those mission objectives, thus undermining long-term peacebuilding as a consequence.

One theme that emerged strongly during discussions with interviewees about the impacts of sexual misconduct by interveners was that it contributed first to the extension of existing cultures and economies of abuse and exploitation and then to their entrenchment in the postwar society and state. For instance, one of the complaints aired multiple times by both local and foreign respondents in Timor-Leste was that peacekeepers "taught" boys how to sexually harass women and girls in the street, and that as a result this has become a much more common aspect of daily life in Dili in particular.[28] It is obviously impossible to draw a direct causal link here, given that harassment certainly existed prior to the peacekeepers' deployment and that sexual violence has been documented as being extensive during the occupation by Indonesia.[29] Nevertheless, it is worth noting that numerous Timorese respondents *believed* that harassment by interveners contributed to those behaviors becoming even further entrenched in Timorese society after independence. Furthermore, a number of international respondents suggested that harassment by Timorese men and boys towards foreign women has increased significantly, possibly because the behaviors of some male interveners in the early missions contributed to the belief that all foreigners were highly sexualized and had "looser" attitudes to sexual interactions. A senior Timorese gender expert argued that some groups of men think "if they [the UN] do this to our women, we'll do it to theirs."[30] This has reportedly impacted the way some foreign women participate in public spaces and engage with local men and boys in their everyday lives while working in Timor.

In a similar vein, one Timorese respondent who had worked extensively with the UN Mission's Conduct and Discipline Unit suggested that the exploitative behaviors of some interveners in establishing relationships based on false promises of marriage contributed to normalizing such exploitative and duplicitous relationships among Timorese men, with some national staff taking a second wife upon moving to Dili for work, with similar implications to those discussed in the last chapter.[31] Similar stories were told of personnel in the Timor-Leste Defense Force.[32] And a national staff member who had worked extensively on issues of violence against women suggested that some Timorese men in Oecusse copied the behaviors of the peacekeepers who had been based there, particularly the Jordanian contingent, perpetrating a number of rapes and trafficking women from across the border with West Timor for sex.[33]

This shows how, in a context where sexual violence and abuse against women and children was already very high, interveners who preyed on already vulnerable people and perpetrated sexual exploitation and abuse contributed to the extension and further entrenchment of cultures of sexual harassment, abuse, and exploitation in local communities.[34] This is not to say that these behaviors were new to Timor-Leste; they were not. But the accounts of those I interviewed suggest that by modeling such behaviors during the transition to independence and peace, which was an opportunity to challenge and shift patterns of discrimination and violence, interveners contributed to creating new postwar patterns of male perpetration of violence and abuse against women and children and associated norms of impunity for such behaviors. This significantly undermines many of the long-term human rights and protection goals of peace operations and the humanitarian and development processes associated with them.

In a similar way, sexual exploitation by interveners contributed to the entrenchment of economies of sexual exploitation and abuse. Although international interveners are not solely responsible for the presence of networked exploitation and abuse, the cases of Bosnia and Timor-Leste demonstrate how an influx of interveners does play a significant role in the proliferation of these forms of networked exploitation and the entrenchment of associated economies. Other contributing factors are direct products of war, namely the collapse of economies, law and order, and traditional social safety nets.[35] Shukuko Kyoma and Henri Myrtinnen have shown that the arrival of UNTAET heralded the development of an internationalized sex industry in Timor-Leste, while Kathleen Jennings and Vesna Nikolić-Ristanović have made similar findings about the development of sex work economies in Bosnia, Kosovo, Liberia and Haiti and concluded that these economies tend to far outlive the peace operations that help build them.[36] These economies both rely on and compel the participation of a broad range of individuals and groups, which contribute to their remarkable longevity, flexibility, and imperviousness to being tamed by legal and judicial frameworks in the future.

My findings align closely with these previous studies: in Bosnia, local experts argued that although there had been some trafficking of Roma people to beg on street corners, sex trafficking was virtually unknown in the country before the arrival of international forces, and that since the drawdown of the international presence and the introduction of antitrafficking laws, the trafficking networks that consolidated themselves by capitalizing on the international presence during peace operations have simply adjusted their business models.[37] For example, one senior Bosnian government official recalled that many existing businesses, such as restaurants, expanded their business model to include prostitution within the spectrum of their services in response to increased demand during the interventions.[38] Now, rather than being a destination country, Bosnia is a source and transit country for human trafficking for both labor and sex, although there is still some trafficking of children into the country from neighboring states for forced labor and begging. Furthermore, as Jennings and Nikolić-Ristanović have shown, the establishment of a robust sex industry in Bosnia to serve the demands of international interveners created a strong organized crime economy that revolved around the sex industry. That industry created income for many people involved and has consequently become "accepted as a complement to or substitute for the inefficient formal economy," continuing to operate in the years since, albeit in modified forms.[39] This highlights how existing networks took advantage of the new economic opportunities ushered in with the arrival of international forces and how they adapted these economies to ensure continued profit when the international presence declined.

Research in Timor-Leste revealed similar findings. Before the arrival of UNAMET, which coordinated and ran the independence referendum in 1999, prostitution did occur in the country but was neither formalized nor visible, according to a number of local experts who have responded to the issues of sexual exploitation in the country.[40] After UNAMET arrived, transactional sex between local girls and women and mission personnel, particularly the Portuguese contingent, led to the development of more extensive transactional sex economies and ultimately to the formalization of those economies. Brothels were opened, as were massage parlors, karaoke joints, and hotels that provided sex services. With time, as the demand for sex grew, criminal networks began to traffic women into Timor-Leste from the region and to work with taxi drivers and local men to procure more Timorese women to work in the sex industry. In some cases, this procurement occurred in real time, in response to the undersupply of women in the venues offering sex for purchase.[41]

The increased supply of sex services and the consolidation of the sex industry in Timor-Leste is reported to also have attracted pedophiles and sex tourists from elsewhere in the world who took advantage of the lack of effective regulation and law enforcement. For example, one international staff member of PRADET, an NGO providing support to victims of domestic violence, sexual assault, child abuse, and human trafficking recounted that, while living in a hotel in 2005–6, staff requested her help in dealing with an eighty-year-old German man who had moved to Dili from Bali and was recruiting young boys off the street for sex in exchange for $1USD or a t-shirt.[42] The case was reported to police, and the man faced trial but was released because he was so old and the judge feared that he would die in jail and cause trouble for the country. The same respondent also recalled at least one international human trafficking network taking advantage of the Timorese context and emerging sex industry to traffic women for sex work elsewhere in the world. In this case, the man responsible posed as a UN worker to gain access to internally displaced persons camps where he recruited women to be trafficked to the Middle East. There is also some emerging evidence of pedophiles using humanitarian work to access vulnerable children, although it is unclear how common this is.[43]

These cases highlight how the entrenchment of economies of sexual exploitation, driven by the influx of international personnel associated with a peace operation, can have far-reaching implications for how others engage with and exploit those economies. Indeed, one international expert suggested this was not uncommon, pointing to the explosion of the sex industry in Cambodia in response to UNTAC's arrival as creating the foundations for the now entrenched sex tourism and trafficking economy in the country.[44] A recent study of peace operations between 2001 and 2011 supported this, finding that the presence of peacekeepers increases the probability that the host state will become a destination for sex trafficking, particularly when the peace operation is large, involves many troop-contributing countries, and operates for a number of years.[45] Moreover, Jennings has shown how, although peacekeeping economies do not always morph into sex tourism economies, they often do as a result of contextual factors and the "entertainment" infrastructure they leave behind.[46] According to Jennings, these factors include an economically disadvantaged population, protourism policies supported by local authorities and international donors, extreme inequality, and state inaction towards the sex industry. Moreover, as the example of the pedophile above suggests, some sex tourists might choose to go to postwar states to exploit the somewhat unregulated environments they offer in order to access forms of sex they would not otherwise be able to in more well-regulated sex industries. This highlights both how the lack of effective rule of law reforms and capacity-building can prolong the existence of opportunities for such economies of exploitation to flourish and also how the complicity and investment of the security sector in such economies can create incentives not to effectively regulate them as part of the peacebuilding process.

In Timor-Leste, the coordinator of Scarlett-Timor recalled that at the height of the intervention some sex workers would receive between $1000 and $2000 USD per encounter from UN staff due to their high disposable incomes, but noted that this dropped significantly with the reduction in the international presence as the peace operations came to an end, with some underage local prostitutes being paid as little as $5 per sexual encounter at the time of interviews.[47] Just as in Bosnia, the sex work industry shifted as a result, targeting primarily local men as purchasers of sex and recruiting ever younger girls into prostitution, with taxi drivers now involved in the recruitment of schoolgirls for sex with older men. In some cases, these taxi drivers convince other girls to trick their friends into getting into the taxis, where they are pressured into engaging in a sex act and then paid high rates, presumably as a way of encouraging them to participate again.[48] These cases show how the structures and logics of economies of sexual exploitation and abuse develop, are reproduced, and are modified in order to maintain the income streams for those involved in organizing the networked forms of exploitation and abuse—whether local men like the taxi drivers who make some extra money through their participation or foreigners who run organized sex trafficking networks globally.

The third and perhaps most insidious way in which sexual misconduct by interveners has long-term effects on the structures of postwar states and societies that are at odds with the goals of peacekeeping is by institutionalizing impunity for sexual abuse and exploitation in the security and judicial sectors and in the practices of particular organizations or companies involved in peace operations. This occurs in two ways: by shaping the internal cultures of organizations such that sexual exploitation and abuse becomes a part of everyday practices; and/or by institutionalizing practices of impunity so that perpetrators of intervener sexual exploitation and abuse and nonintervener sexual violence and exploitation are not held accountable to legal frameworks or misconduct policies by relevant authorities. These implications of sexual misconduct directly undermine core goals of peace operations such as the reestablishment of rule of law and promotion of human rights, including through judicial system development.

The perpetration of sexual exploitation and abuse by interveners—particularly by uniformed peacekeepers who are formally mentoring or training local security sector personnel (as was the case in both Timor-Leste and Bosnia and in most other contemporary peace operations)—sends the message to local police, militaries, and elites that such behaviors are permissible even if formally prohibited. It thereby contributes to embedding a culture of impunity and human rights violations in the security structures of the newly postwar state. My research suggests that this is particularly likely when perpetrators are not held accountable and when key individuals in peace operations and related organizations actively cover up the perpetration of abuse in order to prevent accountability processes being undertaken. In Bosnia, Human Rights Watch found that local police were actively involved in trafficking economies: as traffickers and brothel owners; as employees in brothels; and through facilitating trafficking by granting work permits, falsifying documents, and turning a blind eye to the activities of trafficking networks in exchange for free access to prostitutes.[49] Although some of these behaviors may have predated the intervention, the Human Rights Watch research suggests that they evolved at the same time that interveners became involved in the same networked patterns of exploitation.

For instance, Kathy Bolkovac's whistleblower account of the DynCorp sexual exploitation and abuse scandal in Bosnia illustrates how local police personnel being trained by and working in partnership with IPTF personnel who were involved in networked sexual exploitation became acculturated into both the same practices and the same patterns of ensuring that those involved were not held accountable.[50] As discussed in the previous chapter, some interveners who perpetrated sexual exploitation and abuse were in senior positions and responsible for enforcing codes of conduct, which also contributed to entrenching impunity. The difficulty of addressing the transference of behaviors, particularly around impunity, was brought up by a number of other Bosnian interviewees who had worked as part of the countertrafficking response. For instance, the director of the countertrafficking NGO Emmaus suggested that the poor countertrafficking training provided by IPTF personnel meant that when the IPTF left, local police were left in a vacuum without the capacity or skills to respond to trafficking cases, which undermined the national countertrafficking program. In addition, it meant that if local police conducted raids and found local politicians or other authorities participating in the sex industry, they were either easily threatened into not arresting them or they willingly continued the "boys club" practices of allowing them to go free.[51]

Research in Timor-Leste found similar patterns of intervener misconduct contributing to the institutionalization of impunity for sexual misconduct in the security sector, which severely undermined the development of local justice institutions and the embedding of human rights as a cornerstone of the new state's institutions. For example, Nelson Belo, the director of a local NGO that works on issues of violence by security forces, argued that within a few years of UNPOL leaving Timor-Leste in 2012, his organization saw how patterns of sexual exploitation and abuse by UNPOL were being replicated by Timorese police. This included involvement in and protection of sex trafficking and prostitution networks, sharing profits among police in order to co-opt them into economies of sexual exploitation, and the involvement and protection of senior politicians and officials by these networks.[52] Timorese police have also been implicated in other forms of sexual abuse; for instance, in 2004 six police officers were accused of raping a minor, but investigation of the incident was obstructed by their police colleagues, who also intimidated witnesses and protested outside the courthouse when the trial was in session.[53] Both Timorese police and military personnel have been implicated in the use, harassment, and abuse of Timorese sex workers and the refusal to pay for agreed sexual interactions, while there is evidence that Timorese police extort free sex from sex workers and have in some cases failed to respond adequately to offenses committed against sex workers.[54] While these behaviors are not solely attributable to "training" by their UNPOL counterparts, the behaviors of interveners certainly appear to have played a role in consolidating the security forces' participation in sexual exploitative and abusive practices in the newly independent state and to embedding the cultures of impunity for sexual misconduct that ensure that perpetrators go unpunished. A senior Timorese government official argued further that the fact that the UN's responses to allegations of sexual exploitation and abuse were so poor and allowed perpetrators to go unpunished set a bad precedent in terms of how authorities should deal with crime in general and sexual abuse and exploitation in particular.[55] This sentiment was echoed by a number of other Timorese respondents with professional experience of responses by the security and judicial sectors to sexual violence.

It is important to note here that not all local security sector personnel were acculturated to sexually exploitative and abusive behaviors by the actions of the small groups of intervener perpetrators. In both countries, numerous respondents with expertise in the functioning of the security sector emphasized that policing had improved significantly as a result of the training provided by the UN forces, despite the fact that certain groups within the security sector had adopted cultures of sexual exploitation and abuse and worked to ensure impunity for it. This is crucial to a robust understanding of the impacts of sexual exploitation and abuse: just as sexual misconduct by a small subsection of the intervener community can have far-reaching impacts that undermine the broader goals of a peace operation, the lasting impacts of entrenching cultures of sexual misconduct and impunity in subsections of the police or military in postconflict states can leave an indelible impression on how the security sector works longterm and how it interacts with broader cultures and economies of sexual exploitation and abuse.

In addition to contributing to the institutionalization of impunity for sexual misconduct through the culture and practices of the security sector, sexual exploitation and abuse by interveners contributes to entrenching these practices in a number of less direct ways. First, a number of interviewees, both in Timor-Leste and among the respondents working with the UN and humanitarian sector internationally, suggested that some uniformed peacekeeping contingents took matters into their own hands to circumvent limitations on their sexual interactions while on UN deployment. For instance, one senior foreign military respondent with long-term experience in the peace operations in Timor-Leste confided that one major peacekeeping contingent included a group of nurses who were understood by other contingents not to be nurses but rather embedded sex workers.[56] A number of other peacekeeping experts globally echoed this about at least one other major troop-contributing country and suggested that embedding sex workers within the contingent served dual purposes, namely, increasing the numbers of women deployed and thereby satisfying requirements under UN Security Council Resolution 1325 on Women, Peace and Security while also decreasing allegations of sexual misconduct against local populations by providing outlets for sexual interactions "in house." I have not been able to verify these allegations, but the number of experts who raised them independently of prompts during interviews lends some weight to the claims.

Secondly, impunity for sexual misconduct also becomes embedded as a result of fear of reporting. Megan Nobert, the founder and director of the international NGO Report the Abuse, argued that in South Sudan, both national and international staff were fearful of losing their jobs or being blacklisted if they reported sexual exploitation or abuse, which contributed to cultures of silence and impunity.[57] This has been reported elsewhere—an investigation by the *Independent* of sexual misconduct by peacekeepers in internally displaced persons camps in the Democratic Republic of Congo was told by a local man who worked for the NGO in charge of managing the camp, "Yes, we know that girls go and visit the UN soldiers every night. There is nothing to stop them, and the girls need food. It is best to keep quiet, though. I am frightened that if I say something I may lose my job, and I have children of my own to feed."[58] This fear of reporting was also the case in relation to the UN; a senior UN policing official recalled that during the peace operation in Haiti sexual exploitation by peacekeepers was reported to local police, but they were reluctant to investigate allegations because they worked with and relied on UN peacekeepers for their own security.[59] A senior Bosnian government official made similar claims about the lack of accountability for intervener involvement in trafficking in Bosnia, arguing that some state politicians were involved in covering up the allegations because they worried that the international community would withdraw if the allegations became public.[60] Furthermore, according to two humanitarian experts on organizational responses to sexual exploitation and abuse, general public opinion of the inadequacy of UN responses to allegations and fear of how information provided by witnesses would be used also discouraged reporting by local community members, who often concluded that there was no point in reporting because nothing was done anyway to hold perpetrators accountable and support victims.[61] This was borne out clearly in interviews in both Bosnia and Timor-Leste and has clear implications for reporting rates of sexual violence postconflict more broadly and for public trust in judicial or administrative responses to such reports.

Lastly, when the perpetrators are not held accountable it sends a strong message to other interveners that they too can get away with such behaviors. This is evidenced, for example, by DynCorp's exporting of trafficking practices to every other peacekeeping operation or intervention they have been contracted to support; the importation of sex workers to provide sex to the workers of some Chinese construction companies in Timor-Leste; and the movement of sexual exploitation and abuse with particular individuals who lead contingents or UN missions, described anecdotally in multiple interviews across Bosnia, Timor-Leste, Geneva, and New York.[62] Thus, sexual misconduct and impunity for the behaviors it encompasses become embedded in the structures of intervener communities themselves.

This analysis of the structural impacts of sexual misconduct by interveners demonstrates how an intersecting web of factors operates to institutionalize impunity and contribute to entrenching cultures and economies of sexual exploitation and abuse in postwar states when interveners associated with peace operations perpetrate it in the first instance and their organizations fail to effectively hold them accountable in the second. These structural impacts are unacceptable not only because of the ongoing cycles of violence, abuse, and exploitation they entail but also because they are in clear tension with some of the key goals of peace operations—particularly around the reestablishment of rule of law, including the development of strong judicial institutions and reformed and accountable security sector institutions and the mainstreaming of commitment to and protection of human rights by postwar institutions. The analysis above has demonstrated how all of these are undermined by the structural implications of sexual misconduct. Moreover, the HIPPO Report specifically notes that a "failure to address [human rights] violations contributes to a climate of impunity, which further endangers civilians."[63] My analysis has illustrated how this occurs in peace operations through the perpetration of sexual exploitation and abuse and the failure to hold perpetrators to account, and how it creates ongoing incentives for participation in cultures and economies of both exploitation and impunity for a range of local and international actors. These outcomes in turn erode progress towards the broader peacekeeping goals noted earlier around the reduction of human suffering and the empowerment of women in postconflict societies, which will be discussed in greater detail in the concluding chapter of this book.

Mistrust, Conflict, and Diversion: The Operational Impacts of Sexual Misconduct

The third level on which sexually exploitative and abusive behaviors by interveners in peace operations affect the achievement of the international community's goals in host countries is the operational level: sexual misconduct causes mistrust and conflict between local communities and the peace operation and international community more broadly; leads to a breakdown between organizational units with the peace operation and the related international presence; and diverts critical resources away from essential peacebuilding activities. These operational-level impacts are mutually reinforcing of those identified at the structural and individual/community levels. In Bosnia and Timor-Leste, the international community's goals related to peace, security, and human rights were undermined significantly as a result of these intersecting outcomes, with lasting impacts for the postwar states and societies.

The breakdown of trust between local communities and the international community in Timor-Leste and Bosnia was one of the most significant ways that respondents framed the impacts of sexual misconduct by interveners on operational outcomes. This growing mistrust took a number of forms. For instance, a number of respondents in Timor-Leste said that there is now an expectation that the arrival of foreigners will quickly be followed by the birth of their babies, and that some women are now less willing or not allowed by family members to work with the UN or international NGOs because their families and communities assume that they will engage in sexual relationships in exchange for work.[64] Others recalled that many people were fearful of particular uniformed contingents during the peace operations as a result of particular abuses they had perpetrated—in Dili, of the contingents that were more notorious for street harassment, and in Oecusse, of the Jordanian peacekeepers in general.[65] Numerous respondents also spoke of the anger that many locals felt towards the UN peacekeepers as a result of their sexual misconduct and their disappointment that peacekeepers did not respect their mission to bring peace enough to obey the code of conduct. The lack of accountability for perpetrators who were reported to UN authorities fueled this anger, and the lack of transparency about the processes and outcomes deepened mistrust and, according to some respondents, compounded the traumas of the occupation and the cultures of silence around abuses by authorities. Furthermore, some respondents spoke of the deep disrespect the community felt in the face of the inappropriate sexual behaviors of interveners and the way in which they felt as if their moral code and culture was being disregarded and derided by these behaviors and by the lack of appropriate responses by authorities. Many suggested that their community expected interveners to "be better than this."

These feelings have been echoed by communities elsewhere: during interviews with community members in Liberia in 2004 about the sexual abuse and exploitation of children by peacekeepers, one man complained to Sarah Martin that "this behavior would not be acceptable in the home country of these soldiers. Why are these soldiers playing around with our children?" A Liberian woman went on to say that "these girls that [UN peacekeeping soldiers] go off with are just children. They cannot reason for themselves. They are hungry and want money for school. The peacekeepers give them that. But the peacekeepers are adults. They should act responsibly."[66] This shows how communities might simultaneously understand the economic function of transactional sex for children and their families in the contexts of deprivation and vulnerability in which they find themselves while nevertheless holding higher expectations of the behaviors of interveners sent to protect them.

Interviews in Bosnia aired a different but related set of concerns, in all likelihood because of the different, less visible nature of sexual exploitation and abuse by interveners in the postwar period, the different historical context, and the fact that many of the victims were not Bosnians but rather women from neighboring states. For instance, one Bosnian respondent who worked with the UN during UNPROFOR recalled her deep disappointment when the head of mission and special representative of the secretary-general Jacques Paul Klein appeared on the BBC in response to the allegations of peacekeepers being involved in prostitution and trafficking. She recalled that the staff, especially national staff, were waiting for him to acknowledge what had happened and promise accountability for perpetrators and were shocked and disappointed when he instead denied the problem; as a consequence many of those staff lost faith in his leadership and the veracity of other claims he made about the peace process.[67] Others spoke about how there was little public trust in the institutional responses to misconduct, which, as mentioned above, led to a general reluctance to report abuses by interveners to relevant authorities.[68] Furthermore, researchers who had studied the experiences of Bosnians during the war and its aftermath found that many local people became very critical of the international community as a result of the very different standards of behavior, capacities, and qualifications of personnel in different uniformed units.[69] The sense that the UN peace operation was not coherent and that the different elements of the mission were not working well together contributed to overarching mistrust and dissatisfaction with the mission.

The mistrust that sprung directly from intervener sexual misconduct was compounded by what many locals perceived as the inequality between the international community and the local community as demonstrated by the employment conditions and treatment of local translators and national staff employed by the UN and NGOs and the broader behaviors of the international community. For example, a number of interviewees mentioned the Christmas gala hosted at the UN base each year during the siege of

Sarajevo, when no one else had electricity, heating, or enough food. During the gala, the Bosnian police were required to stand outside in the freezing weather and protect the celebration. This was seen as deeply inconsiderate and disrespectful of the situation of the besieged local community and of Bosnians in general. "And yet they [the peacekeepers] would exchange sex with girls for a can of tuna," one respondent said, pointing out how offensive it was for peacekeepers to be engaging in exploitative transactional sex when they were so well fed and looked after.[70] Hasan Nuhanović, the Bosnian translator working with the Dutch contingent at Srebrenica, recounted how translators and other men working for the mission were prohibited from eating at the base's cafeteria whereas the young Bosnian women working on the base were permitted to do so, and it was implied that there were sexual relationships between those women and peacekeepers on the base. Nuhanović spoke at length of how this illustrates the lack of empathy, sympathy, and respect the peacekeepers had for the civilians they were mandated to protect and the way the perceptions of these forms of discrimination and racism deeply affected subsequent interactions between local populations and the international interveners deployed to the country.[71] In short, sexual misconduct was seen in the context of a range of other interlinked disrespectful and harmful practices that interveners engaged in—and together, they seeded a deep mistrust of interveners in segments of the local population.

Respondents in Timor-Leste also bought up questions of sexism, discrimination, and racism in relation to employment practices. Such discriminatory practices produced a range of inappropriate, exploitative, and problematic interactions between locals and international personnel, some of which were closely linked to sexual exploitation and others of which related more generally to the dynamics between local and international staff in workplaces. For instance, it is fairly commonplace across peace operations for women to be employed to work as maids or housekeepers for international interveners. In Haiti, Paul Higate and Marsha Henry were told that "[male] international staff always seem to look for a younger girl that they can 'employ' in their house . . . that is exploitation, because he has financial power and in his home country he can never employ a teenager like that."[72] This came up multiple times in interviews in Timor-Leste as well: sometimes the arrangement was simply for housekeeping, but other times there was an expectation that sexual services would also be provided, as the previous chapter showed. The biases and power dynamics that underpin this form of exploitation also give rise to workplace policies that distinguish between local and international staff in terms of workplace rights and remuneration. Most Timorese respondents mentioned at some point that unfair salary arrangements meant national staff were paid significantly less than their international counterparts for similar jobs and did not receive the same per-diems for travel away from headquarters even though their living costs were just as high. Furthermore, national staff were in some cases limited in their use of business vehicles, which was considered particularly galling in light of the dangerous and sometimes illegal on-road behaviors of some international personnel in official vehicles. Others complained that they felt as if Timorese staff were treated as second class and not considered as smart or as qualified for certain jobs, despite their professional and educational backgrounds.[73] This not only caused tension and mistrust between the local and international communities but also created an artificial economy, pushing the price of living in Dili up significantly with impacts for the Timorese community in the capital, and also meant that once the large international presence wound down the local economy was severely impacted.

This shows how patterns of mistrust arise as a result of both sexual misconduct and other, often intersecting practices and arrangements that amplify the power differential between local communities and international interveners. As Séverine Autesserre has shown, the structure of inequality permeates relationships between interveners and their local counterparts, which strengthens boundaries between the two groups and antagonizes local populations; my analysis has shown how the structure of inequality manifests both in sexual exploitation and abuse and in nonsexual practices of exploitation or discrimination.[74] The consequent breakdown of trust between a host-population and the international community deployed to serve and protect it has clear operational implications. The importance of local participation and buy-in to the effectiveness of peace operations has been well established in the literature and practice on peacekeeping.[75] Richard Caplan has shown how the legitimacy (and therefore success) of peace operations depends on the accountability of peace operations, particularly to local populations, and how trust is a crucial aspect of this.[76] Andrew Goldsmith and Vandra Harris have illustrated how long-term cooperation and compliance with a policing operation relies on the trust of the local population and how in the absence of such trust local individuals and groups may directly defy international personnel or resist, disengage, or attempt to manipulate them, which can undermine their capacity to achieve mission objectives.[77] Autesserre has shown how the structure of inequality in peace operations decreases their effectiveness by reinforcing boundaries between expatriates and their local counterparts and fueling local resentment of interveners and feelings of being disrespected and disregarded, which undermine local engagement in and ownership and authorship of peacebuilding.[78] Ultimately, all of this goes to show that when interveners engage in behaviors that erode the trust the local population has in them and in the peace operation more broadly, it fundamentally undermines their capacity to achieve mission objectives, which rely on the cooperation, consent, and buy-in of the host community.

A related operational impact of sexual misconduct by interveners is that it has in some cases led to a peace operation becoming a direct target of violence. One senior international official with experience in Cambodia, Bosnia, and Timor-Leste recalled that in Cambodia, rapes perpetrated by a group of Bulgarian peacekeepers led to an attack on peacekeepers that resulted in multiple deaths.[79] The same official recalled that in Bosnia, some peacekeepers were relocated elsewhere because they were in danger of revenge attacks after perpetrating sexual exploitation and abuse. In Liberia, a Molotov cocktail was thrown into a UN checkpoint operated by the Bangladeshi contingent, allegedly because local men were angry that UN troops were engaging in sexual relationships with local women.[80] Hasan Nuhanović, the Bosnian translator who worked with UNPRO-FOR during the war, recalled a case of conflict between the Canadian contingent he worked for and the local police force: the peacekeepers allowed a group of local women into the base regularly to trade sex for food and other material goods, which made local men angry that they were not allowed onto the base to trade other goods with peacekeepers. The men complained to the local police chief, who approached the Canadian commander and said that he had arrested the twelve to fifteen women involved because prostitution was illegal and that he expected the commander to arrest and repatriate the Canadian peacekeepers involved. The commander refused, saying that he was already low on personnel, and as a result the relationship between the two collapsed and they did not speak to one another for a month, even though coordination between the peace-keepers and local police was crucial to the mission's work.[81] A number of individuals in the UN bureaucracy who had worked in peace operations globally further argued that sexual misconduct or even the appearance of inappropriate relationships with certain groups can undermine a mission's impartiality in the eyes of local communities, creating risks to both mission personnel and objectives. Their anecdotal experiences have been confirmed by Kate Grady's research.[82] Grady found that sexual exploitation and abuse can affect local perceptions of impartiality when peacekeepers patronize brothels selling women who have been trafficked by a party to the conflict, thereby financially supporting that group. She also found that reports of sexual misconduct by interveners have been used as a propaganda tool by parties to a conflict seeking to pursue their own conflict interests by undermining UN authority: such groups argued that sexual interactions between peacekeepers and locals from a particular group illustrated the UN's partiality to that particular group.

In addition to causing conflict and mistrust between the local population and the international presence in a host country, sexual misconduct by interveners appears to also seed mistrust and conflict between organizational units within the international community. A significant number of the international staff I interviewed, both in the case study countries and at international headquarters, recounted a reluctance to work with colleagues who they knew had engaged in sexual exploitation or abuse (particularly transactional sex) or with organizations that had a reputation for not ensuring accountability for perpetrators. Direct conflict also emerged in some cases: the *Australian* reported that after an Australian soldier blew the whistle on the abuse of children by Jordanian peacekeepers in Oecusse, the Jordanians threatened the whistleblower and other Australian peacekeepers in an armed confrontation, leading to the whistleblower being evacuated and Australia sending reinforcements to protect the Australian peacekeepers still stationed in Oecusse.[83] Although this seems to be a rare case of outright conflict between peacekeeping units, one senior military official with experience in numerous interventions globally suggested that it was not uncommon for there to be a breakdown between national contingents that upheld strict rules of conduct and those that tolerated sexual misconduct by their personnel.[84] Another interesting instance of conflict between organizational units as a long-term result of sexual exploitation and abuse was recounted to me in Timor-Leste. A senior foreign military official with long-term experience of the peace operations in the country recalled that a particular Fijian unit engaged in sexual misconduct during an early deployment in Timor-Leste, and when a Fijian soldier from a different unit was placed in a senior position more than ten years later, he found it difficult to be accepted and establish strong working relationships with his Timorese counterparts because of the behaviors of Fijians in the past and suspicions that he would behave in similar ways. These cases, although different in nature and intensity, demonstrate how sexual misconduct by interveners can undermine the operational outcomes of peace operations by seeding conflict when cooperation between the different elements of a peace operation and integrated responses have been shown to be crucial to a mission effectively undertaking its mandated duties.[85]

One final operational impact that sexual misconduct by interveners has is to divert critical resources away from core peacebuilding tasks that are fundamental to the long-term objectives of peace operations. Madeline Rees, the head of the Office of the High Commissioner for Human Rights in Bosnia after the war, was at the forefront of pushing for an institutional response to the sexual exploitation and abuse perpetrated by peacekeepers that Kathryn Bolkovac revealed. Reflecting on the lessons she learned from her experience working in Bosnia, Rees has told researchers:

> I got very frustrated dealing with trafficking when I was there. I was supposed to work on post-conflict issues. We could have made much more progress on those issues if we (and here I refer to the women's NGOs as well the "good" parts of the international community and government), hadn't had to spend 50 per cent of our time working on trafficking. Working with the Bosnian government was great, they wanted to listen to us. But what was happening to all the other issues around transitional justice while we were doing that?[86]

This suggestion that intervener misconduct in Bosnia delayed crucial other work was echoed by a number of interviewees who had worked with international and national organizations in their response to sexual exploitation and pointed out that it diverted resources and attention away from addressing the ramifications of extensive conflict-related sexual violence during the war. A Bosnian expert in human rights law and gender equality argued along the same lines, claiming that one of the biggest challenges facing the country today is the lack of public policy, legislation, and support mechanisms related to sexual violence and sexual harassment and implying that these issues might have been addressed had the UN and international community set an example about the importance of addressing sexual violence by pursuing a robust response to intervener sexual exploitation and abuse.[87] Although this issue was not raised in Timor-Leste, a senior UN policing official in New York argued, "Sexual exploitation and abuse doesn't impact our credibility so much as it means that we can't get things fixed faster wherever we are working," and suggested that delays in "getting things fixed" can then have a significant impact on the UN's credibility.[88] This shows how the imperative to respond to sexual misconduct using existing resources and personnel within a peace operation can divert the attention of key staff and operational units away from the core business of the operation, including pursuing the overarching mission strategy, ensuring accountability for wartime crimes (including sexual violence), strengthening the effectiveness and accountability of the security sector, and supporting local efforts to embed human rights frameworks and policies in the postwar state and legislative structures. Delays in these core tasks can have significant impacts for the outcomes peace operations are able to achieve.

This discussion has demonstrated how sexual abuse and exploitation by interveners can have significant operational impacts by seeding mistrust of the international mission, thus provoking conflict both between the local community and international personnel and between elements of a mission, and by diverting attention and resources away from critical peacebuilding tasks and towards responding to misconduct. What is particularly striking is how these operational-level impacts intersect with and mutually reinforce those impacts identified earlier at the structural and individual/community levels in peace operations. Taken together, these three levels of impacts represent significant obstacles to the international community's capacity to achieve its goals in peace operations and cast doubt on the credibility of the stated values that animate them.

An interesting contradiction emerged during discussions, though. The accounts provided by local respondents about the impacts of sexual misconduct suggested that such behaviors are in deep tension with the goals and principles underpinning peace operations and that they affected mission outcomes in important ways. Yet, on the whole, local respondents in both Timor-Leste and Bosnia argued that sexual exploitation and abuse did not undermine the international community's efforts to stop the violence and establish security. Most suggested that the fact that security was established relatively successfully (despite some crises) in their country was evidence of how sexual exploitation and abuse did not affect or undermine the overarching outcomes of the peace operation. This reflects a fairly narrow view of what the core goals of peace operations are: security was valued by local respondents over and above other goals that the international community might itself believe to be equally important, such as the protection of human rights, the pursuit of justice and accountability, and the establishment of rule of law and robust and democratic postwar security institutions. This shows a fundamental tension between how the purposes of peace operations are understood by the recipients of those missions and how they are understood by the international community, and it shows how the behaviors of the international interveners can affect the fundamental justifications they articulate themselves for their missions in contrast to those that local communities interpret to be most important. Furthermore, it illustrates a tension in how the various elements of peace operations are understood to relate to one another; peacekeeping doctrine, as discussed earlier, holds that the establishment of lasting peace and security is contingent on the achievement of goals relating to justice, rule of law, democracy, and inclusivity. This suggests that greater work needs to be done to communicate the broad goals of peace operations and to engage local communities in understanding the connection between the establishment of security and broader political, social, and justice-related goals in peace operations.

This chapter has shown how sexual exploitation and abuse perpetrated by interveners in peace operations can have serious implications for the outcomes of peace operations and how it undermines the broader goals of such operations, which revolve around assisting in the establishment of peace and security and the protection of human rights and vulnerable groups. The experiences in Bosnia and Timor-Leste illustrate how sexual misconduct by interveners directly violates these goals in the short-term while also contributing to the entrenchment of practices and economies that outlast peace operations and thereby undermine efforts towards them in the much longer term as well. The impacts of such misconduct operate on multiple levels: for individuals and their communities; for the structures, economies, and cultures of postwar states and societies; and for the capacity of missions to effectively undertake their mandated activities and achieve their stated goals. One fairly obvious conclusion arising from this analysis is that, in perpetrating sexual exploitation and abuse, interveners commit human rights violations, consolidate structures and processes that facilitate further exploitation and abuse, and spark conflict with actors who object to such behaviors; thus these outcomes are not in line with general expectations of the impacts peacekeepers should have on local populations and host states.

More important, this chapter has illustrated that the implications of sexual misconduct by interveners have clear and long-term consequences for the outcomes of the peace operations into which they are deployed. In other words, sexual exploitation and abuse by interveners undermines the capacity of the international community to achieve mission objectives and leads to outcomes that are in direct tension with the broader goals around establishing lasting peace, security, and respect for human rights that animate the peacekeeping project. In fact, in the cases studied, such behaviors contributed to the expansion and consolidation of patterns of human suffering and cultures and economies of gendered exploitation, abuse, and impunity, which long outlasted peace operations. Sexual exploitation and abuse was a significant source of mistrust between local communities and the international intervention, particularly as it intersected with other behaviors that amplified and exploited the power imbalance between international interveners and local communities. Furthermore, it caused direct and indirect conflict, both within a mission and between locals and international personnel. And last, it diverted critical (and scarce) resources away from core peacebuilding issues and towards the response to intervener misconduct. These outcomes undermined the ability of international personnel to effectively achieve their goals, both directly and indirectly, through undermining community confidence in the purpose and credibility of the peace operation. Moreover, this analysis has shown that even a limited number of cases of the more violent forms of sexual abuse can seriously affect public opinion on interveners, and even those forms of sexual misconduct considered less egregious

by the international community—namely transactional sex—can significantly affect peacebuilding outcomes and perceptions of the legitimacy
of a peace operations.

Jeni Whalan's study of how peace operations work showed that in
order to achieve their transformative goals, peace operations depend first
and foremost on their capacity to obtain and maintain local compliance
and cooperation. She argues that this can only occur when peace operations are perceived by local communities to be legitimate:

> When local actors perceive a peace operation to be legitimate, they are more
> likely to act in ways that enable the operation to achieve its goals. The belief
> that a peace operation, its personnel, and its goals are "right" provides nor-
> mative reasons for local actors to cooperate; meanwhile, the perception that
> an operation is illegitimate—is unfair, partial, untrustworthy, self-interested,
> disrespectful—provides reasons for local actors to resist it.[89]

This highlights the fundamentally social power relationship between
local communities and international personnel and the importance of a
social contract between local communities and interveners—ultimately,
that "people within a society will assent to power concentrated in the
form of a government on the condition that the government protects their
individual and collective rights."[90] This depends on the construction of
a moral basis for the authority and political power of a peace operation,
which is central to local perceptions of legitimacy: the analysis above demonstrates how sexual misconduct by interveners directly undermines local
perceptions of legitimacy and willingness to cooperate and comply with
peace operations. The perpetration of sexual exploitation and abuse, and
the failure to hold perpetrators accountable, throws into question the international community's commitment to norms of human rights, accountability, and rule of law—which, given that the international community
is attempting to embed these norms in postwar societies, reveals a deep
hypocrisy in the peacekeeping project.

The peacekeeping moment is one of great promise and opportunity,
during which the international community can work to support local
communities in the transition from violence towards peaceful modes of
social and political organization and competition. This opportunity is lost
when interveners perpetrate sexual exploitation and abuse against local

populations, consolidating instead patterns of impunity, suffering, and violence in postwar societies and state structures and limiting the capacity of the international community to convince local actors of the legitimacy of its goals and methods in the peace operation. This analysis raises a critical question: do these impacts of sexual misconduct stop at the level of a mission in which the abuses are perpetrated or can they impact the international community's capacity and credibility, with broader consequences for the international peacekeeping project? It is to that question that the next chapter turns.

4

LEGITIMACY IN CRISIS

The Impacts of Sexual Misconduct on Capacity and Credibility

Having established in the last chapter how the perpetration of sexual exploitation and abuse by international interveners impacts the international community's capacity to achieve its objectives in specific missions, I turn in this chapter to the question of whether such behaviors have implications beyond specific missions. What are the global political implications of sexual misconduct scandals? Does sexual exploitation and abuse undermine the international community's credibility in the eyes of the people and communities around the world just as it undermines credibility at the local level? Does it affect operational capacities at the international level? And, perhaps most important, does it affect perceptions of the legitimacy of the global peacekeeping and peacebuilding project? In answering these questions, this chapter shifts from a local- and operational-level analysis to one focused primarily on the institutional- and macro-level impacts of sexual misconduct by interveners.

This chapter shows that sexual misconduct in individual missions has far-reaching impacts that reduce international capacities to engage effectively in peace operations and diminish the perceived legitimacy of the international community engaged in peacekeeping and peacebuilding, thereby undermining the international community's capacity to pursue the broader aspirational goals that animate peacekeeping. By analyzing the perspectives and experiences of international interveners themselves and by tracking international responses to the 2015 peacekeeper sexual abuse scandal in the Central African Republic and the 2018 Oxfam sexual exploitation scandal in Haiti, this chapter demonstrates that such behaviors undermine the capacity and perceived legitimacy of the international community in a number of mutually reinforcing ways. Sexual exploitation and abuse compromises perceptions of impartiality and diminishes the confidence interveners themselves have in their organization and the international peacekeeping project, leading to staff attrition. It seeds conflict between different organizational or peacekeeping units as a result of perceived misbehaviors and undermines the morale of peacekeepers and humanitarians. Furthermore, with growing pressure for UN compensation and support for victims of sexual misconduct by peacekeepers, sexual exploitation and abuse policy responses may put further financial pressure on already underfunded UN peacekeeping operations and divert resources from other central peacekeeping tasks. Perhaps most critical, sexual exploitation and abuse presents a challenge to the established processes of legitimation that the UN and the international community pursue in order to maintain the perception of moral authority in the eyes of the world's states and peoples that is foundational to its continued work. This can result in reduced financial and other support for peace operations and related work and provide fodder for anti-intervention campaigners, which immediately affects capacity in missions and creates a cycle whereby diminished credibility further undermines capacity, which in turn further diminishes perceptions of credibility. This has serious implications for the future of peacekeeping and peacebuilding, suggesting that sexual misconduct is an issue of the utmost importance to the core competences and collective goals of the international community.

This chapter proceeds in two sections. The first addresses the question of capacity, investigating how sexual exploitation and abuse by interveners affects the capacity of the international community internationally to achieve its goals relating to the promotion of peace and security. The second discusses the global political implications of such behaviors, including for the international community's perceived credibility as peacemaker and peacebuilder and for the peacekeeping and peacebuilding project more broadly. It considers how sexual misconduct presents a challenge to the established processes of legitimation that the UN pursues in order to maintain its moral authority in the eyes of the world's states and peoples, and tracks through case studies how this creates a mutually reinforcing downward spiral of capacity and perceived credibility.

Undermining Capacity?

The previous chapter demonstrated how, by diverting resources away from critical peacebuilding tasks and undermining trust between the international interveners and the local population in contexts where interveners were deployed, sexual exploitation and abuse by interveners undermined their capacity to achieve central mission goals. Research undertaken with members of the international community of interveners suggested that the impacts on capacity were much broader and, in many ways, much more insidious and far-reaching than might be assumed at first glance because of the ways in which sexual misconduct undermines perceptions within the intervener community about the legitimacy of their own work and creates additional financial pressures on an already over-stressed UN system.

Many of those who opt to work with the international community in peace operations—as civilian peacekeepers, military experts, and individual police in UN missions (as distinct from uniformed contingents deployed by states) or as part of the broader nonpeacekeeping presence—do so because they are committed to the values and goals that underpin humanitarian and peacebuilding efforts. A study of humanitarian health workers found that the most common motivating factor for undertaking such deployments was a feeling of responsibility for others—a moral obligation—which outweighed considerations of personal risk and inconvenience when deploying into emergency contexts.[1] Other research has similarly highlighted the importance of moral motivations for humanitarian workers, based on values such as humanity, altruism, solidarity, empathy, and democracy, and the fact that the strong motivation to help others outweighs motivations that drive other forms of professional activity, such as financial gain and the desire to develop professional expertise.[2] Indeed many of these values are enshrined in the humanitarian principles as articulated in the Red Cross and NGO Code of Conduct and in the 1991 UN General Assembly Resolution 46/182. These core principles include the humane treatment of and respect for all individuals, the primacy of the humanitarian imperative (the right to receive and offer humanitarian assistance wherever it is needed), impartiality in the delivery of assistance, and independence.[3] The perpetration of sexual exploitation and abuse by those involved in humanitarian work and peace operations clearly violates the first three of these principles, so it is unsurprising that, during interviews, many respondents credited the tension between their own personal commitment to these principles and knowledge of sexual exploitation or abuse perpetrated by colleagues as having serious consequences for morale and confidence in their organizations and mission.

A number of women respondents spoke of how their knowledge of sexually inappropriate behaviors by colleagues affected the confidence they had in their own organization and in the peacekeeping project more broadly. For instance, one expatriate woman who had worked in Timor-Leste since independence argued that while many people in the international missions cared deeply about the protection and needs of Timorese communities, they had to work alongside people who did not and who failed to even recognize the exploitative nature of some of their interactions with local individuals, particularly relationships characterized by massive power imbalances.[4] Another told me that she lost respect for her colleagues when she saw UN vehicles parked outside of brothels and that sexual exploitation and abuse by interveners fundamentally tarnished the reputation of the international community in her eyes.[5] Both suggested that this affected their working relationships with colleagues they knew to be engaging in sexual misconduct, with tangible consequences for work outcomes. A senior male staff member at UN headquarters in New York similarly argued that the impact of sexual exploitation and abuse on UN staff is high and "hard to come to terms with" if you are part of the UN system: "How do you explain it to your kids, when you know the UN was supposed to be better than this?"[6] This sentiment was amplified when respondents felt that their organization failed to take allegations of sexual misconduct seriously and appropriately hold perpetrators accountable. One interviewee in Geneva recalled being told by senior leaders in her organization that she was "exaggerating the problem" when she raised issues of sexual abuse and exploitation by staff, and that, when forced to respond, management was primarily concerned with organizational risk and reputation rather than accountability to victims.[7] A number of respondents working with major international organizations said that there were particularly strong feelings of disappointment among staff when senior leaders refused to believe that their staff would perpetrate sexual misconduct and clung to the assumption that all staff were motivated by altruistic values and the principles in the humanitarian code of conduct that they had signed. This echoes the sentiment expressed by Bosnian respondents working with the UN mission when mission leadership refused to acknowledge the widely known involvement of peacekeepers in sexual exploitation discussed in the last chapter. Individuals involved in supporting victims were particularly distressed by what they described as systematic victim-blaming in the aftermath of allegations, particularly in cases of transactional sex or involvement in prostitution and in investigative processes that were not victim-centered and often failed to report back to victims on the outcomes of their allegations.[8]

Taken together, the reluctance of senior leaders to accept that humanitarian personnel also perpetrate sexual exploitation and abuse, insufficient responses to allegations, poor or retaliatory responses to whistle-blowers, and a culture where certain behaviors are simply accepted despite being exploitative appear to undermine the confidence staff have in their organization and in the peacekeeping project. This has significant consequences for staff morale more broadly: many of the expatriate staff interviewed, particularly women, noted that they were disheartened as a result of these factors and mentioned that they knew colleagues who had left the mission or sector altogether as a consequence. One former senior NGO staff member who had been her organization's focal point for the prevention of sexual exploitation and abuse recalled that she realized with time that there was a "hierarchy of evils" whereby agencies decide which behaviors are worse.[9] However, she pointed out that in the absence of an understanding of the impacts of sexual exploitation and abuse on women and children, it was easy for such behaviors to be considered a lesser form of evil and one that agencies could devote fewer resources towards addressing. This was particularly true for those acts that involve some level of consent or transaction, which makes their exploitative nature hard to ascertain. After attempting but failing to shift these cultures and establish strong mechanisms to address sexual exploitation and abuse, she left the sector. A group of Geneva-based experts on sexual exploitation and abuse argued that the fact that child protection policies have strong commitment of donors and organizational leadership but that the same is not true of sexual exploitation and abuse policies shows how this hierarchy works in practice.[10]

Sarah von Billerbeck's research has shown that the UN frames its identity first in terms of its operational role responding to conflicts globally and second in terms of its normative role in developing, upholding, and promoting norms and UN principles at the international level.[11] These define how UN staff see themselves and the "worthiness and rightness of their role in post-conflict situations."[12] My interviews with UN staff and others associated with peace operations showed how sexual misconduct by interveners challenges both of these perceptions: by undermining operational effectiveness, as demonstrated in the previous chapter, and by directly violating the norms and principles the international community claims to be driven by in peace operations. It is no wonder that by fundamentally challenging staff's beliefs about the rightness and justness of their work and the international project they are a part of, sexual exploitation and abuse leads to staff attrition and disengagement with their organization's mission and, as a result of this drain on human resources, diminishes the international community's capacity to effectively respond to conflicts through peace operations.

Another way in which sexual misconduct undermines the capacity of the international community more broadly than within specific missions is by diverting already scarce resources towards response mechanisms such as institutional support to victims. In 2016, Secretary-General Guterres established the Trust Fund in Support of Victims of Sexual Exploitation and Abuse, which became operational the following year. The trust fund does not provide compensation to victims but rather engages in community outreach and supports projects to provide specialized services and assistance to victims and children born of sexual exploitation and abuse. It currently works in three countries that experienced high rates of sexual exploitation and abuse perpetrated by peacekeepers: the Democratic Republic of Congo, the Central African Republic, and Liberia. Nineteen countries have voluntarily contributed to the trust fund, which, as of mid-2017, had a total of US $2 million available, approximately $317,000 of which derives from payments withheld from UN personnel against whom sexual misconduct allegations had been substantiated.[13] While this work is undeniably important, a number of UN policymakers expressed concern during interviews that it would compete with other similar areas of work for funding from donor states, such as the funding for gender-based violence in conflict and the Trust Fund for Victims at the International Criminal Court.[14] The trust fund may also divert critical funding away from sexual exploitation and abuse prevention responses if member states are unwilling to increase the overall amount of their contribution to these issues. Competition for funding of these "non-essential" activities is likely to only intensify with the downward pressure already being applied to the UN peacekeeping budget, particularly by the United States. Furthermore, victim assistance funds, which are used to provide support ranging from emergency accommodation and medical care to HIV prophylaxis tests and psychological counseling, generally through contracting local service providers, are not drawn from a separate fund but rather from the existing budget of each peacekeeping mission.[15] Ultimately, these responses to sexual exploitation and abuse undermine the capacity of the international community by diverting resources away from tasks that are critical to peacebuilding in order to address the long-term consequences of misconduct by peacekeepers for their victims. This is not to suggest that providing such redress is wrong—quite the opposite, it is fundamental to the UN's embodiment of principles of human rights and protection. Rather, it shows how sexual misconduct affects the distribution of already scarce resources with inevitable impacts for the capacity of the international community to fulfill fundamental activities. More effective prevention strategies might obviate the need for as many resources to be devoted to redress mechanisms.

Undermining Legitimacy?

The previous chapter demonstrated how the perpetration of sexual exploitation and abuse by international interveners has significant impacts on local perceptions of a mission's credibility, with demonstrable operational impacts. However, given that peace operations are underwritten by a language of morality and an aspirational political project revolving around values of justice, human rights, and peace, these operations also depend on and reflect the perceptions diverse global audiences have of the legitimacy of this project. The different audiences that judge the legitimacy of peacekeeping include neighboring and regional states, the domestic constituencies of intervening states, and the international community of interveners—including both state and non-state actors. The research undertaken for this book has illuminated how perceptions of legitimacy in these broader audiences affect the way states engage in and support the international peacekeeping project, which in turn affects the capacity of the international community in peace operations.

Scholars who have examined the way legitimacy operates in peace operations have found that the perceived legitimacy of peacekeeping derives from a number of sources and strategies. These include the alignment of peace operations with international legal norms and broadly liberal international principles that underpin the purpose of the UN; the expectation that peace operations result in positive outcomes for societies experiencing violence and conflict; the presence of an international consensus on peacekeeping operations (through the mandate provided by authorizing bodies); and evidence that peacekeeping actors and policy are learning from past experiences and improving the effectiveness of their work as a result.[16] In other words, perceptions of legitimacy tend to rest on assessments of whether an organization or its actions reflect what is considered right, proper, and fair and the extent to which operational outcomes align with the rhetoric and norms used to justify operations in the first place.[17]

The UN and associated actors actively engage in strategies of legitimation to promote the images inherent in the sources of legitimacy just listed. Discursive strategies are a cornerstone of this, by which the UN depicts its actions as representative of the shared principles and core goals that underpin the organization's mandate, namely the promotion of peace and human rights through efforts to prevent and resolve violent conflict in the world. The full range of UN actors participate in these legitimation strategies, including the secretary-general and the secretariat, the UN Security Council, the General Assembly, and the range of UN funds and agencies. They do so through a combination of public communications outreach (such as the UN websites), official statements, ceremonies, events, and regular debates or meetings that link UN operations to the organization's mandate and principles as set out in the charter. The previous chapter illustrated how this operates in practice in peace operations, whereby the UN articulates why the inclusion of particular operational mandates such as rule of law reflect the UN's core goals around the promotion of peace and human rights and are therefore appropriate activities for peacekeepers to undertake. Success in fulfilling these operational mandates is then used to reinforce claims of the legitimacy of UN peacekeeping and the values underpinning it.[18]

However, sexual exploitation and abuse by peacekeepers fundamentally undermines the hard work that has gone into these legitimation strategies by revealing the disconnect between the values underpinning peacekeeping and its (albeit unintended) outcomes. Sexual misconduct scandals, revelations about chronically poor institutional responses to allegations, and an awareness that the rhetoric of a zero-tolerance policy towards sexual exploitation and abuse has not translated into effective prevention or response mechanisms in peace operations all undermine the legitimation strategies that UN actors engage in and rely on to maintain global support for the peacekeeping project. They also affect support for the UN more generally, given that the UN's mandate, as set out in the charter, is to "save succeeding generations from the scourge of war" and "reaffirm faith in fundamental human rights, in the dignity and worth of the human person."[19] Pursuing these goals through peacekeeping is central to the UN's narratives of its identity and legitimacy.[20]

The diminished legitimacy of the UN in the eyes of intervening states and their domestic constituencies as well as in the eyes of the international community of interveners more broadly has led to some states reducing their financial and personnel contributions to UN peace operations. The same effect has been felt by other organizations implicated in sexual misconduct by interveners. Reduced support has direct implications for the capacity of individual missions and organizations, which then further undermines the effectiveness of the legitimation strategies discussed above. This effects are amplified by the fact that the UN's credibility and value (and that of the broader international community engaged in peace and humanitarian operations) is already under extreme scrutiny as a result of myriad other challenges and failures. This is despite peacekeeping, peacebuilding, and related humanitarian services being relatively oversubscribed—with the numbers of peacekeepers deployed and the peacekeeping budget at an all time high.[21]

So, how do these effects play out in practice? A close look at the international responses to the 2018 Oxfam sexual exploitation scandal in Haiti and the 2016 peacekeeper sexual abuse scandal in the Central African Republic illuminates the global political implications of sexual exploitation and abuse scandals. It shows the ways in which they challenge established processes and strategies of legitimation that the UN and other organizations rely on to maintain the global perceptions of their moral authority, which are critical to continued support, funding, and operational effectiveness.

The 2018 Oxfam Haiti Sexual Exploitation Scandal

The Oxfam sexual exploitation scandal of early 2018 demonstrates how quickly trust in even well-established and well-respected humanitarian organizations like Oxfam can be lost and how quickly public perceptions of their moral authority and legitimacy can be damaged, leading to lasting long-term consequences for the operation of those organizations and the sector as a whole.

When the *Times* broke the story that a number of Oxfam Great Britain (Oxfam GB) staff in Haiti, including the director of operations, had engaged in transactional sex with local Haitian women while deployed to the country as part of the 2010 earthquake response, both donor governments and the general public reacted swiftly.[22] On the same day that the story broke, the UK government demanded that all evidence of the case be handed over to the Charity Commission, and within a few days the government had launched a statutory inquiry into the organization, questioned Oxfam's moral leadership, and threatened to cut off funding for Oxfam if it could not account for its handling of the claims, which prompted the resignation of Oxfam GB's deputy chief executive.[23] Oxfam GB's chair of trustees made a public statement acknowledging that staff within the organization had been coming forward with concerns over staff recruitment and vetting in this case, suggesting that the trust staff had in their own organization was severely impacted by the scandal.[24] The European Commission demanded full clarity and transparency from Oxfam about the case and declared that it was ready to "cease funding any partner not living up to high ethical standards," and a number of major corporate sponsors made similar threats.[25] A week after the news broke, the UK's international development secretary Penny Mordaunt announced that Oxfam had "a long way to go before they can regain the trust of the British public, their staff and the people they aim to help" and that the organization had agreed to withdraw from any new UK government funding bids until the Department for International Development was satisfied that they could meet the expected standards around protection.[26] Roughly 8 percent of Oxfam GB's income comes from the UK government, so this was a significant cut.[27] Furthermore, within ten days of the scandal breaking in international media, Oxfam GB confirmed that it had lost the support of 7,094 direct supporters, representing roughly 3.5 percent of donations received through direct debits, and it is likely that this number continued to rise although exact data is not available.[28] Within two weeks of the story breaking, Haiti suspended Oxfam GB's operations in the country and opened an investigation into the misconduct claims, chiding the organization for failing to inform Haitian authorities of the allegations at the time they were made.[29] It is worth noting, however, that there are plausible reasons why these allegations were not passed on, including the additional risk potentially posed to the women involved given that prostitution is illegal in Haiti.

The ramifications of the scandal were not limited to Oxfam GB. The Swedish International Development Cooperation Agency temporarily suspended a joint project with Oxfam pending an investigation of the case, resulting in a halt to a humanitarian project that assisted two hundred fifty thousand people in Iraq, the Central African Republic, and the Democratic Republic of Congo.[30] The European Commission halted the signing of all new development and humanitarian contracts with Oxfam affiliates while it completed an assessment of the organization's policies to prevent, detect, and respond to allegations of misconduct—and extended this review to all two hundred organizations that it provides funding to.[31] The UK government similarly announced measures to review funding arrangements and accountability mechanisms of all NGOs and cut funding to any that failed to declare safeguarding concerns and refer them to relevant authorities.[32] The US Agency for International Development reiterated its zero-tolerance policy on sexual misconduct and announced a review of all current agreements with Oxfam.[33] Australia's foreign minister Julie

Bishop asked Oxfam Australia to suspend funding to all operations of its UK counterpart, which accounted for approximately a quarter of the Australian Department of Foreign Affairs and Trade's funding for Oxfam Australia and affected projects in South Sudan and projects for Syrian refugees in Jordan and Lebanon.[34]

Although Sweden resumed funding for Oxfam after a month, by May Oxfam GB had announced that it would have to make approximately one hundred staff redundant as a result of other large donors pausing new and expected funding.[35] This would significantly impact the organization's capacity. Although EU funding was reapproved in June, Haiti permanently banned Oxfam GB from operating in the country later that month on account of its "violation of [Haiti's] laws and serious breach of the principle of human dignity," although it has allowed other Oxfam affiliates to continue their humanitarian work.[36] Given the findings of the previous chapter, it is conceivable that this decision will affect the way the local community and government trust and engage with the Oxfam staff still in Haiti even though they are not from Oxfam GB, with implications for how effectively the organization can carry out its humanitarian projects in the country.

This case shows how quickly and severely allegations and cases of sexual exploitation and abuse by interveners can affect perceptions about the legitimacy of the organizations those interveners work for, and the multiple audiences affected, including donor governments and the general public. It illustrates how this can result directly in reduced funding or contributions to the organizations implicated as well as others in the same sector, thereby limiting operational capacities. In fact, a number of experts have suggested that the Oxfam scandal might diminish public trust in the humanitarian sector overall, leading to a decrease in direct donations to humanitarian organizations, including from major philanthropists, and pressure for governments to spend less on international development.[37] Moreover, negative public perceptions about the UN and humanitarian sectors broadly were fueled by sensationalist media coverage of the Oxfam crisis that suggested, without evidence, that pedophiles were deliberately infiltrating humanitarian organizations and peace operations in numbers on par with the sex tourism industry in order to gain access to vulnerable children to exploit and abuse.[38] The social media reaction to those claims, despite the lack of evidence provided for them, confirmed how even just suspicions of misconduct by peacekeeping or humanitarian staff can lead to a direct reduction in financial contributions to the humanitarian sector.

This is not to suggest that organizations should continue to receive funding when they fail to put in place the appropriate safeguards to prevent sexual misconduct by their personnel or hold perpetrators accountable—the new oversight mechanisms imposed by the UK and European Commission in the aftermath of the Oxfam scandals are vitally important to ensure organizations have appropriate policies. Rather, it illustrates how such scandals undermine organizations' claims of legitimacy, which are their primary basis for leveraging support from both the general public and official donors. The sexual exploitation of Haitian women by Oxfam GB staff and the organization's failure to prevent those staff from finding employment in other similar contexts stood in stark contrast with its stated vision of "a just world without poverty . . . where people are valued and treated equally" and its purpose to "help creating lasting solutions to the injustice of poverty."[39] Quite the opposite: it showed that some staff were not challenging "the structural causes of the injustice of poverty," as Oxfam International's mission statement holds, but rather exploiting the poverty of those they had been sent to work with and for in order to exploit and abuse them. This case has demonstrated how, by undermining Oxfam's claims to legitimacy and global perceptions of the organization's moral authority, the scandal seriously affected the operational capacities of both Oxfam and the broader humanitarian sector to continue their vital work with the world's most vulnerable communities.

The 2015 Peacekeeper Sexual Abuse Scandal in the Central African Republic

Just as the Oxfam scandal demonstrates the risks sexual misconduct poses to global perceptions of the legitimacy of humanitarian organizations, the global reaction to the sexual abuse scandal in the Central African Republic in 2015 illustrates how such misconduct challenges the UN's strategies of legitimation, which are critical to maintaining member states' financial and political support for peace operations. It also shows how the Central African Republic scandal became a watershed moment for the UN, with the secretariat, Security Council, and member states increasingly talking about legitimacy in order to garner support for stronger mechanisms to ensure accountability for the perpetration of sexual exploitation and abuse. Perhaps most important, this case illustrates just how significant the global political implications of sexual misconduct are. The reactions to the scandal illustrate how sexual exploitation and abuse puts at risk the future of UN peacekeeping and peacebuilding efforts, the end result of a cycle whereby diminished perceptions of credibility reduce the capacity of peace operations, which in turn further undermines the international community's ability to leverage perceptions of legitimacy.

The scandal broke when the NGO AIDS-Free World leaked to the *Guardian* an internal UN report on the violent sexual abuse of children in the Central African Republic by French Sangaris soldiers deployed under a Security Council mandate to support the peace operation and UN peacekeepers from Chad and Equatorial Guinea.[40] The scandal revolved around not just the sadistic and violent nature of the abuses perpetrated but also the fact that the report had been ignored and suppressed for nearly a year by multiple UN offices and agencies. The scandal also hinged on the harsh treatment of the whistleblower, Anders Kompass, the UN human rights official who passed the report on the investigation of allegations to French officials after UN authorities across multiple agencies and departments had failed to act on it for nearly a year. Kompass was condemned by UN officials for leaking the report and suspended from his job, and an internal investigation into his conduct was launched, eventually exonerating him of all charges.[41] Even Zeid Ra'ad Al Hussein, the architect of the UN's 2005 comprehensive policy on sexual exploitation and abuse and, by 2015, the UN's high commissioner for human rights, was himself implicated in the harsh treatment of Kompass.[42]

In the months that followed, AIDS-Free World published further leaked documents and reports of peacekeeper sexual misconduct in Central African Republic and elsewhere, and there was a flurry of news media reports on the issue globally.[43] The particularly horrific nature of the allegations and the fact that the peacekeepers involved allegedly preyed on the most vulnerable children in the communities they had been sent to protect sharpened the global reaction in a way that previous sexual misconduct scandals had not, which may also reflect intensifying global attention to institutional child abuse and gender-based violence. Shortly after the report was leaked, the French president François Hollande pledged to "show no mercy" to French troops found to have been involved in sexual exploitation and abuse while deployed in the Central African Republic, and declared that any sanctions should reflect the gravity of the crimes and set an example of France's zero-tolerance attitude towards such behaviors.[44] In contrast, the Central African Republic's justice minister, Aristide Sokambi, told media, "I deplore the fact that we haven't been joined about this investigation" despite it occurring in the Central African Republic against its citizens, and instructed the public prosecutor to begin an inquiry and collect evidence in parallel to the French investigations.[45]

The scandal also created pressure and momentum within the UN system for addressing what Ban Ki-moon eventually came to describe in the aftermath of the revelations as the "cancer in our system."[46] The response to the scandal reflected, for the first time, an increasing awareness of the impact that sexual exploitation and abuse has on global perceptions of UN legitimacy. Although statements about sexual misconduct affecting the credibility of the UN had been made many times before, it was only in the aftermath of this particular scandal that such statements gradually began to show a genuine engagement with how exactly sexual exploitation and abuse affects perceptions of UN legitimacy and the implications for peacekeeping. Tracking the development of this new discourse after the Central African Republic scandal is helpful in understanding the ways in which sexual misconduct affects UN strategies of legitimation and global perceptions of legitimacy more broadly.

While the UN's response initially focused on what it alleged was misconduct by Kompass in releasing the report, about a month after the first revelations the secretary-general acknowledged the UN's failures in responding to the allegations and announced an external review into the UN's handling of the issue.[47] UN staff expressed their disappointment and distress at the scandal through the president of the UN's staff association, who wrote to the secretary-general calling for the resignation or termination of employment of the two senior officials in charge of internal investigations "since their actions are an embarrassment to the UN in general, their offices, [and] their fellow staff members."[48] Shortly after, in June 2015, the High-Level Panel on Peace Operations released its report, which (albeit briefly) noted "serious deficiencies" in UN responses to sexual exploitation and abuse and a "culture of enforcement avoidance."[49] It went on to recommend that the secretary-general name the contributing country of personnel against whom allegations of sexual misconduct are made; until then, the nationalities of alleged perpetrators had been kept confidential for reasons that will be discussed below.

The momentum continued to build. In August 2015, the secretary-general demanded the resignation of General Babacar Gaye, the Senegalese head of the UN Multidimensional Integrated Stabilization Mission in the Central African Republic (MINUSCA), over the mishandling of dozens of sexual misconduct allegations against UN and affiliated forces in the country. He went on to brief the Security Council and police- and troop-contributing countries in a closed session, in which he announced his intention to begin naming and shaming countries whose peacekeeping personnel face credible allegations of sexual exploitation and abuse, in a sharp turnaround from previous policy.[50] His speech was a marked shift in tone from previous addresses by Ban and his predecessor Kofi Annan on the issue of sexual misconduct by peacekeepers. It was a powerful call for member states to take greater responsibility for ensuring the prevention of and accountability for sexual exploitation and abuse by their personnel and an acknowledgement that while the UN could not effectively address such misconduct without the cooperation of member states, it also had the most to lose in terms of perceived legitimacy from any failures in accountability. He argued forcefully that "by not responding to allegations quickly, responsibly or thoroughly, the work of thousands can be upended by the indecent acts of a few," and that "even one case of sexual exploitation and abuse erodes the trust of the most vulnerable population we are sent to safeguard." He finished by calling for greater action "to protect civilians and uphold the values of the United Nations." In directly referring to the risks sexual misconduct poses to peacekeeping success and failure, the trust of local communities, and the UN's values and mission, the secretary-general was actively invoking the ways in which it threatens the strategies of legitimation that the UN relies on to maintain support for its work. He was doing so in order to prompt stronger action from member states to prevent and ensure accountability for sexual exploitation and abuse perpetrated by their citizens.

Negotiations within the UN and among member states about appropriate responses to sexual misconduct continued in the aftermath of this powerful speech. They focused initially on the implications of sexual exploitation and abuse for UN capacity before shifting towards statements about the effects for UN legitimacy. A month later, the Security

Council adopted Resolution 2242, which pledged better integration of the Women, Peace and Security agenda into the council's work, called for greater gender analysis and technical expertise in peace operation planning and implementation and a revised strategy to double the numbers of women in peace operations over five years, and urged police- and troop-contributing countries to better prevent, investigate, and prosecute sexual misconduct by their peacekeepers.[51] This was followed by two Security Council presidential statements. The first, in November 2015, connected sexual misconduct to the effectiveness of UN peace operations with "the Security Council [affirming] that proper conduct by, and discipline over, all personnel deployed in United Nations peace operations are crucial to their effectiveness," and making immediate reference to sexual exploitation and abuse after this statement.[52] The second, in December of the same year, called for better consultative processes and mechanisms between the Security Council, troop- and police-contributing countries and the UN secretariat to improve mission planning and implementation, including on issues of sexual exploitation and abuse.[53]

The Central African Republic scandal was, in many ways, a watershed moment for member states at the UN and for the Security Council, who realized that the UN's reputation and credibility suffered no matter what uniform offending troops wore and that sexual exploitation and abuse by peacekeepers was relevant to discussions of peace operation effectiveness. This realization prompted a stronger collective response that appealed to the need to address the crisis of UN legitimacy that the scandal heralded. This was a major shift: ten years earlier, when the Security Council first addressed sexual misconduct in response to the release of the Zeid Report, it "condemned, in the strongest terms, all acts of sexual abuse and exploitation committed by peacekeepers," but framed the issue as "primarily the responsibility of managers and commanders."[54] In subsequent years, sexual exploitation and abuse was sometimes raised in annual Women, Peace and Security debates but never dealt with substantively. In contrast, in meetings in the lead-up to the adoption of Resolution 2272 in March 2016, which gave the secretary-general authority to repatriate units or contingents that failed to address sexual misconduct by their personnel, most Security Council members directly, and for the first time, referred to the legitimacy and credibility deficit that UN peacekeeping suffered as a result of such behaviors.

In his opening statement to the meeting, the secretary-general argued that sexual exploitation and abuse perpetrated against vulnerable people by the UN personnel authorized to protect them "tarnishes the credibility of United Nations peacekeeping operations, and the United Nations as a whole. The impact is not limited to the location of the abuse but reflects on the efforts of tens of thousands of peacekeepers and civilian staff working tirelessly to save lives and protect people around the world in difficult and often dangerous conditions."[55] Other states echoed these sentiments. The US argued that by "[undermining] the credibility of peacekeeping missions everywhere, as well as the legitimacy of the United Nations writ large," sexual exploitation and abuse "undermines our ability to address effectively the serious threats of our time." China claimed that sexual exploitation and abuse tarnished the UN's image and undermined the reputation of peacekeeping operations, while Senegal pointed out that it "[overshadowed] the praiseworthy efforts and the heroic work accomplished by [peacekeepers], sometimes at the cost of their lives." Malaysia characterized "the Blue Helmets as the embodiment of all the aspirations of all the world for peace," and cautioned that "the expectations of the international community and the local populations who they are sent to protect are extremely high" and threatened by sexual misconduct. Venezuela claimed that sexual exploitation and abuse damaged the moral support of UN peacekeeping operations and the "legitimacy and work of our Organization." The UK and New Zealand reflected that the reputation of peacekeeping, the Security Council, and the UN are undermined by sexual exploitation and abuse, particularly when a blind eye is turned to allegations. France and Uruguay worried that it tarnished the global perception of peacekeepers, most of whom do not perpetrate such abuses, while India emphasized the importance of "regaining our collective reputation as exemplars of universal idealism."

Some states also directly linked sexual misconduct to operational outcomes and thereby to the legitimacy crisis of UN peacekeeping. The US representative claimed that "in addition to being a heinous abuse, sexual exploitation and abuse erode the discipline of military and police units and [undermines] the confidence of local communities in peacekeepers, both of which are critical to fulfilling Security Council mandates. . . it undermines our ability to address effectively the serious threats of our time." The French, responding to the fears by major troop-contributing countries that Resolution 2272 would stigmatize whole contingents and their home countries, affirmed that peacekeepers "should know that we do not wish to stigmatize them for the actions of others; on the contrary, we want to assure them that they can continue to do their work with the effectiveness it needs." Perhaps most powerfully, the UK representative appealed to the aspirational goals of the UN and the ways in which sexual misconduct undermines them. He said,

> In the midst of conflict and chaos, peacekeepers bring safety and hope to those most in need, to those in the darkest moments of their lives. To fulfil that crucial role, peacekeepers need the trust of those they seek to protect. When a girl looks up to a Blue Helmet, she should do so not in fear, but in hope. Every time that a peacekeeper fails to live up to our principles or fails to uphold the integrity and decency that is expected of the United Nations, that trust is undermined.

These statements reflect how the Central African Republic scandal and its aftermath led to growing recognition within the Security Council and the UN that sexual exploitation and abuse presents a fundamental challenge to UN strategies of legitimation of the organization and its overarching purpose and of peacekeeping as a central project by which the organization pursues that purpose. In other words, they recognized that sexual misconduct is bad for the UN's public relations and were prompted to act to address this. As noted above, the UN's strategies of legitimation rely on two central claims: its moral leadership, based on its embodiment of widely accepted and shared norms and values; and its operational effectiveness. In their explicit recognition that sexual misconduct affects both of these claims, members of the Security Council acknowledged the ways in which it challenges processes of legitimation and threatens to severely diminish the perceived legitimacy of UN peace operations and the UN overall, sparking a mutually reinforcing downward spiral of capacity and perceived legitimacy. Sexual exploitation and abuse simultaneously undermine operational effectiveness and the credibility of UN claims to moral authority, affecting how member states engage with UN peacekeeping, leading to reduced support and contributions, and in turn further undermining operational effectiveness.

The way the US Senate responded to the Central African Republic scandal illustrates these secondary implications for the capacity and perceived legitimacy of UN peacekeeping. Shortly after Resolution 2272 was adopted by the Security Council, the US Senate Foreign Relations Committee held a special hearing to discuss sexual misconduct in peace operations, during which senior senators criticized the secretary-general's failure to prevent such behaviors and noted that the US was the largest single contributor to the UN peacekeeping budget even though it contributed few personnel. Senators also suggested that they might bypass the administration's efforts to address sexual exploitation and abuse in the UN and pass legislation to withhold funding from UN peacekeeping and withhold bilateral aid from countries who failed to hold their own peacekeepers accountable for misconduct while deployed under UN auspices.[56] Senator Bob Corker, the chairman of the committee, said, "I am disgusted by the actions of UN peacekeepers that American taxpayers are paying for, and I hope that somehow we'll figure out a way to reel this in."[57] The US representative to the United Nations for UN management and reform, Isobel Coleman, echoed the need for the US to take direct bilateral action in addition to supporting UN reform processes, telling the hearing that "clearly, given the shocking scale and gravity of the SEA [sexual exploitation and abuse] incidents being reported from CAR [Central African Republic] and other missions, [recent UN actions to address sexual exploitation and abuse] are necessary but by themselves are not sufficient to address the crisis."[58] One of the experts called to testify before the committee went further, recommending that Congress push for a UN policy that bars states from providing troops to peacekeeping operations if they fail to hold perpetrators accountable for sexual exploitation and abuse or substantially reduces the reimbursement they receive for the provision of peacekeepers rather than simply withholding some of the monthly compensation of accused personnel.[59] This last measure, if taken, would likely ignite significant conflict with troop-contributing countries, and might result in reduced voluntary contributions to peace operations.

A year later, a resolution was introduced into the US House of Representatives flagging lawmakers' ongoing concern about allegations of sexual misconduct by UN peacekeepers. It again noted that the US had "an obligation to hold the United Nations accountable and assist the body in addressing issues of sexual abuse and exploitation," and called for Congress to urge the president to use the role of the US within the UN to reform and improve sexual exploitation and abuse policy and to directly encourage other UN member states and TCCs to fully investigate and ensure accountability for perpetrators.[60] Although this matter has not since progressed, these discussions and proposals highlight how seriously US lawmakers took the issue of sexual misconduct in peace operations in the aftermath of the Central African Republic scandal. They illustrate how sexual exploitation and abuse by interveners in a peace operation diminished the perceived legitimacy of UN peacekeeping (and the UN) in the eyes of US lawmakers, particularly those already critical of the organization. This case also underscores the capacity of US lawmakers to significantly alter US participation in peacekeeping in the future if sexual misconduct is not addressed in a manner that they consider satisfactory and that restores their perceptions of the UN's legitimacy. If taken, the actions threatened would reduce the UN's operational capacity in peace operations globally. Moreover, a withdrawal of US support would further diminish the UN's ability to leverage support on the basis of claims of moral authority and operational effectiveness and might in fact fuel anti-UN sentiments globally.

Sexual Misconduct in the Context of Other Challenges to UN Legitimacy

A related issue is that there are some indications that countries may reduce their contributions of soldiers to UN peacekeeping operations as a result of public backlash for misconduct and fears that they might perpetrate it again or engage in other forms of misconduct. This of course has implications for the capacity of UN peacekeeping and therefore also its perceived legitimacy if operational outcomes suffer. Although this has not yet occurred, other cases of peacekeeper abuses and failures that undermined public perceptions of peacekeeping legitimacy have led to such a drawdown of peacekeeping contributions. Given that this chapter has demonstrated how sexual exploitation and abuse affect perceptions of peacekeeping legitimacy, considering the effects of a number of instructive past legitimacy crises in peacekeeping illuminates some of what is at stake if sexual misconduct in peace operations continues unabated.

Perhaps one of the most significant crises in UN peacekeeping related to the failure of Dutch UN peacekeepers at Srebrenica to prevent the genocide of over eight thousand Bosniaks after the enclave the peacekeepers were mandated to protect was overrun by Serb militias in 1995. After the genocide, the Dutch government reduced its previously high personnel contributions to UN peacekeeping to virtually zero as a result of collective public trauma over the role the Dutch battalion played in the Srebrenica massacres, government and military mistrust of UN command and control structures, and a strong perception in the Dutch Ministry of Defence (and more generally) that UN peace operations were ineffective.[61] It was eight years before this began to shift somewhat: larger contributions were made to the missions in Liberia (2003–4) and Lebanon (2006–8), but these consisted of maritime components only, severely limiting the interaction between Dutch peacekeepers and local populations.[62] By contrast, the Netherlands maintained a substantial contribution to non-UN military operations, particularly NATO missions, such as that in Kosovo and ad hoc multinational operations in Afghanistan and Iraq.[63] It was not until 2013 that the Netherlands returned to a large-scale involvement in UN peacekeeping, deploying the largest European contribution to the UN Multidimensional Integrated Stabilization Mission in Mali (MINUSMA), with 450 Dutch troops. In addition, it provided the UN special representative to the mission, special operations forces, an intelligence unit, numerous helicopters, police officers, civilian experts, and officers to the staff of the force commander—in doing so, the Netherlands ensured its influence over the military operations of MINUSMA.[64] This shows how severely the Srebrenica failure affected the Netherlands' willingness to participate in UN peace operations—it took fifteen years for the country to return to peacekeeping in a significant way as a result of the crisis in trust and legitimacy that resulted from Dutch peacekeepers' involvement in Bosnia. Similarly, when details of Canadian peacekeepers' involvement in the torture and murder of the Somali teenager Shidane Arone emerged in November 1994 after a publication ban was lifted, public and government perceptions of the military and its involvement in UN peacekeeping resulted in a significant decrease in Canadian contributions to UN missions—going from one of the highest contributors of personnel to one of the lowest and resulting in a 25 percent cut to Canada's military budget.[65]

In both cases, there is evidence that the soldiers' complicity in these atrocities negatively affected public perceptions of and support for their militaries, with implications for their countries' participation in global peace operations.[66] Although broader data on this is not available, these trends, along with what we know of the reactions to the Oxfam and Central African Republic scandals, suggest that sexual misconduct scandals may similarly lead to a drawdown of troop and other contributions to UN peace operations as a result of the ways in which they undermine perceptions of peacekeeping legitimacy and effectiveness. This suggestion may seem incongruous with the general trend at UN peacekeeping pledging conferences for member states to promise increased contributions to UN peace operations, however, shifts in public perceptions of legitimacy in the wake of sexual misconduct scandals in recent years along with global shifts in attitudes towards member state funding of the UN and peace operations more broadly suggest that past growth in support for peacekeeping may be unsettled by sustained global attention to sexual exploitation and abuse in peacekeeping.[67]

Local Perceptions of Legitimacy

The international reactions to recent sexual misconduct scandals illuminate how sexual exploitation and abuse can directly affect the capacity of the international community's peacebuilding efforts by challenging established processes used by the international community to maintain the perception of legitimacy among multiple audiences that is critical to ensuring ongoing global support for peace operations. This has tangible implications for the international community's ability to pursue its goals, which presents a further obstacle to legitimation strategies.

However, interviews with policymakers and practitioners for this project suggest that there is another crucial way in which perceptions of UN and peacekeeping legitimacy are undermined, one that affects primarily audiences that have been recipients of international peace operations. In both Timor-Leste and Bosnia, a number of respondents invoked the idea that sexual exploitation and abuse by interveners was simply something that host communities needed to "suffer" or "endure" in return for the albeit important peacekeeping work of the international mission.[68] They argued that this affected their respect and support for the UN's role in responding to other crises and to the organization's potential reengagement in their country if violence resumed. A group of staff at a major international humanitarian organization argued that in their work they had seen how these feelings, along with sexual misconduct scandals in general, could have a "ripple effect," particularly into neighboring or regional countries that had also been recipients of peace operations or other international intervention.[69] These experts suggested that this undermined the trust those communities had in the UN and their willingness to share concerns with the international community of interveners about security or other challenges they faced in the contexts of peace operations deployed to protect them. Multiple international staff across both the UN and NGO sector echoed this. Furthermore, direct experiences of sexual exploitation or abuse seemed to compound the perception of some individuals and groups that the international community was not genuinely interested in supporting the communities they professed to serve, which further delegitimized the international peacekeeping project and systems in their eyes.[70] These misgivings by communities who received peacekeeping operations are likely to become more important in the political landscape of peacekeeping over time: as host societies move further away from violent conflict, they become the states to whom the international community might look to contribute personnel for peace operations elsewhere. However, their perceptions of peacekeeping legitimacy, which stem from their own experiences of misconduct by interveners, are likely to shape the way they engage in the peacekeeping project in the future.

A Growing Rift between the Global North and South?

One final issue worth noting here is how the perceived racism of UN and international responses to sexual exploitation and abuse by interveners in peace operations can impact the way governments and the domestic public in troop-contributing countries perceive the legitimacy of the UN and its peacekeeping project. A senior diplomat to the UN recalled that during negotiations and debates in the aftermath of the Central African Republic scandal—in both General Assembly and Security Council meetings—many troop-contributing countries were acutely aware of the racial dynamics of reporting on sexual exploitation and abuse scandals and of the international debates about appropriate policy responses, and they were worried about the reputation of all people from their country being tarnished by generalizations about their nationals being rapists.[71] This was particularly the case because countries that contribute the largest numbers of troops and police to UN peacekeeping are generally less developed and nonwhite, and are therefore often already subject to prejudices about the violent nature of their people or cultural treatment of women. The diplomat in question recalled that a major concern during informal discussions was how these generalizations would be received by both global audiences and the TCCs' own citizens. The diplomat suggested that this would lead to greater misgivings among the governments and constituencies of major TCCs about their support for UN peacekeeping and their willingness to put their soldiers' lives at risk if they would be subjected to racialized generalizations about their propensity to sexual violence as a result of the behaviors of just a few personnel, particularly given the low personnel contributions from Global North states.

It was perhaps because of these concerns that some TCCs, notably Nigeria, Rwanda, and India, threatened in the past to withdraw their troops from peacekeeping if they were named publicly in relation to alleged abuses—sexual exploitation and abuse as well as other forms of misconduct.[72] In fact, in 2015, between the Central African Republic scandal breaking and Resolution 2272 being adopted, these threats forced the UN to withhold information about the nationalities of peacekeepers implicated in the abuse and rape of street children and women in CAR and to refuse to identify as Rwandan the police peacekeepers implicated in the killing of civilians in Mali in the secretary-general's official statement about the incident.[73] According to the journalist Chris McGreal, a UN source said that although the Rwandan government did withdraw the police unit in question and promise to hold perpetrators accountable, it threatened to withdraw its peacekeepers from the separate peace operation in Darfur if it was named publicly in relation to the incident.[74] In the Security Council debates around Resolution 2272, the secretary-general explained why he had overturned the policy of keeping the nationalities of alleged perpetrators confidential. He affirmed that "the honour and reputation of troop contributing countries should be respected" but argued that the policy of confidentiality on the nationality of alleged perpetrators "is not very helpful" and that "sometimes we need to make it known to the public so that [the TCCs] will also be motivated to improve their way of conducting business."[75] Nevertheless, during Security Council negotiations, numerous troop-contributing countries, including Egypt, Senegal, Pakistan, and India, opposed the policy of naming and shaming and the provisions contained within Resolution 2272 for the repatriation of units or contingents implicated in systematic and widespread sexual exploitation and abuse. They argued that it amounted to collective punishment, tarnishing the reputation of whole contingents on account of the behavior of just a few individual personnel. Pakistan further cautioned that "any action by [the Security Council] that could lead to a generic blaming of peacekeepers is bound to negatively impact the morale of the troops on the ground," implying that mission outcomes may be affected. It is worth noting that this concern about tarnished reputations is not limited to Global South member states concerned about racism: in his response to the initial leaking of the Central African Republic report, the French Defence Minister Jean-Yves Le Drian said that he had felt "disgust" and "betrayal" and declared that the acts, if true, "sullied our flag" and betrayed "comrades, the image of France and the army's mission."[76]

These responses by major troop-contributing countries illuminate a critical tension in the UN's response to sexual exploitation and abuse, namely that the concerns of TCCs that their international reputation will be tarnished if reports of their personnel's involvement in sexual misconduct are made public may drive the obfuscation of details of such misconduct by the UN. This ultimately undermines the UN's credibility in the eyes of the international community of states and the global public. Because of resourcing constraints, the UN is beholden to these states and there is a strong impetus to keep them involved in peacekeeping, just as there is a strong impetus to maintain the effectiveness of the organization's legitimation strategies more generally, even though these two pressures may operate in tension. This is likely to pose a significant challenge to the implementation of Resolution 2272, which provides the secretary-general with the Security Council's backing to repatriate units or national contingents where there is credible evidence of their involvement in widespread and systematic sexual exploitation and abuse, or where the TCC has failed to take appropriate steps to investigate and hold perpetrators accountable.[77] There have already been some instances where the Conduct and Discipline Unit is alleged to have failed to disclose information about allegations.[78]

Some of the concerns troop-contributing countries have around this issue may be about the racialized dynamics of peacekeeping, whereby poorer southern countries provide the boots on the ground and accept the risks to their troops and police inherent to doing so while wealthier northern countries provide resources and set policy agendas. However, some of the concerns may also be grounded in the benefits countries accrue through contributing troops, particularly in terms of remuneration and access to military equipment and training, which does not flow directly to personnel but rather makes its way into the defense forces or governments of troop-contributing states. While it remains to be seen how these issues play out, there were some reports in 2015 that the UN had begun to suspend payments for peacekeeping troops to TCCs that failed to respond to credible allegations of sexual misconduct, although it is unclear how widely this has been implemented to date.[79]

This issue shows how the legitimation strategies that the UN relies on to maintain support for peacekeeping are contingent on context and audience and sometimes conflict with one another. On the one hand, strengthening accountability mechanisms through Resolution 2272 was an attempt to bolster perceptions of UN and peacekeeping legitimacy by addressing an issue that undermined existing legitimation strategies emphasizing the alignment of peacekeeping and its outcomes with core UN values and goals. On the other hand, in doing so, the Security Council and secretariat were perceived by the governments and publics of many southern troop-contributing countries as unfairly apportioning blame for sexual exploitation and abuse and generalizing the behaviors of a few personnel to whole contingents or nationalities, thereby threatening perceptions of the alignment of the policy (and process by which it was developed) with core UN values and principles.

Conclusion: Eroding the UN's Moral Authority

This chapter has demonstrated how sexual exploitation and abuse by interveners undermines both the operational capacity and the perceived legitimacy of the international community as it engages in peace operations. Crucially, it has demonstrated how such behaviors challenge the existing strategies the UN and the international community rely on in order to maintain the perceptions of their legitimacy and moral authority in the eyes of multiple audiences globally, which are foundational to the continued support for peace operations. This chapter has also shown how capacity and perceived legitimacy are locked in a mutually reinforcing relationship—as one diminishes, so does the other, thus in turn further diminishing the first. Most importantly, it has shown how sexual misconduct and its effects contribute to the erosion of the UN's moral authority, not just in relation to peacekeeping but also as it relates to the UN's role as the chief proponent of global peace and security and as a forum for all states to work together as equals towards these goals.

The uneven responses to sexual exploitation and abuse within the UN system and the treatment of whistleblowers amplify this erosion of perceived legitimacy. For instance, despite statements from the highest levels of the UN, including the various secretary-generals and the Security Council, about the UN's commitment to ensuring accountability for sexual misconduct across the UN system, this has not translated into reality. This was illustrated perhaps most starkly by the sexual abuse scandal in the Central African Republic. As the scandal progressed, media reporting and document leaks to Code Blue Campaign revealed not only the initial UN failure to act on allegations that French Sangaris soldiers had sexually abused children but also the noncooperation of French military officials with a Security Council mandated inquiry into human rights violations in the country. Reports went on to show the apparent knowledge of French military officials about their troops' participation in sexual exploitation and abuse. Furthermore, the report's leak led to the whistleblower being targeted for punishment, rather than the troops involved. And lastly, the case against troops allegedly involved was eventually dismissed despite evidence collected by medical and other NGOs that supported allegations because of the "unreliability" of children's' testimonies and because the quality of evidence collected by the UN originally apparently did not meet French prosecutorial standards.[80] All of these revelations played out in the global media and laid bare the chasm between the stated values and commitments of the UN and its member states around human rights, prevention of sexual exploitation and abuse, and protection of vulnerable groups and their responses to allegations of sexual misconduct in practice. This chasm poses a serious challenge to established UN legitimation strategies, as discussed above.

This illuminates a fundamental challenge facing UN policies and systems—its genetic defect—which holds it hostage to a combination of various interests from its member states, bureaucratic imperatives to protect its image and demonstrate its centrality to the project of international peace and security, and bureaucratic limitations under which the secretariat operates, particularly in relation to resources and authority over peacekeeping personnel. As an organization driven by and accountable to state interests that does not have authority over the conduct of uniformed peacekeepers contributed by member states to peace operations, the UN is structurally limited in its capacity to effectively enforce accountability for sexual exploitation and abuse. But it also has a strong incentive to demonstrate that existing policies are working in order to justify funding allocations and troop contributions by member states and maintain political support for peacekeeping. This generates a pressure to report on successes that operates at both the UN and individual levels. For example, as discussed in chapter 2, Jacques Paul Klein, head of the UN Mission in Bosnia and Herzegovina, was complicit in suppressing revelations that peacekeepers were involved in trafficking because it was in his interest to assert that he was maintaining order and standards of conduct so as to protect his reputation and employment opportunities.[81] The suppression of Anders Kompass's original report into sexual exploitation and abuse in the Central African Republic and the backlash to his whistleblowing by UN officials who had previously been strong advocates of robust accountability for sexual exploitation and abuse provide another example. This showcases a fundamental tension in the way UN peacekeeping works: the UN bureaucracy is in the position of auditing and reporting on itself in relation to breaches of conduct, but at the same time bureaucratic imperatives to demonstrate order, control, and success (which are also central to UN legitimation strategies) militate against robust investigations and reporting. Furthermore, it highlights the limitations the UN secretariat faces in holding uniformed peacekeepers accountable for sexual misconduct, even though their inability to do so is framed as a failure on the UN's part rather than a reflection of the limited authority the UN has over uniformed personnel and its limited capacity to pressure troop-contributing countries to fully implement UN codes of conduct regarding sexual exploitation and abuse.

Ultimately, the Central African Republic scandal also laid bare the conflicting interests that troop-contributing countries have in peace operations and the limitations of UN authority. The French response demonstrated an unwillingness to prioritize accountability for sexual misconduct over other interests such as the protection of its soldiers and operational imperatives. When French personnel were sent to investigate allegations of Sangaris involvement in child abuse, it took them five months to reach the village where the abuse allegedly occurred, in part because Operation Sangaris allegedly could not spare a helicopter to transport them there due to other operational priorities.[82] Most troop-contributing countries have also been steadfastly opposed to any mechanisms that would give the UN or independent actors jurisdiction over their troops—which, in addition to the obvious issues, means that it will remain difficult for UN actors to gather evidence of a standard and form permissible in the judicial systems of member states in cases of sexual exploitation and abuse allegations. Indeed, Pakistan has argued at the Security Council against "intrusive and prescriptive calls on Member States to review their criminal procedures and legislation," implying that such suggestions are disrespectful and out of line with the principle of noninterference in the internal affairs of member states.[83] Furthermore, Keith Allred's research suggests that troop-contributing countries rarely prosecute personnel alleged to have perpetrated sexual exploitation or abuse in order to avoid international and national embarrassment.[84]

A number of UN officials and staff suggested to me in discussions that the Central African Republic scandal punctured the belief held by many who worked at the UN that progress was being made on issues of sexual exploitation and abuse, a belief based on the falling rates reported by the Conduct and Discipline Unit.[85] Instead, it demonstrated that there has been little change in the culture of peacekeeping and in the attitudes of many troop-contributing countries to ensure accountability for their own uniformed personnel deployed into peace operations. Furthermore, officials within the UN Department of Peacekeeping Operations as well as diplomats to the UN acknowledged the reluctance within the UN to openly discuss sexual misconduct because it is bad for the UN's reputation.[86] This again shows how the impact of sexual exploitation and abuse at the institutional level is twofold: it affects both the perceptions staff have of their own organization and the perception multiple global audiences have of the UN's legitimacy and the alignment of peacekeeping with its stated values and goals. It reveals also that the impetus to cover up or obfuscate allegations of sexual misconduct may be driven not only by the interests of troop-contributing countries and bureaucratic imperatives within the UN but in some cases also by well-meaning staff who are committed to the UN's mission and concerned about the way the UN's legitimacy will be affected by exposés. As Jose Ramos-Horta, former president of Timor-Leste and co-chair of the HIPPO panel, said to me, "The UN is not a superpower. It only has its moral authority, and if you undermine that, you're finished.'[87] There appears to be an acute awareness of this among at least some UN officials and staff.

Conclusion

One Problem among Many? An Integrated Response to Sexual Exploitation and Abuse

In July 1995, in one of the most notorious failures of UN peacekeeping, Dutch peacekeepers at the Potočari base near Srebrenica in northern Bosnia refused to allow Bosniaks to take refuge in their base in the UN-designated safe area when Serb militias overran the town they had been deployed to protect. Subsequently, more than eight thousand Bosniaks, largely men and boys, were killed by the militias in the worst genocide on European soil since World War II. During interviews in Bosnia, nearly all those I spoke to suggested at some point that it was naive to single out the impact sexual exploitation and abuse by interveners had on peacebuilding outcomes and on the relationship between the local and international communities. They argued that a more important factor was the responsibility UN peacekeepers had, in their eyes, for atrocities such as the Srebrenica genocide, when they failed to protect civilians in the designated safe area, or other instances where peacekeepers showed disrespect or disregard for those they had been sent to protect. They also talked about the graffiti left behind at the UN barracks at Potočari, which was offensive towards Bosniaks in the enclave and particularly Bosniak women. In other words, after sharing the stories and details about the ways in which sexual misconduct affected peacebuilding outcomes in their country—the stories that have animated most of this book—they were at pains to reiterate that it was just one of the interconnecting factors that affected the relationship between their communities and the international community.

This book set out to understand the way sexually abusive and exploitative behaviors by interveners in peace operations affect the outcomes of those operations and the capacity and credibility of the international community, both within specific operations and more broadly. In demonstrating the significant long-term consequences of such behaviors, this book has revealed the intersections between them and many of the other challenges facing UN peace operations today, including the failure of peacekeepers to fulfill protective mandates, such as at Srebrenica; the growing rift between the Global North and South over the distribution of the burden of peacekeeping; and the competing interests at play in peace operations, including between the UN and troop- and police-contributing countries. In this concluding chapter, I draw these issues together by considering how intervener cultures interact with the broad range of factors that challenge and undermine the effectiveness of peace operations, including by giving rise to the perpetration of sexual exploitation and abuse against local communities. In light of this, I then consider the key insights the book has revealed about the nature and impacts of sexual misconduct by interveners in peace operations and suggest how the international community might better address this issue and its complex, interlinked implications in the future. I reflect on the major shortcomings of policy on sexual exploitation and abuse to date, including the individualization of sexual exploitation and abuse, which relegates responses primarily to conduct and discipline policies rather than addressing the broader and systemic issues at play. I then consider the extent to which recent policy shifts might avoid replicating past mistakes in terms of sexual exploitation and abuse policy, particularly in the aftermath of the peacekeeper sexual abuse scandal in the Central African Republic and the Oxfam sexual exploitation scandal in Haiti. I argue that sexual exploitation and abuse in peace operations fundamentally undermines the international community's operational capacity to effectively build peace after civil wars and sustainably alleviate human suffering in crises and that it poses a significant risk to the perceived legitimacy of the peacekeeping project and the UN more broadly at a time when the organization already faces a deepening political and legitimacy crisis. Ultimately, recognizing the mutually reinforcing ways in which sexual exploitation and abuse by interveners undermines peacekeeping and peacebuilding outcomes and developing an effective and robust response to such misconduct and other interlinked peacekeeping challenges based on that understanding is crucial to the pursuit of global peace, order, and justice.

Racism, Respect, and Responsibility in Peace Operations

During my interviews in Bosnia, many respondents suggested that the lack of empathy and responsibility—and, in some cases, the racism—that interveners felt towards the groups they were sent to protect contributed to the high levels of sexual misconduct, particularly transactional sex economies, in UN safe areas during the war. Chapter 2 illustrated how these factors operated to shape the forms that sexual misconduct took in Bosnia. However, when discussing these factors, respondents also often raised other problematic behaviors and interactions between interveners and locals during the peace operations, drawing parallels with sexual exploitation and abuse. Local experiences of the international intervention in the Srebrenica safe area illustrate the intersection between these various factors and the ways they combine to challenge the effectiveness of UN peacekeeping, shedding light on the intervener cultures that set the scene for the perpetration of abuse and exploitation. They show how the factors that give rise to such misconduct in peace operations also give rise to other forms of behavior and actions by interveners, including operational choices that conflict with the values and mandated goals of those missions. Seeing the interconnections between these factors and their outcomes is crucial to developing a robust response to sexual exploitation and abuse, as the rest of this concluding chapter will illustrate.

The derogatory and sexualized graffiti about Bosniak women at the Dutch UN peacekeepers' base at Potočari near Srebrenica is now infamous and was often raised in discussions of peacekeeper behaviors as illustrative of peacekeepers' feelings towards locals. It features prominently in memorials to the genocide at Srebrenica, including the memorial set up in the

Potočari base and at the Galerija 11/07/95, the memorial museum to the events at Srebrenica in central Sarajevo. Perhaps the most famous piece of graffiti is one piece, scrawled on the inside of the factory the soldiers lived in, which reads, "*NO TEETH. . .? *A MUSTACHE. . .? *SMEL [sic] LIKE SHIT? BOSNIAN GIRL!" It is common in museums and in the streets of Sarajevo to see an image in which the graffiti has been superimposed over a defiant young Bosnian woman's face. The artist Šejla Kamerić created the piece in 2003 as part of the commemoration for victims at Srebrenica. Nearly all of the people I met with to discuss the impacts of sexual exploitation and abuse by interveners, both local and expatriate, raised this piece of graffiti as an example of the disrespect peacekeepers felt and showed towards the Bosnians they had been sent to protect. It is worth noting that over the summer prior to fall of Srebrenica, the Bosnian Serb forces had systematically restricted the UN humanitarian convoys into the enclave, with only one convoy per month allowed in to feed the population of approximately thirty-nine thousand civilians.[1] The militias prohibited salt from being included in the convoys, which prevented residents from preserving the food they were able to grow, and as a consequence of the limited humanitarian deliveries, malnutrition and starvation in the enclave spread. The Serb militias also denied water, electricity, and medical supplies to the inhabitants of Srebrenica.[2] It was in this context that Dutch peacekeepers, who had themselves been denied rotational personnel replacements by the Serb militias and key equipment supplies and had limited access to water for showering, scrawled the graffiti mocking local women for the outward physical signs of malnutrition and starvation.

On nearby walls in the same barracks, large-scale pornographic graffiti depicted semi-naked women with large breasts, multiple sex acts between men and women portrayed as prostitutes, bestiality involving a man and a horse, and one sex act involving a woman and a highly sexualized peacekeeper tank. One wall was painted as if it was the entry to a sex bar. The Dutch peacekeepers also left a lot of non-sexualized graffiti, depicting various cartoons, calendars, religious iconography, and some further statements about how bad local Bosniaks smelled.[3]

This intersection of sexually inappropriate behaviors and more general disrespect and lack of empathy was borne out in other discussions, most notably in Hasan Nuhanović's recollections of his time working as a local translator for UNPROFOR in the Srebrenica safe area. He recalled during his interview the widespread suspicion among locals that the young Bosnian women who worked as cleaners and cooks at the Potočari base were engaging in transactional sex with the Dutch peacekeepers living there; a number of other interviewees suggested the same, as noted in chapter 1.[4] Nuhanović further recounted in his book that the women were searched every day when they left the base. One time he witnessed this search, during which some of the women were found to have a few oranges and small packs of butter in their pockets that they had taken to give to their families, who were starving. As a consequence, the whole group was fired immediately.[5] So, while peacekeepers would engage in transactional sex with the women and would write graffiti that (at least implicitly) recognized the deprived situation in which Bosnians were living (only two humanitarian convoys had made it through that summer, leaving locals starving and without access to water for washing), they strictly enforced rules about food being carried out of the base.

Nuhanović's own experiences add layers of what he perceived to be racism to this mix of factors that characterized interactions between peacekeepers and locals in the Srebrenica safe area. He recounted, among other things, being hungry every day at work because of the lack of food in Srebrenica but being barred from eating in the canteen with the peacekeepers he worked alongside, even though the local women staff were invited to join them and even though the peacekeepers knew that Bosniaks in the enclave were starving. Furthermore, when Serb militias overran the safe area in July 1995 and civilians were forced out of the Potočari peacekeeper base where they had taken refuge, Nuhanović begged the Dutch leadership to allow his parents and his nineteen-year-old brother to stay with him on the base to avoid certain death, but they refused. As his family prepared to leave, the commander called to Nuhanović's father and offered him the choice to either stay on the base, or leave with his wife and son; he left, and all three were killed by the Bosnian Serb militias in the following days.[6] This cruel choice—to stay in safety and watch his wife and son pushed into the hands of the Serb militias at the base's gates, where people had been killed the night before, or to leave with them—is emblematic of the disregard the peacekeepers showed for the dignity and humanity of Bosniaks at Srebrenica. The same disregard characterized the graffiti on the base and instances of sexual exploitation in the safe area during the peacekeepers' deployment.

Although anecdotal, Nuhanović's personal account of both working within and being subject to the UN peace operation at Srebrenica demonstrates the intersections between the factors that contribute to the perpetration of sexual exploitation and abuse by interveners and those that contribute to broader challenges facing peacekeeping, such as the failure of peacekeepers to fulfill their protective mandates towards civilians even while deployed in the name of peace, justice, and human rights. This is particularly the case when his account is considered in parallel to the issues of the graffiti left by Dutch peacekeepers on the walls of their base at Potočari, and the accounts of sexual misconduct by interveners in Bosnia discussed in chapter 2. These accounts together illustrate the way gender orders and structures (such as militarized masculinities) intersect with local contexts (including the material situation of local communities and the power differential between locals and interveners), international dynamics (such as the authority and structure of the international mission, which meant the Dutch peacekeepers were unable to maintain a strong defense against the Bosnian Serb militias), and systemic factors (such as racism and sexism). Chapter 1 illustrated how these factors interact to create the intervener cultures and economies in which interveners perpetrate sexual exploitation and abuse, but research in Bosnia demonstrated how the same factors and cultures also produce other behaviors that are disrespectful to local communities and lead to operational choices that do not reflect core peacekeeping goals, such as the protection of civilians from harm. In other words, the same factors that lead to the perpetration of sexual misconduct by interveners in peace operations also lead to other problematic behaviors by interveners, and looking at these various behaviors in isolation is counterproductive to effectively addressing any of them.

As Séverine Autesserre has shown in her ethnographic work on intervener cultures, the everyday practices of interveners shape the work of peace operations from the bottom up.[7] These practices range from the social habits of international interveners to security procedures and their approaches to collecting and analyzing information on violence or the conflict into which they are deployed. They include informal and personal interactions as well as formal professional interactions and, ultimately, they "enable, constitute and help reproduce the strategies, policies, institutions and discourses" that animate peace operations.[8] This book has demonstrated how this causality operates in relation to the sexual interactions of interveners with local individuals across many contexts; the experiences at Srebrenica illustrate how it operated in one particular peacekeeping site. It has shown how their sexual behaviors—including both sexual exploitation and abuse and the murkier forms of consensual relationships characterized by unequal power dynamics—intersect with the other aspects of intervener cultures and behaviors to produce dynamics and outcomes that conflict with the goals of peace operations and fundamentally undermine peacebuilding.

In a Nutshell: The Nature and Impacts of Sexual Exploitation and Abuse in Peace Operations

Each time a sexual misconduct scandal breaks in global media, UN and world leaders condemn it in the strongest possible terms and claim that such behavior by interveners undermines the capacity and credibility of the international community in peace operations. However, despite these widely accepted claims, there has, to date, been very little understanding of how the impacts of sexual exploitation and abuse by interveners operate, whether they are similar across different peace operations where such behaviors has been perpetrated in different patterns, and the extent to which their operational impacts contribute to the broader challenges of peace process failure facing the international community. This book has provided the first comparative account of the impacts of sexual exploitation and abuse in peace operations on peacebuilding outcomes in individual missions, on the capacity of the international community in peace operations more broadly, and on the perceived legitimacy of the UN and international community's involvement in peace processes through peacekeeping and peacebuilding operations. It has done so while also shedding light on the perpetration of sexual misconduct by civilian interveners and considering the ways in which it intersects with other significant peacekeeping challenges, such as the failures of peacekeepers to enact their protective mandates, the perpetration of nonsexual abuses by interveners, and the emergent fractures between the Global North and South over peacekeeping policy and the distribution of responsibility for enacting it. The experiences of sexual exploitation and abuse in the peace operations in Bosnia and Timor-Leste have been the foundation upon which much of this analysis has been built, but have been complemented by extensive research with the international community of interveners in New York and Geneva as well as analysis of the experiences and impacts of such behaviors in other peace operations. This investigation has produced a range of findings that are of relevance not only to the emerging scholarly debates about sexual exploitation and abuse but also to the community of policymakers and practitioners grappling with the phenomenon and challenges of responding to such misconduct in practice in peace operations. These findings can be broadly divided into two themes: those related to the nature of sexual misconduct and those related to its impacts, both of which have implications for policy responses that will be discussed in the final section of this chapter.

The Nature of Sexual Exploitation and Abuse

This book has shown that the nature of sexual misconduct in peace operations is diverse and encompasses a broad set of behaviors that have less in common than the overarching label of sexual exploitation and abuse might suggest, although they are united by the sexual nature of the behaviors involved. It identified four distinct but intersecting types of behavior: opportunistic sexual assault, planned and sadistic abuse, transactional sex, and networked abuse and exploitation. Only some of these are criminal; some involve monetary or other transactions, and they all involve varying levels of planning, violence, and consent. They are produced by different constellations of permissive factors and choices being made by perpetrators (and, sometimes, victims), even though they occur in similar contexts, and there are areas of overlap between them. Perhaps most important, this book demonstrates how a range of local contextual factors intersected with international, normative, and systemic factors to create the conditions in which sexual misconduct is perpetrated in these distinguishable forms in peace operations. Understanding the intersections and interactions of these factors is vital if robust policy responses are to be developed and deployed in individual peace operations and across the UN system of peacekeeping overall. Furthermore, an awareness of the intersections between sexual exploitation and abuse by interveners and conflict-related sexual violence in a particular context is critical to understanding the broader conditions of peace operations in which certain groups or individuals are particularly vulnerable to being abused or exploited by interveners when a peace operation is deployed.

This book has also shown that although it is often assumed that sexual exploitation and abuse is predominantly perpetrated by military peacekeepers, this is not borne out in the evidence, which shows that uniformed and civilian peacekeepers, humanitarian personnel, and others associated with peace operations are all implicated. While scholars and policymakers have given significant attention to understanding why soldiers perpetrate sexual violence—including through developing accounts of militarized masculinities and the legacies of military prostitution—similar attention has not been devoted to understanding why civilian personnel also perpetrate sexual exploitation and abuse, despite the fact that they are responsible for greater numbers of misconduct allegations per capita in peace operations. In drawing parallels to the available data on sexual harassment and abuse within the humanitarian sector, this book has shown that understanding the organizational and intervener cultures in the humanitarian sector are vitally important to understanding and responding to the perpetration of sexual misconduct by humanitarian or civilian personnel. Furthermore, understanding the patterns and permissive factors around sexual harassment and violence perpetrated by civilian interveners against their colleagues is helpful in understanding the patterns of sexual misconduct by civilian interveners against local communities. Key trends included the pervasiveness of sexual harassment, which falls outside the category of sexual exploitation and abuse but is closely linked to the behaviors it encompasses, the prevalence of sexual aggression and assault in social and shared accommodation contexts, and the fact that perpetrators are often in a position of authority over their victim. In addition, systems for reporting and responding to allegations of harassment and abuse within the civilian intervener community are inadequate in the first instance and are further undermined by organizational cultures that fail to take allegations seriously and tend to blame victims. This leads to low reporting rates and consolidates intervener cultures whereby impunity for perpetrators prevails. And lastly, factors including a "boys will be boys" culture, high rates of drug and alcohol consumption as stress-relief mechanisms, and the absence of strong law and order mechanisms in the contexts into which peace operations are deployed contribute to creating the contexts in which both sexual harassment and abuse within the civilian intervener community and sexual exploitation and abuse against local communities are perpetrated.

These trends regarding the nature of sexual misconduct perpetrated by uniformed and civilian interveners were borne out in the detailed accounts developed of such behaviors in the peace operations in Bosnia and Timor-Leste. These two cases reinforced the importance of recognizing the distinct but interconnected forms of sexual exploitation and abuse in order to understand the varying constellations of factors that give rise to them in each context, and the different impacts they have for the outcomes of peace operations. They also showed that the ways in which local communities experience such misconduct is deeply culturally and historically contingent, which means that what are considered inappropriate sexual behaviors by interveners can vary significantly between contexts. This poses a particular challenge for codes of conduct, which are uniform across peace operations but which may not encompass the forms of behaviors considered particularly egregious by local communities (such as, in Timor-Leste, consensual relationships that were based on false promises about the future of the relationship), or may overemphasize behaviors considered less problematic in other contexts (such as transactional sex in Bosnia). These case studies also illustrated the chronic underreporting of sexual misconduct by interveners as a result of cultures of silence and inadequate response mechanisms. Lastly, they confirmed trends in the patterns of perpetration, with transactional sex and networked abuse and exploitation by far the most common forms of sexual misconduct while opportunistic sexual assault and planned, sadistic abuse were relatively less common. Ultimately though, the cases studies showed that even a limited number of instances of the more violent forms of sexual abuse can contaminate public opinion of interveners among locals, and that even the form of sexual misconduct considered less egregious by the international community—namely transactional sex—has significant implications for peacebuilding outcomes and perceptions of the international community's legitimacy.

Impacts of Sexual Exploitation and Abuse

Just as the nature of sexual exploitation and abuse is diverse, so too are the implications its perpetration has for peacebuilding outcomes in individual missions and for the international community's capacity and credibility on a global scale. The international community deploys peace operations to conflict-affected contexts in pursuit of peace, security, and justice. Through peacekeeping, the international community aims to protect civilians from violence, reduce human suffering, build stable and prosperous societies, promote and protect human rights, support women's political participation, and strengthen rule of law and security institutions, thereby contributing to consolidating lasting peace. This book has shown how the perpetration of sexual exploitation and abuse by interveners in peace operations undermines both the values that animate peace operations and the international community's capacity to achieve its stated goals in missions. The impacts of sexual misconduct operate on three key levels.

First, sexual exploitation and abuse by interveners compounds poverty and human rights abuses on the individual and community level. Perpetrators prey on individuals who are already the most vulnerable in their societies, including young women and children and victims of conflict-related sexual violence. The experience of abuse and exploitation heightens the vulnerabilities of these individuals, particularly in contexts where they are stigmatized by family and community as a result or where police responses may also involve human rights violations, as is the case for women involved in prostitution. In producing these outcomes, sexual misconduct violates the UN's raison d'être, which, according to the UN Charter, is to "reaffirm faith in fundamental human rights, in the dignity and worth of the human person."

Second, sexual misconduct by interveners has significant long-term structural impacts on the cultures, economies, and institutions of host societies that undermine the international community's goals related to strengthening rule of law and promoting human rights as part of establishing a stable peace. Sexual exploitation and abuse contributes to the entrenchment and extension of cultures of abuse and exploitation and the economies associated with them. These cultures and economies long outlast peace operations, both relying on and compelling the participation of a broad range of individuals and groups (including the security sector), and adapting the way they operate to reflect changed economic opportunities when the international presence declines. Perhaps most important, the failure of international interveners to ensure (and model) accountability for misconduct contributes to the institutionalization of impunity for sexual exploitation, sexual abuse, and other forms of sexual violence in the security and judicial sectors of postwar states and in the practices and cultures of particular organizations or companies involved in peace operations. This is compounded by cultures of silence around sexual violence and the fear of reporting it to authorities—which can be a product both of poor experiences of accountability processes in the past and of conflict-related sexual violence. These outcomes not only affect the establishment and consolidation of rule of law and protection and promotion of human rights but also erode progress towards broader long-term goals around reducing human suffering, building prosperous and stable societies, and supporting women's empowerment in postwar societies.

Third, sexual exploitation and abuse has severe implications for operational outcomes. It causes mistrust and conflict between local communities and international interveners, which can result in an unwillingness to cooperate with the peace operation as well as the direct targeting of international staff. It amplifies local feelings of disappointment in and disrespect by the international community, which may be the result of disparities in employment conditions and material wealth between locals and interveners. Sexual misconduct also leads to a breakdown of relationships between different units or organizations in the international response, which has in some cases resulted in violent confrontations between interveners. Furthermore, dealing with sexual exploitation and abuse has directed operational resources away from core peacebuilding tasks that are crucial to the long-term objectives of peace operations, routing them instead towards investigation and accountability mechanisms.

Taken together, these outcomes affect local perceptions of the legitimacy of a peace operation that are critical to efforts to foster local participation in and ownership of the peace processes the international community is supporting through peace operations. In order to achieve mission goals, peace operations depend on their capacity to obtain and maintain local compliance and cooperation, and this relies on their ability to claim a moral basis for their authority and political power.[9] Sexual exploitation and abuse directly undermines this, thereby diminishing local perceptions of the legitimacy of a peace operation as well as local willingness to cooperate and comply with its work. It also reveals a deep hypocrisy in the peacekeeping project: how can the international community credibly claim to be promoting norms of human rights, justice, account-ability, and rule of law when their own personnel violate these norms with relative impunity?

This leads to the final major finding that this book has revealed: sex-ual misconduct affects the capacity and credibility of the international community—not just at the mission level, but also at the global level. Abuses perpetrated by interveners in individual missions have far-reaching impacts that reduce the international community's capacities in peace operations and diminish the perception among multiple audiences of the legitimacy of the international community's engagement in those opera-tions and of the internationalist peacekeeping project itself. It does this in two mutually reinforcing ways. First, sexual exploitation and abuse un-dermines the confidence interveners themselves have in their organization and the peacekeeping project, leading to decreased morale, staff attrition, and poor working relationships and even outright conflict between differ-ent organizational units. It also puts further financial pressure on already underfunded peace operations, diverting critical resources away from core mission tasks. These outcomes undermine the immediate operational ca-pacity of the UN and the broader international community in effectively engaging in peace operations.

Second, and more critical, the perpetration of sexual exploitation and abuse against the world's most vulnerable people by those sent to protect them presents a fundamental challenge to the strategies and processes of legitimation that the UN and the international community rely on in order to maintain support for their work from both the governments and pub-lics of member states. These strategies emphasize the alignment of peace operations with international legal norms and broadly accepted principles that underpin the UN's mission as well as the alignment of operational outcomes with core UN goals. In other words, they stress that peace op-erations do what they are supposed to do—namely, reduce human suf-fering and build peace in conflict-affected societies—and that they do so in service of the goals set out in the UN Charter—namely the promotion of peace, security, and human rights. When interveners perpetrate sexual exploitation and abuse, they directly undermine these strategies of legiti-mation, at a time when the international community's moral authority in peace operations is already under intense scrutiny. Diminished percep-tions of legitimacy reduce the willingness of donors to fund or otherwise support peace operations and their related work—as the Oxfam scandal in Haiti and peacekeeper scandal in the Central African Republic illustrated. Reductions in support immediately affect operational capacity, the results of which further diminish perceptions of legitimacy and create a vicious cycle of diminished capacity and credibility in peace operations. If sexual misconduct is not effectively addressed and its implications for perceptions of the legitimacy of peace operations continue unabated, the inevitable cycle of scandals will present a major challenge to the international peacekeeping and peacebuilding project at a time that the project is perhaps more vital (and more under attack) than ever.

Prevention and Accountability: Towards an Integrated Policy Response

This leads us to the question of how this book's findings about the nature and impacts of sexual exploitation and abuse might inform better policy responses. This book has shown that sexual exploitation and abuse is a complex issue, produced by the interaction of a wide range of local, international, normative, and systemic factors. It results in a mutually reinforcing set of consequences that together undermine peacebuilding outcomes and the capacity and perceived legitimacy of the international community in peace operations. In the process, this book has also suggested how difficult an issue sexual exploitation and abuse is to address: the behaviors it encompasses are varied and multifaceted, only some are criminal, and some of the behaviors considered sexual misconduct by local communities may not fall under the official definition of prohibited sexual interactions. They intersect in numerous ways with other aspects of intervener cultures, including racism, the perceptions peacekeepers have of the communities they have been sent to protect, organizational cultures, and the still contested balance between peacekeepers' responsibilities and the acceptable risks they should shoulder in discharging those responsibilities. Furthermore, developing policy responses at the international level have been fraught, not least because of the limited authority the UN has over uniformed personnel deployed into peace operations. This book has shown that the appropriate regulation of the sexual behaviors of interveners is contested not just at the local level within units, organizations, and missions (even where the policies are relatively clear) but also in troop-contributing countries at the highest levels of UN policy development and within scholarly discourse. Moreover, the processes of strengthening and implementing accountability mechanisms for perpetrators and their superiors have been fraught with conflict among UN member states and between member states, troop-contributing countries, and the secretariat. This has been characterized by division between the Global South, which shoulders the burden of peacekeeping personnel contributions, and the Global North, which shoulders the financial burden of the peacekeeping project, over the appropriate ways to hold troop-contributing countries responsible for ensuring accountability for sexual misconduct perpetrated by their personnel.

So why have policies failed to effectively prevent and ensure accountability for sexual exploitation and abuse, and how might they be approached in the future to better respond to the challenges that these broader contextual and political factors present? Three themes help explain the failures of the last fifteen years of policy development since the zero-tolerance policy was adopted and provide a basis for thinking about whether recent developments might herald better outcomes and what steps might lead to more robust policies in the future.

First, the development of sexual exploitation and abuse policies has been largely reactive: policy has been developed at the international level in response to misconduct scandals that have played out in the global media, such as the scandal in the Central African Republic or the more recent Oxfam scandal in Haiti. In response to global outrage, new rounds of policies have embodied global statements of principle, commitment, and intent, such as the zero-tolerance rhetoric and statements about a "cancer" in the UN system, rather than addressing the technical, conceptual, or implementation weaknesses of earlier policies.[10] As Nicola Dahrendorf's report on the challenges of addressing sexual exploitation and abuse in the UN peace operation in the Democratic Republic of Congo has shown, new policies developed in the aftermath of scandals have been launched into a vacuum; peace operations have neither the capacity nor the expertise to implement them properly, and competition for resources within these operations means that leadership may prioritize other areas of work, as will be discussed shortly.[11] Policies have, in other words, been revised and "improved" without due regard for why they were not able to prevent the behaviors that sparked outrage in the first place.[12]

Second, sexual exploitation and abuse policies—from the zero-tolerance policy to the adoption of Resolution 2272—reflect an individualized understanding of the problem and target individual compliance primarily through standards of conduct, recruitment standards and training, and threats of punishment.[13] As a result, they fail to address the complex mix of contextual, normative, and systemic factors that operate in distinct ways on the ground to produce sexual exploitation and abuse (discussed in chapter 1). In other words, sexual misconduct is understood primarily as an issue of rules not being adequately conveyed, understood, and obeyed rather than a diverse set of behaviors that involves varying levels of agency and consent and reflects local conditions and vulnerabilities as well as gendered expectations of sexual behaviors, opportunism, violence, and the cultures interveners bring with them on deployments. Policy responses, particularly as developed in the aftermath of misconduct scandals, have tended to focus on strengthening sexual exploitation and abuse prevention training, reporting, and investigating procedures and capacity rather than on considering whether the train-and-punish model is the most appropriate response to this complex issue. Furthermore, the compliance-based approach, which has served as the foundation for sexual exploitation and abuse policy, assumes that robust accountability mechanisms deter rules breaches—a logic for which there is little evidence in relation to conflict-related sexual violence more broadly and which, moreover, is undermined by the low rates of criminal charges or material punishments for perpetrators.[14]

Perhaps most crucial, the train-and-punish approach obscures the challenge that mid- to high-ranking officials—in the UN, in troop-contributing countries, and in other organizations—pose when they either refuse to deal with allegations or are simply too occupied with "hard security" issues to take "gender issues" seriously and provide adequate resources and support to accountability processes. The way that allegations of sexual abuse in the Central African Republic have been dealt with over the last three years illustrates this challenge and is worth considering here. In 2014–15, the internal UN report documenting the violent sexual abuse of children by French Sangaris soldiers as well as by UN peacekeepers from Chad and Equatorial Guinea was suppressed and ignored by multiple UN offices and agencies, including senior UN officials such as Zeid Ra'ad Al Hussein, for almost a year before being leaked to AIDS-Free World, at which point the UN was forced by international outcry to take action.[15]

Despite vows from the French president François Hollande to "show no mercy" to the soldiers involved in the rapes, in early 2017 French judges decided not to bring charges against anyone, with a spokesperson citing challenges in basing a case solely on the accounts of children involved without independent evidence.[16] This raises the question of whether the outcome would have been different had the UN taken steps to properly investigate the allegations when first reported. It also raises questions around the priorities of the French officials, given the challenges French investigators faced trying to access the sites of alleged abuse when military leadership would not transport them by helicopter for months because of other operational demands, as I discussed in the previous chapter.

In February 2016, after Secretary-General Ban Ki-moon committed to "doing more" to protect civilians from sexual exploitation and abuse by peacekeepers, the UN announced that 120 peacekeepers from the Republic of Congo would be immediately repatriated due to the gravity of the sexual misconduct allegations against them.[17] However, the troops in question were not repatriated until more than a month after the investigation had occurred because senior UN officials were concerned about the risks of instability related to the mid-February presidential election in the Republic of Congo and did not want the unit to be repatriated until after the election. According to one UN official, there were allegations of at least nine more cases of sexual exploitation and abuse perpetrated by the contingent slated for repatriation, seven of which involved children, in the intervening period between when their repatriation was announced and when it actually occurred.[18] This privileging of "hard" security concerns over "soft" security issues such as sexual misconduct throws into question the extent to which military and other UN officials are willing to genuinely implement more heavy-handed sexual exploitation and abuse policies such as those laid out in Resolution 2272, which was formally adopted shortly after the initial repatriation announcement just discussed.

In his first week in office in 2017, Secretary-General Antonio Guterres committed himself to making protection from sexual exploitation and abuse one of his key priorities, declaring, "Such acts of cruelty should never take place. Certainly, no person serving within the United Nations in any capacity should be associated with such vile and vicious crimes."[19] Yet despite the secretary-general's strong commitment and attempts to build political will at all levels of the secretariat and among member states, new revelations about sexual misconduct in the Central African Republic in mid-2017 suggest that some officials continue to block effective policy. The Code Blue Campaign at AIDS-Free World published leaked confidential UN documents from mid-May that included a detailed report of sexual and other misconduct by the Congolese battalion in the UN Multidimensional Integrated Stabilization Mission in the CAR (MINUSCA) and an official facsimile from the force commander noting that despite the repatriation of the former battalion commander and troops in 2016 the battalion had not improved and remained "notorious for SEA misconducts, fuel trafficking and poor discipline," and requesting that they be repatriated if Congo could not immediately improve the unit's standard.[20] The letter was sent to Lt. Gen. Loitey, military advisor for peacekeeping operations in the Office for Military Affairs at the Department of Peacekeeping Operations. Loitey sat, at the time, on the secretary-general's newly established High-Level Task Force overseeing the UN's reformed approach to sexual exploitation and abuse policy. Nevertheless, no action was taken by the secretariat until June 20, 2017, two weeks after the leaked documents were published and over a month after the force commander had sent his memo to UN Headquarters.

These three examples demonstrate that one of the most significant challenges to effective sexual exploitation and abuse policy remains the unwillingness of officials to enforce it, despite significant policy development in recent years and despite the growing awareness of the impacts sexual exploitation and abuse has for global perceptions of the UN's legitimacy. This challenge is papered over by the individualized, train-and-punish approach to sexual misconduct that has been pursued to date. These examples also illustrate the UN's tendency, discussed above, to respond to sexual exploitation and abuse when prompted by public outcry and media revelations rather than proactively, as well as the inherent tension resulting from the UN's need to maintain a positive relationship with troop-contributing countries while also pursuing the accountability of their personnel for misconduct.

Putting aside the issue of the lack of will to fully enforce sexual exploitation and abuse policies, the third, related theme that helps explain the failure of such policies is that the individualized approach to understanding sexual misconduct has isolated policy from other relevant thematic agendas and operational frameworks by focusing on conduct and discipline. Relegating sexual exploitation and abuse to the conduct and discipline arena has meant first and foremost that policy has not addressed the contextual factors that create an environment in which communities are particularly vulnerable to abuse and exploitation by peacekeepers. Peace operations are deployed into contexts characterized by deprivation, displacement, economic necessity, and the breakdown of social support networks as a result of war, and this book has shown how the small number of interveners who perpetrate sexual exploitation and abuse capitalize on these contextual factors and prey on those who are most vulnerable, predominantly women and children. Although contextual factors are only one piece of the puzzle of why interveners perpetrate sexual exploitation and abuse, the international community's prevention efforts could helpfully be broadened from focusing on predeployment training to preemptively addressing the risk factors for sexual misconduct in the operational contexts into which they deploy interveners. Rapidly and systematically addressing deprivation in the areas where large groups of interveners are based would likely affect, and possibly curtail, the development and consolidation of transactional sex economies. For instance, the funding and rapid deployment of food security programs through the World Food Programme could mean young girls like Faela, whose story was discussed in chapter 1, do not need to exchange sex with peacekeepers for meager amounts of food to keep their babies alive. Attention could also be devoted to reducing the opportunities deployed peacekeeping personnel have to exploit local people. One senior military official deployed into multiple peace operations suggested that the Australian army had found success in limiting instances of sexual misconduct by either banning or severely limiting alcohol consumption by their military peacekeepers through a combination of standing orders and careful rostering arrangements that reduced opportunities for large groups of personnel to drink or leave base for recreation together.[21] Ensuring adequate accommodation and recreation arrangements—and equity in these among different groups of peacekeepers—may also help prevent instances of sexual exploitation and abuse. Obviously, addressing these contextual factors will only go so far towards improving the prevention of sexual misconduct by interveners, but integrating prevention of sexual exploitation and abuse efforts with broader considerations of the operating environment of peace operations would help mainstream efforts to both prevent and respond to the phenomenon more effectively.

More critical, this book has shown how the causes and consequences of sexual exploitation and abuse intersect with broader issues of gender, protection, and human rights in peace operations. However, despite these synergies, sexual exploitation and abuse policy has been isolated from the Women, Peace and Security (WPS) agenda and framework, as well as those related to conflict-related sexual violence and the protection of civilians. It is notable that Resolution 2272 was not listed as a WPS resolution, even though it has clear synergies with that part of the Security Council's body of work and includes a mandate for WPS mechanisms to include sexual misconduct allegations in reporting to the secretary-general.[22] In fact, sexual exploitation and abuse remains listed on the UN Peacekeeping website as a conduct and discipline issue only. It is, moreover, siloed from references to protection of civilians and WPS in mission mandates, and it was not included in the annual secretary-general's reports on conflict-related sexual violence and children and armed conflict until after the scandal in the Central African Republic.

It is important to note that, although it took some time for those working in the WPS policy space to recognize issues of sexual exploitation and abuse as within the purview of WPS, this has changed significantly in recent years. For example, the 2015 Global Study on the Implementation of UN Security Council Resolution 1325 on Women, Peace and Security gave significant attention to sexual exploitation and abuse, arguing strongly that a greater presence of women in peace operations was crucial to reducing incidences of sexual misconduct; this argument has since been reiterated by Secretary-General Guterres.[23] It is interesting to note that a recent study by Sabrina Karim and Kyle Beardsley on Women, Peace and Security in postconflict states suggested that representation alone would yield only limited benefits given that it would not necessarily reform the dysfunctional institutional cultures at the root of the problems of women's disempowerment in peace operations and the phenomenon of sexual exploitation and abuse by peacekeepers. Instead, they found that a more holistic approach focusing on embedding the norm of "equal opportunity" in all aspects of peacekeeping would more effectively address the challenges stemming from power imbalances.[24] Nevertheless, despite these moves from the WPS side, it appears that most policy development related to sexual exploitation and abuse continues to be pursued in ways isolated from the larger WPS body of work.

So what are the impacts of delinking sexual exploitation and abuse policy from other relevant frameworks and thematic agendas within the UN? First, by dealing with sexual exploitation and abuse as an individualized conduct and discipline issue only, policies and their implementers are constrained in addressing the structural gender inequalities that shape the choices made by perpetrators (and sometimes, their victims, as chapters 1 and 2 illustrated). The challenges of the UN's policy regarding transactional sex are illustrative of this lack of sensitivity to gender experiences and constructs. The zero-tolerance bulletin explicitly prohibits any "exchange of money, employment, goods, or services for sex." However, peace operations are normally deployed into contexts where the intersection of conflict-related sexual violence and associated stigma, gender inequality, and material deprivation creates the conditions for "survival" sex economies to emerge and flourish. A key characteristic of transactional sex is that it "involves a level of agency and negotiation" even though it is negotiated in the context of often-extreme deprivation, desperation, and insecurity.[25] Without the benefit of a gender analysis as part of their training materials, guidelines, and approaches to sexual misconduct, interveners can have trouble making sense of the way this agency operates for local people and its implications for regulating sexual interactions between interveners and locals. So, for instance, despite receiving mandatory training on the UN code of conduct that prohibits transactional sex, some peacekeepers have argued to Paul Higate that their sexual "transactions" were acceptable because women "enthusiastically" competed to attract their attention, or because the "donated" food, resources or money made the women involved more secure.[26] That some parents encouraged their child's participation in transactional sex as a way of securing their family's economic survival may bolster this impression.[27] This illuminates the disconnect between the list of rules that peacekeepers are expected to follow, which is conveyed in mandatory predeployment training, and their understanding of why those rules are important. Situating sexual exploitation and abuse policy within a gendered analysis of power, context, vulnerability, and agency—such as that embodied in the WPS framework—would not only give interveners the language and concepts necessary to understand the multiple dimensions of transactional sex and better navigate their interactions with locals but would also help eschew the "women as victims" mentality that the policy currently reinforces.

Another implication of the isolation of sexual exploitation and abuse policy from the WPS frameworks is the tension created between protection and participation in the implementation of those policies. One of the most controversial provisions in the zero-tolerance bulletin asserts that "sexual relationships between United Nations staff and beneficiaries of assistance, since they are based on inherently unequal power dynamics, undermine the credibility and integrity of the work of the United Nations and are strongly discouraged."[28] Putting aside the unenforceability of this provision, this suggests that no adults in conflict-affected communities have the capacity to consent in the context of unequal power dynamics, which is infantilizing and disempowering.[29] The discussion in chapter 2 of the complexities of consensual adult transactional sex in Bosnia and Timor-Leste illustrated the fallacy of assuming that local women were not making considered choices, even if elements of exploitation were involved. Given that the zero-tolerance policy is primarily understood to apply to relationships between intervener men and local women (although relationships with local men fall under the same rule, the power dynamics between international women and local men tend to be understood as having less problematic power differentials, and the dynamics of homosexual relationships seem not to be considered at all), the policy undermines the values that underpin the WPS framework.[30] These hold that women can exert agency even in the context of the particular vulnerabilities they face in conflict and postconflict contexts, and that they have valuable contributions to make to local and national processes of decision-making and peace-making.

It is hardly surprising that there have been so few gains in convincing peacekeepers and policymakers to ensure the full and active participation of women in peace processes if the same people receive training that reinforces the idea that adult women in conflict contexts are so vulnerable that they cannot make choices for themselves about relationships they enter into. Ultimately, the current conduct and discipline approach to sexual exploitation and abuse fails to equip peacekeepers with the concepts and language required to navigate the complexities of relationships with locals, including distinguishing between exploitative and nonexploitative relationships.

This discussion raises two crucial issues for policymakers, the first of which is how to improve training and prevention approaches in order to provide peacekeepers with the conceptual foundations to understand why certain forms of interactions with locals are problematic and may be exploitative even if consent appears to be present and how to co-opt supervisors and managers into supporting robust discussions about these interactions and decisions while on deployment. During interviews, a senior military official from a Global North troop-contributing country suggested that the most effective way he had found to address the issue of relationships between his soldiers and local women was to have informal conversations over an evening meal or beer with men he had noticed were becoming close to local women about the different cultural perceptions of those relationships and the men's long-term intentions, particularly in terms of the expectations that the women involved and their families might have of romantic relationships, and how the women would be perceived if the relationship ended.[31] This approach diverges radically from the train-and-punish approach to sexual exploitation and abuse policy and provides an opportunity for personnel to consider the gender and power dynamics of their interactions with locals and the different implications those interactions might have for all parties involved. Complementing formal gender and prevention of sexual exploitation and abuse training with opportunities for these sort of conversations may be a useful way to develop more robust understanding among personnel about the complexities of and power dynamics inherent to sexual relationships with locals while on deployment in a peace operation.

The literature on conflict-related sexual violence provides a number of further pointers as to how approaches to the prevention of sexual exploitation and abuse might be improved. Elisabeth Wood's study of when wartime rape is rare suggests that if leaders judge sexual violence to be counterproductive to their interests and if the organizational hierarchy is strong enough to restrain sexual violence by individual combatants or particular units, little sexual violence will be observed.[32] She argues that leaders may take this position for a number of reasons, including when an armed group is particularly dependent on civilians for their activities and recognizes the importance of maintaining the support of those civilians. Additionally, showing deference to international law by prohibiting such sexual violence can support aspirations for international recognition and concerns about maintaining the support of financial backers. Amelia Hoover Green's in-depth study of why some combatants and armed groups carefully limit the scope and types of violence they use while others do not suggests that restraint among fighters occurs when they know why they are fighting and believe in the cause and when they understand the ways in which their behaviors affects the purposes of their war, which comes about when commanders or leaders invest in political education.[33] These findings are of great relevance to the sphere of sexual exploitation and abuse policy, given the close parallels between conflict-related sexual violence and sexual exploitation and abuse by interveners in peace operations. They highlight the importance of ensuring that leaders—at all levels and within all organizations in a peace operation—understand the ways in which sexual misconduct by their personnel undermines their interests, including by compromising their mission's values and goals, affecting operational capacity, and undermining local and international perceptions of the legitimacy of their work. They also underscore how critical it is to have a robust and responsive organizational hierarchy that has both the capacity and commitment to ensure that prevention and accountability mechanisms related to sexual misconduct are strong and effective. And finally, they bring to the fore the critical importance of political education among interveners in peace operations about why they have been deployed, how their actions affect broader mission goals and outcomes, and to what end certain behaviors have been proscribed or discouraged. This reiterates the importance of moving beyond the train-and-punish model of policy towards one more integrated with core mission goals and business.

The second critical issue for policymakers that the discussion above raises is the question of whether current definitions of prohibited and discouraged behaviors, as contained in the zero-tolerance bulletin, strike an appropriate balance between setting up protective mechanisms that limit what peacekeepers are permitted to do and undermining the agency of local individuals in establishing adult, consensual relationships with peacekeepers. The zero-tolerance bulletin is, in essence, an administrative policy developed in 2003 in response to major sexual misconduct scandals that has attained quasi-legal standing: it is being used as a basis for legal accountability processes despite not having the internal coherence and clarity that would normally be expected of legal regulations.

Revising it in order to improve clarity of the rules and resolve contradictions with other frameworks may set the foundations for more effective policy implementation in the future. Moreover, the discussion in chapter 2 of local perceptions of the behaviors that constitute sexual exploitation and abuse shows how culturally and historically contingent experiences of sexually inappropriate behaviors are and highlights the need for more flexible policy frameworks that can respond to the particularities of the specific contexts into which peacekeepers are deployed in order to prevent the negative peacebuilding outcomes that this book has demonstrated result from sexual misconduct by international interveners.

A final implication of the isolation of sexual exploitation and abuse policy from other frameworks is that it has been disconnected from the extensive policy and operational work being done on issues of conflict-related sexual violence. As discussed in chapter 1, there are important differences between sexual exploitation and abuse by interveners and conflict-related sexual violence; primarily that conflict-related sexual violence is perpetrated as part of violent conflicts by individuals and groups within those conflicts, whereas sexual exploitation and abuse is perpetrated by those sent to protect civilians from harm during and after conflicts. However, there are also important areas of overlap in terms of policy responses that could help strengthen sexual exploitation and abuse policy if the connections are made and lessons learned in relation to conflict-related sexual violence are translated into the sexual exploitation and abuse policy response. UN Security Council Resolutions 1820 (2008) and 1888 (2009) firmly established conflict-related sexual violence as a crime that is preventable and punishable under international human rights law, and these resolutions have led to work to strengthen criminal accountability for conflict-related sexual violence, responsiveness to survivors, and judicial capacity. Key obstacles regarding accountability for sexual exploitation and abuse include the difficulties of collecting evidence in relation to allegations that satisfy legal standards and generating political will to hold perpetrators criminally accountable under national legal frameworks. The operational and policy work being done under the conflict-related sexual violence umbrella is already addressing these challenges, but the connection has not yet been made to sexual misconduct accountability mechanisms. Indeed, the first recommendation of the

Independent Review of the sexual exploitation and abuse scandal in the Central African Republic was that

> The most significant step the UN can take to improve its responses to allegations of sexual exploitation and abuse by peacekeepers is to acknowledge that such abuses are a form of conflict related sexual violence that must be addressed under the UN's human rights policies. To acknowledge and operationalize the UN's obligations to protect victims, report, investigate, and follow up on allegations, and ensure that perpetrators are held accountable, the SEA and human rights policy frameworks must be harmonized under a unified policy framework.[34]

Relinking sexual exploitation and abuse policy with WPS and conflict-related sexual violence frameworks on both conceptual and operational levels would be a significant step in reorienting it away from the individualized, conduct and discipline framing of the problem, which is a key reason policies have been ineffective to date. This would help on two fronts: prevention and response policies would benefit from being situated within the WPS frame of gender, power, and protection issues, while accountability mechanisms would be strengthened by closer integration with conflict-related sexual violence frameworks. In other words, links to conflict-related sexual violence would strengthen the grounding of sexual exploitation and abuse policy in human rights and accountability frameworks, while links to WPS would provide the crucial grounding in feminist analysis, which is required for individuals to navigate the inevitably complex interpretation and implementation of such policies in practice.

If sexual exploitation and abuse policies and training drew on the language of gender and power and the conceptual framework around women's roles and vulnerabilities in conflict and peace processes—which are the foundation of the WPS agenda and currently absent from sexual exploitation and abuse policy discourse—peacekeepers would be equipped with an understanding of why the rules on sexual misconduct are important rather than simply what the rules are. Furthermore, couching sexual exploitation and abuse policy within the broader WPS framework and language would give peacekeepers and those involved in accountability processes for sexual misconduct a conceptual framework for how to navigate the sometimes complicated negotiation of relationships with local individuals and communities, particularly sexual relationships that are consensual but sometimes involve transactions and where consent does not rest on equal, nonhierarchical power relations. Importantly, this conceptual framework would help prevent the infantilization and disempowerment of women by foregrounding their agency while providing peacekeepers with an understanding of the gendered, racialized, and economic context in which it may be exercised. Equipping peacekeepers with a language of power dynamics—which can encompass gender, race, and economics—and a lens through which to make sense of their own role and position in peacekeeping contexts, is crucial to preventing and ensuring accountability for sexual exploitation and abuse. It would provide all personnel involved—including military, policy, and civilian peacekeepers; the UN secretariat; troop-contributing countries; and UN funds and agencies—with a better grounding from which to understand why certain behaviors are unacceptable in the context of peacekeeping operations, to identify sexual exploitation and abuse, and to hold perpetrators accountable for violations of the zero-tolerance policy. The current sexual exploitation and abuse policy approach provides a list of prohibited and discouraged behaviors, which belies the reality that navigating the permissibility or exploitative nature of sexual interactions that take place in the complex and unequal contexts into which peace operations are deployed is, in practice, much less clear-cut.

While prevention and response policies would benefit greatly from being couched within the language and concepts of WPS, accountability processes and mechanisms would be significantly improved through a closer integration with conflict-related sexual violence frameworks, which would assist in addressing the practical, political, and legal challenges to holding perpetrators accountable. Recognizing those types of sexual misconduct that are criminal—for instance sexual abuse, sexual exploitation of children, and trafficking—as forms of conflict-related sexual violence, which requires a robust, human rights based criminal legal response and demands the foregrounding of victim needs, might be an important step in strengthening current accountability mechanisms. This could be done while still recognizing the important differences between sexual exploitation and abuse by interveners and conflict-related sexual violence but also acknowledging that conflict and conflict-related sexual violence form the backdrop that shapes the context in which sexual exploitation and abuse economies develop and against which interveners participate in sexual misconduct against local communities. The Office of the Special Coordinator for SEA has already undertaken work to streamline and standardize reporting, data collection, and referral processes, which is an important step in this direction and would be bolstered by explicit connections with similar work being done in relation to conflict-related sexual violence.[35] Furthermore, if integrated also into the work of the special representative on sexual violence, sexual exploitation and abuse policy would benefit from the political mobilization the representative undertakes to ensure states hold their citizens accountable for crimes of sexual violence in conflict contexts.

At a glance: Advice to policymakers

- *Reframing "the problem."* Policy frameworks should move away from the individualized understanding of sexual exploitation and abuse, which identifies "the problem" as one of individual personnel engaging in prohibited behaviors, and rules not being adequately conveyed, understood, and obeyed; "the solution" in this model is understood to be strengthening the train-and-punish model of response. Instead, sexual exploitation and abuse should be understood in more complex terms: it is a diverse set of behaviors that involves varying levels of agency and consent and reflects local conditions and vulnerabilities as well as gendered expectations of sexual behaviors, opportunism, violence and the cultures that interveners bring with them into peace operations. These contextual, normative, and systemic factors intersect in different ways in different peace operations to produce different patterns of sexual exploitation and abuse by interveners. This means also that local communities may have different expectations of sexually appropriate and inappropriate behaviors by interveners, regardless of what formal codes of conduct outline. Policy needs to be responsive to these complexities and the particularities of each context in order to improve the effectiveness of prevention and response mechanisms.

- *Committed and accountable leadership.* Leadership at all levels in peace operations and the organizations associated with them needs to ensure that sexual exploitation and abuse policies are enforced, even where doing so presents operational or reputational challenges in the short term. Ensuring that mid- to high-level officials understand the ways in which sexual exploitation and abuse perpetrated by their personnel undermines their and their organization's interests—including by compromising their mission's values and goals, affecting operational capacity, and undermining local and international perceptions of the legitimacy of their work—is critical to shifting attitudes to ensure greater commitment to preventing misconduct and holding perpetrators accountable. Furthermore, ensuring that officials who fail to enforce accountability for sexual exploitation and abuse are held accountable themselves is crucial to establishing robust and credible sexual exploitation and abuse policy and processes.

- *Proactive and integrated policy development.* Policy development should be pursued proactively, rather than in response to major scandals, and should consider first the shortcomings in and implementation challenges to existing policy frameworks. The policy field does not need to be further crowded but rather sharpened and better aligned with the other relevant policy frameworks, particularly those related to sexual exploitation and abuse; Women, Peace and Security; and conflict-related sexual violence. In particular, sexual exploitation and abuse prevention and response policies would benefit from being aligned with the language and concepts provided by the WPS framework relating to gender, power, agency, and protection issues. Sexual exploitation and abuse accountability processes and mechanisms would be greatly improved through integration with conflict-related sexual violence frameworks, which are more advanced in addressing the practical, political, and legal challenges to holding perpetrators accountable. Moreover, recognizing those types of sexual exploitation and abuse that are criminal as forms of conflict-related sexual violence that require a criminal legal response foregrounding victim rights and needs would significantly strengthen current accountability frameworks.

- *Integrated training and political education.* Complementing rules-based training with ongoing opportunities for discussion and political education about the mission and their role in it is critical to ensuring that personnel understand not only *what* rules govern their behaviors while on deployment but also *why* they have been deployed, *how* their everyday actions affect broader mission goals and outcomes, and *to what end* certain behaviors have been proscribed or discouraged. Critically, such an integrated training approach would help interveners see the intersections between sexually exploitative and abuse behaviors and the broader challenges facing peace operations.
- *Recognition that sexual exploitation and abuse is one (important) problem among many.* In order to better address the broader challenges facing peacekeeping, policymakers and personnel in peace operations must understand the intersections between the factors that give rise to sexual exploitation and abuse and those that lead to peacekeepers failing in their protection responsibilities more broadly. Considering sexual misconduct in the context of nonsexual abuses against local populations and addressing it as a critically important piece of the puzzle of peacekeeping success are important steps towards addressing the dynamics of intervener cultures that have serious implications for the success or failure of peace operations. Moreover, a multifaceted response can embed efforts towards the prevention of sexual exploitation and abuse within general operational context considerations in order to anticipate and address the contextual factors that contribute to setting the scene for the perpetration of sexual misconduct, for instance by ensuring that the deployment of peacekeepers is closely linked to a humanitarian response that addresses food security and economic necessity.

Understanding the patterns of sexual exploitation and abuse, the factors that give rise to it, and its impacts on the capacity and credibility of the international community is crucial to developing effective prevention and response policies globally. This book has shown how the perpetration of sexual misconduct by international interveners undermines the operational capacity of the international community to effectively build peace after civil wars and sustainably alleviate human suffering in crises. It has also demonstrated that sexual exploitation and abuse poses a significant challenge to the established processes of legitimation that are critical to maintaining support for the UN, the broader international community involved in peace operations, and the multilateral peacekeeping project itself. This has serious ramifications for the nature and dynamics of peace operations in the future. Effectively preventing and responding to sexual misconduct is therefore crucial to continued international efforts to promote and secure global peace, order, and justice, but the current policy approach is fundamentally flawed as a result of framing the problem as an individualized form of misconduct by interveners.

This book has shown that, ultimately, sexual exploitation and abuse by interveners is not a standalone issue. Recognizing and mobilizing the connections and parallels it has with other areas of the international community's work in conflicts and peace processes will provide a stronger foundation from which a robust, multifaceted response can be built that more effectively reflects the complexities of the context, causes, and consequences of sexual misconduct by interveners in peace operations. Moreover, the individualized approach to sexual exploitation and abuse policy, which leads to the train-and-punish model of policy response, belies the fact that rules are both negotiated and negotiable in the specific contexts they are expected to regulate, as the detailed analysis of the way sexual misconduct and associated accountability measures operated in Timor-Leste and Bosnia illustrated. In order to effectively prevent and ensure accountability for sexual exploitation and abuse, policymakers must recognize this and pursue responses that are less rules-based, refocusing instead on identifying the intersecting causes of such behaviors, in particular the decisions being made by perpetrators and victims and the contexts and economies in which those choices are made.

Perhaps most important, though, if policymakers and intervener communities recognize the ways in which sexual misconduct undermines the international community's capacity to achieve core mission goals—including the protection and promotion of lasting peace, human rights, and justice—they may be able to generate greater political will at all levels of the international community to take these behaviors seriously. This would not only go some way to ensuring a more robust and effective approach to prevention and accountability by shifting the cultures within the international community that have shaped the development and implementation of sexual exploitation and abuse policies to date but would also strengthen cohesion around the values, principles, and goals of the peacekeeping project. In other words, just as the consequences of sexual exploitation and abuse by interveners are felt far beyond individual victims, pursuing a robust and integrated response would have positive ramifications far beyond just preventing such misconduct and holding individual perpetrators accountable. Such a response would fundamentally improve the capacity of the international community to support conflict-affected societies as they move from war towards a lasting peace based on justice, human rights, and accountability and, in doing so, bolster global perceptions of the value and legitimacy of the UN in addressing violent conflict in the world today.

NOTES

Introduction

1. AIDS-Free World, "The UN's Dirty Secret: The Untold Story of Child Sexual Abuse in the Central African Republic and Anders Kompass," May 29, 2015, http://www.codeblue campaign.com/carstatement/; Marie Deschamps, Hassan B. Jallow, and Yasmin Sooka, *Taking Action on Sexual Exploitation and Abuse by Peacekeepers: Report of an Independent Review on Sexual Exploitation and Abuse by International Peacekeeping Forces in the Central African Republic*, UN External Independent Panel, 2015.

2. Jasmine-Kim Westendorf and Louise Searle, "Sexual Exploitation and Abuse in Peace Operations: Trends, Policy Responses and Future Directions," *International Affairs* 93, no. 2 (2017): 365–87.

3. Thelma Awori, Catherine Lutz, and Paban Thapa, *Final Report: Expert Mission to Evaluate Risks to SEA Prevention Efforts in MINUSTAH, UNMIL, MONUSCO, and UNMISS* (November 3, 2013), 1, https://static1.squarespace.com/static/514a0127e4b04d7440e804 5d/t/55afcfa1e4b07b89d11d35ae/1437585313823/2013+Expert+Team+Report+FINAL.pdf, accessed May 6, 2019. This report was never officially released by the UN, but is available at the link above.

4. Secretary-General, Report of the Secretary-General on Special Measures for Protection from Sexual Exploitation and Sexual Abuse A/69/779 (February 13, 2015), 1, http://reliefweb .int/report/world/special-measures-protection-sexual-exploitation-and-sexual-abuse-report-secretary. Secretary-General, Remarks of the Secretary-General at the Informal Meeting of

the General Assembly (January 16, 2018), https://www.un.org/sg/en/content/sg/speeches/2018-01-16/remarks-informal-meeting-general-assembly.

5. For accounts of institutional reluctance to respond transparently to allegations of sexual exploitation and abuse in Bosnia and the Central African Republic, see Kathryn Bolkovac and Cari Lynn, *The Whistleblower: Sex Trafficking, Military Contractors, and One Woman's Fight for Justice* (New York: Macmillan, 2011); AIDS-Free World, "The UN's Dirty Secret."

6. Cynthia Enloe, *Maneuvers: The International Politics of Militarizing Women's Lives* (Berkeley: University of California Press, 2000); Henri Myrttinen, "Disarming Masculinities," *Disarmament Forum* 4 (2003): 37–46; Sandra Whitworth, *Men, Militarism, and UN Peacekeeping: A Gendered Analysis* (Boulder: Lynne Rienner Publishers, 2004); Paul Higate and Marsha Henry, "Engendering (in) Security in Peace Support Operations," *Security Dialogue* 35, no. 4 (2004): 481–98; Paul Higate, "Peacekeepers, Masculinities, and Sexual Exploitation.," *Men and Masculinities* 10, no. 1 (2007): 99–119; Marsha Henry and Paul Higate, *Insecure Spaces: Peacekeeping, Power and Performance in Haiti, Kosovo and Liberia* (London: Zed Books, 2009); Marsha Henry, "Sexual Exploitation and Abuse in UN Peacekeeping Missions: Problematising Current Responses," in *Gender, Agency, and Coercion*, ed. Sumi Madhok, Anne Phillips, and Kalpana Wilson (Houndmills: Palgrave Macmillan, 2013), 122–42.

7. Kathleen M. Jennings and Morten Bøås, "Transactions and Interactions: Everyday Life in the Peacekeeping Economy," *Journal of Intervention and Statebuilding* 9, no. 3 (2015): 281–95. This article is part of a special issue edited by the same authors entitled "Service, Sex and Security: Everyday Life in the Peacekeeping Economy." The other articles in the collection are relevant also to this discussion.

8. Kathleen M. Jennings, "Service, Sex, and Security: Gendered Peacekeeping Economies in Liberia and the Democratic Republic of the Congo," *Security Dialogue* 45, no. 4 (2014): 313–30; Kathleen M. Jennings, "Unintended Consequences of Intimacy: Political Economies of Peacekeeping and Sex Tourism," *International Peacekeeping* 17, no. 2 (2010): 229–43; Kathleen Jennings and Vesna Nikolić-Ristanović, "UN Peacekeeping Economies and Local Sex Industries: Connections and Implications," MICROCON Research Working Paper No. 17, 2009, http://papers.ssrn.com/sol3/papers.cfm?abstract_id=1488842.

9. Dianne Otto, "Making Sense of Zero Tolerance Policies in Peacekeeping Sexual Economies," in *Sexuality and the Law*, ed. Vanessa Munro and Carl Stychin (Abingdon: Routledge-Cavendish, 2007), 259–82; Olivera Simić, *Regulation of Sexual Conduct in UN Peacekeeping Operations* (New York: Springer, 2012); Gabrielle Simm, *Sex in Peace Operations* (Cambridge: Cambridge University Press, 2015); Jena McGill, "Survival Sex in Peacekeeping Economies: Re-Reading the Zero Tolerance Approach to Sexual Exploitation and Sexual Abuse in United Nations Peace Support Operations," *Journal of International Peacekeeping* 18 (2014): 1–44.

10. Lisa Carson, "Pre-Deployment 'Gender 'Training and the Lack Thereof for Australian Peacekeepers," *Australian Journal of International Affairs* 70, no. 3 (2016): 275–92; Sarah Smith, "Accountability and Sexual Exploitation and Abuse in Peace Operations," *Australian Journal of International Affairs* 71, no. 4 (2017): 405–422.

11. Sabrina Karim and Kyle Beardsley, *Equal Opportunity Peacekeeping: Women, Peace, and Security in Post-Conflict States* (Oxford: Oxford University Press, 2017).

12. Ragnhild Nordås and Siri Rustad, "Sexual Exploitation and Abuse by Peacekeepers: Understanding Variation," *International Interactions* 39 (2013): 511–34; Sabrina Karim and Kyle Beardsley, "Explaining Sexual Exploitation and Abuse in Peacekeeping Missions: The Role of Female Peacekeepers and Gender Equality in Contributing Countries," *Journal of Peace Research* 53, no. 1 (2016): 100–115; Bernd Beber et al., "Peacekeeping, Compliance with International Norms, and Transactional Sex in Monrovia, Liberia," *International Organization* 71, no. 1 (2017): 1–30; Megan Bastick, Karin Grimm, and Rahel Kunz,

Sexual Violence in Armed Conflict: Global Overview and Implications for the Security Sector (Geneva: Geneva Centre for the Democratic Control of Armed Forces, 2007).

13. Kelly Neudorfer, "Reducing Sexual Exploitation and Abuse: Does Deterrence Work to Prevent SEAs in UN Peacekeeping Missions?," *International Peacekeeping* 21, no. 5 (2014): 623–41; Westendorf and Searle, "Sexual Exploitation and Abuse in Peace Operations."

14. Kate Grady, "Sex, Statistics, Peacekeepers and Power: UN Data on Sexual Exploitation and Abuse and the Quest for Legal Reform," *Modern Law Review* 79, no. 6 (2016): 931–60; Róisín Burke, "Attribution of Responsibility: Sexual Abuse and Exploitation, and Effective Control of Blue Helmets," *Journal of International Peacekeeping* 16, no. 1 (2012): 1–46; Marco Odello and Róisín Burke, "Between Immunity and Impunity: Peacekeeping and Sexual Abuses and Violence," *International Journal of Human Rights* 20, no. 6 (2016): 839–53; Cassandra Mudgway, "Sexual Exploitation by UN Peacekeepers: The 'Survival Sex' Gap in International Human Rights Law," *International Journal of Human Rights* 21, no. 9 (2017): 1453–76.

15. Kelly Neudorfer, *Sexual Exploitation and Abuse in UN Peacekeeping: An Analysis of Risk and Prevention Factors* (Lanham, MD: Lexington Books, 2014); Olivera Simić, "Does the Presence of Women Really Matter? Towards Combating Male Sexual Violence in Peacekeeping Operations," *International Peacekeeping* 17, no. 2 (2010): 188–99.

16. This data is available at the UN's Conduct and Discipline Unit website at https://conduct.unmissions.org/sea-data-introduction.

17. Secretary-General, Secretary-General's Bulletin: Special Measures for Protection from Sexual Exploitation and Sexual Abuse, ST/SGB/2003/13 (October 9, 2003), https://oios.un.org/resources/2015/01/ST-SGB-2003-13.pdf, 1.

18. Westendorf and Searle, "Sexual Exploitation and Abuse in Peace Operations."

19. Séverine Autesserre, *The Trouble with the Congo* (Cambridge: Cambridge University Press, 2010); Séverine Autesserre, *Peaceland: Conflict Resolution and the Everyday Politics of International Intervention* (Cambridge: Cambridge University Press, 2014).

20. Kate Grady, "Sexual Exploitation and Abuse by UN Peacekeepers: A Threat to Impartiality," *International Peacekeeping* 17, no. 2 (2010): 215–28; Jennings, "Unintended Consequences of Intimacy"; Jennings and Nikolić-Ristanović, "UN Peacekeeping Economies and Local Sex Industries."

21. See for example Secretary-General, Special Measures for Protection from Sexual Exploitation and Abuse: A New Approach, A/71/818 (February 28, 2017), para. 1.4, https://undocs.org/A/71/818; Secretary-General, Special Measures 2003, sec. 3(d); Jane Connors, "UNMISS ASG VRA Media Briefing (Transcript)," UNMISS, December 8, 2017, https://unmiss.unmissions.org/unmiss-asg-vra-media-briefing-near-verbatim-transcript.

22. Jennings and Nikolić-Ristanović, "UN Peacekeeping Economies and Local Sex Industries"; Bolkovac and Lynn, *The Whistleblower*.

23. For the full set of data on sexual exploitation and abuse allegations and investigations in UN missions, see the UN's page on sexual exploitation and abuse, accessed May 6, 2019, https://conduct.unmissions.org/sea-data-introduction.

24. Autesserre, *Peaceland*; Jasmine-Kim Westendorf, *Why Peace Processes Fail: Negotiating Insecurity After Civil War* (Boulder: Lynne Rienner, 2015).

25. Mats Berdal, *Building Peace After War* (London: International Institute for Strategic Studies, 2009), 27.

1. The History and Nature of Sexual Misconduct in Peace Operations

1. Avi Selk and Eli Rosenberg, "Oxfam Prostitution Scandal Widens to at Least Three Countries," *Washington Post*, February 13, 2018, https://www.washingtonpost.com/news/worldviews/wp/2018/02/13/oxfam-prostitution-scandal-widens-to-at-least-three-countries/;

Sean O'Neill and Leila Haddou, "Oxfam Sex Scandal: Sacked Staff Found New Aid Jobs," *Times*, February 10, 2018, https://www.thetimes.co.uk/article/new-shame-for-oxfam-h5nq8lmfn.

2. In fact, the high rates of sexual exploitation and abuse in MINUSTAH contributed to the establishment of an expert team to report on risks to sexual exploitation and abuse prevention efforts in UN peacekeeping. Thelma Awori, Catherine Lutz, and Paban Thapa, *Final Report: Expert Mission to Evaluate Risks to SEA Prevention Efforts in MINUSTAH, UNMIL, MONUSCO, and UNMISS* (November 3, 2013), unreleased United Nations report, https://static1.squarespace.com/static/514a0127e4b04d7440e8045d/t/55afcfa1e4b07b89d11d35ae/1437585313823/2013+Expert+Team+Report+FINAL.pdf.

3. UN Security Council, UN Security Council Resolution 1542, S/RES/1542 (2004) (April 30, 2004), http://www.un.org/en/ga/search/view_doc.asp?symbol=S/RES/1542(2004).

4. Oxfam Great Britain, *Haiti Investigation Final Report FRN5 (Confidential)* (London: Oxfam Great Britain, 2011), 3.

5. Secretary-General, Secretary-General's Bulletin: Special Measures for Protection from Sexual Exploitation and Sexual Abuse, ST/SGB/2003/13 (October 9, 2003), https://oios.un.org/resources/2015/01/ST-SGB-2003-13.pdf; Inter-Agency Standing Committee, "Six Core Principles Relating to Sexual Exploitation and Abuse" (IASC, June 13, 2002), http://www.pseataskforce.org/en/tools. See also the range of policies and standards from across the UN and humanitarian sector at the IASC Task Team resources page (http://www.pseataskforce.org/en/tools).

6. Sandra Whitworth, *Men, Militarism, and UN Peacekeeping: A Gendered Analysis* (Boulder: Lynne Rienner Publishers, 2004), 67.

7. Whitworth, *Men, Militarism*, 68.

8. UNAIDS, "AIDS and the Military," UNAIDS Best Practices Collection (Geneva: UNAIDS, 1998), 2.

9. Judy L. Ledgerwood, "UN Peacekeeping Missions," Analysis from the East-West Center, Asia Pacific Issues (Honolulu: East-West Center, March 1994), http://www.seasite.niu.edu/khmer/ledgerwood/PDFAsiaPacific.htm; Olivera Simić, *Regulation of Sexual Conduct in UN Peacekeeping Operations* (New York: Springer, 2012), 41.

10. Simić, *Regulation of Sexual Conduct*, 41–42; Gabrielle Simm, *Sex in Peace Operations* (Cambridge: Cambridge University Press, 2015), 88–94.

11. Examples of such behaviors were detailed by multiple Bosnian interviewees who had worked with the UN and humanitarian community deployed in Bosnia during the war and are detailed in chapter 3.

12. Simić, *Regulation of Sexual Conduct*, 42.

13. Human Rights Watch, "Hopes Betrayed: Trafficking of Women and Girls to Post Conflict Bosnia and Herzegovina for Forced Prostitution," *Human Rights Watch* 14, no. 9 (D) (November 2002): 41–43, http://www.hrw.org/legacy/reports/2002/bosnia/.

14. Human Rights Watch, "Hopes Betrayed," 42.

15. Secretary-General, Investigation into Sexual Exploitation of Refugees by Aid Workers in West Africa, A/57/465, October 11, 2002, 9–11.

16. Secretary-General, Investigation into Sexual Exploitation of Refugees, 1.

17. United Nations General Assembly, Resolution Adopted by the General Assembly: Investigation into Sexual Exploitation of Refugees by Aid Workers in West Africa, A/RES/57/306 (May 22, 2003), 1–2, http://www.un.org/en/ga/search/view_doc.asp?symbol=A/RES/57/306. Emphasis in original.

18. Secretary General, Special Measures 2003.

19. Dianne Otto, "Making Sense of Zero Tolerance Policies in Peacekeeping Sexual Economies," in *Sexuality and the Law*, ed. Vanessa Munro and Carl Stychin (Abingdon: Routledge, 2007), 259–282; Simić, *Regulation of Sexual Conduct*.

20. Kate Grady, "Sex, Statistics, Peacekeepers and Power: UN Data on Sexual Exploitation and Abuse and the Quest for Legal Reform," *Modern Law Review* 79, no. 6 (2016): 935–41.

21. Jasmine-Kim Westendorf and Louise Searle, "Sexual Exploitation and Abuse in Peace Operations: Trends, Policy Responses and Future Directions," *International Affairs* 93, no. 2 (2017): 365–87.

22. The two most comprehensive examples are Ragnhild Nordås and Siri Rustad, "Sexual Exploitation and Abuse by Peacekeepers: Understanding Variation," *International Interactions* 39, no. 4 (2013): 511–34; and Sabrina Karim and Kyle Beardsley, *Equal Opportunity Peacekeeping: Women, Peace, and Security in Post-Conflict States* (Oxford: Oxford University Press, 2017).

23. Grady, "Sex, Statistics," 942. On the underreporting of sexual exploitation and abuse, see also Corinna Csaky, *No One to Turn to—The Under-Reporting of Child Sexual Exploitation and Abuse by Aid Workers and Peacekeepers* (London: Save the Children UK, 2008); Kathleen M. Jennings, *Protecting Whom? Approaches to Sexual Exploitation and Abuse in UN Peacekeeping Operations* (Oslo: Fafo, 2008), http://lastradainternational.org/lsidocs/fafo_approaches_abuse_0309.pdf; Nordås and Rustad, "Sexual Exploitation and Abuse by Peacekeepers," 530.

24. Interview with a UNHCR expert in accountability to affected populations and prevention of sexual exploitation and abuse, Geneva, September 23, 2016.

25. AIDS-Free World, "Leaked Files Reveal Hidden Scope of UN Sex Abuse," September 13, 2017, http://www.codebluecampaign.com/press-releases/2017/9/13; AIDS-Free World, "Another 41 Allegations of Peacekeeper Sex Abuse Undisclosed by the UN," April 13, 2016, http://www.codebluecampaign.com/press-releases/2016/4/13.

26. Nordås and Rustad, "Sexual Exploitation and Abuse by Peacekeepers."

27. Jacqui True, *The Political Economy of Violence against Women* (Oxford: Oxford University Press, 2012), 114–15; Nicola Henry, "Theorizing Wartime Rape," *Gender and Society* 30, no. 1 (2016): 44–56.

28. Elisabeth Jean Wood, "Conflict-Related Sexual Violence and the Policy Implications of Recent Research," *International Review of the Red Cross* 96, no. 894 (2014): 473.

29. Secretary General, Special Measures 2003.

30. Nordås and Rustad, "Sexual Exploitation and Abuse by Peacekeepers," 518.

31. United Nations Conduct in UN Field Missions, "Sexual Exploitation and Abuse Data," June 23, 2016, https://conduct.unmissions.org/table-of-allegations; Secretary-General, Special Measures for Protection from Sexual Exploitation and Abuse, A/72/751 (February 15, 2018), 15–16, https://conduct.unmissions.org/sites/default/files/a_72_751_0.pdf.

32. Secretary-General, Special Measures 2018, sec. Annex 1; United Nations Conduct and Discipline Unit, "Sexual Exploitation and Abuse: Table of Allegations," Conduct in UN Field Missions, April 5, 2017, https://conduct.unmissions.org/table-of-allegations.

33. Human Rights Watch, "Central African Republic: Rape by Peacekeepers," February 4, 2016, https://www.hrw.org/news/2016/02/04/central-african-republic-rape-peacekeepers.

34. Kevin Sieff, "The Growing U.N. Scandal over Sex Abuse and 'Peacekeeper Babies,'" *Washington Post*, February 27, 2016, http://www.washingtonpost.com/sf/world/2016/02/27/peacekeepers/.

35. "Fear over Haiti Child Abuse," *BBC News*, November 30, 2006, http://news.bbc.co.uk/2/hi/6159923.stm.

36. Craig Dodds, "SA Soldiers' Shame in the DRC," *IOL News*, June 13, 2013, http://www.iol.co.za/dailynews/news/sa-soldiers-shame-in-the-drc-1531660; Human Rights Watch, "We'll Kill You If You Cry: Sexual Violence in the Sierra Leone Conflict," January 16, 2003, http://www.hrw.org/en/reports/2003/01/15/well-kill-you-if-you-cry.

37. Elisabeth Jean Wood, "Armed Groups and Sexual Violence: When Is Wartime Rape Rare?," *Politics & Society* 37, no. 1 (2009): 131–61, https://doi.org/10.1177/00323292083297 55; Sara Meger, "Rape of the Congo: Understanding Sexual Violence in the Conflict in the Democratic Republic of Congo," *Journal of Contemporary African Studies* 28, no. 2 (2010): 119–35, https://doi.org/10.1080/02589001003736728; Dara Kay Cohen, *Rape during Civil War* (Ithaca, NY: Cornell University Press, 2016).

38. Joakim Kreutz and Magda Cardenas, "Women, Peace and Intervention: How the International Community Responds to Sexual Violence in Civil Conflict," *Canadian Foreign Policy Journal* 23, no. 3 (2017): 260–76.

39. Sandra Whitworth, "Gender, Race and the Politics of Peacekeeping," in *A Future for Peacekeeping?*, ed. Edward Moxon-Browne (Houndmills: Macmillan Press Ltd, 1998), 176–91; Cynthia Enloe, *Maneuvers: The International Politics of Militarizing Women's Lives* (Berkeley: University of California Press, 2000).

40. "One in Four Men Rape," *IRIN*, June 18, 2009, http://www.irinnews.org/report/849 09/south-africa-one-four-men-rape; United Nations Conduct and Discipline Unit, "Status of Allegations."

41. Karim and Beardsley, *Equal Opportunity Peacekeeping*, 101–5.

42. AIDS-Free World, "The UN's Dirty Secret: The Untold Story of Child Sexual Abuse in the Central African Republic and Anders Kompass," May 29, 2015, http://www.codeblue campaign.com/carstatement/; Marie Deschamps, Hassan B. Jallow, and Yasmin Sooka, *Taking Action on Sexual Exploitation and Abuse by Peacekeepers: Report of an Independent Review on Sexual Exploitation and Abuse by International Peacekeeping Forces in the Central African Republic* (UN External Independent Panel, 2015).

43. AIDS-Free World, "Shocking New Reports of Peacekeeper Sexual Abuse in the Central African Republic," March 30, 2016, http://www.codebluecampaign.com/press-releases/ 2016/3/30.

44. AIDS-Free World, "Shocking New Reports."

45. Sherene Razack, "From the 'Clean Snows of Petawawa': The Violence of Canadian Peacekeepers in Somalia," *Cultural Anthropology* 15, no. 1 (2000): 127–63.

46. Emily Wax, "Congo's Desperate 'One-Dollar U.N. Girls,'" *Washington Post*, March 21, 2005, http://www.washingtonpost.com/wp-dyn/articles/A52333-2005Mar20.html.

47. Human Rights Watch, "Central African Republic: Murder by Peacekeepers," June 7, 2016, https://www.hrw.org/news/2016/06/07/central-african-republic-murder-peacekeepers.

48. Cynthia Enloe, "Wielding Masculinity inside Abu Ghraib: Making Feminist Sense of an American Military Scandal," *Asian Journal of Women's Studies* 10, no. 3 (2004): 89–102.

49. United Nations, A Comprehensive Strategy to Eliminate Future Sexual Exploitation and Abuse in United Nations Peacekeeping Operations, A/59/710 (March 24, 2005). For a similar assessment of the prevalence of exploitative sexual relationships and sex with prostitutes in peacekeeper sexual exploitation and abuse, see Secretary-General, Special Measures for Protection from Sexual Exploitation and Sexual Abuse, A/61/957 (June 15, 2007), 13–15, https://undocs.org/A/61/957.

50. Secretary General, Special Measures 2003.

51. Otto, "Making Sense," 260–61.

52. Sieff, "The Growing U.N. Scandal.'"

53. Kate Holt and Sarah Hughes, "Sex and Death in the Heart of Africa," *Independent*, May 25, 2004, http://www.independent.co.uk/news/world/africa/sex-and-death-in-the-heart-of-africa-564563.html.

54. Wax, "Congo's Desperate 'One-Dollar U.N. Girls.'"

55. "Fear over Haiti Child Abuse."

56. UNHCR and Save the Children UK, Sexual Violence & Exploitation: The Experience of Refugee Children in Guinea, Liberia and Sierra Leone (February 2002), 4, https://www.savethechildren.org.uk/content/dam/global/reports/health-and-nutrition/sexual_violence_and_exploitation_1.pdf.

57. Shukuko Koyama and Henri Myrttinen, "Unintended Consequences of Peace Operations in Timor Leste from a Gender Perspective," in *Unintended Consequences of Peacekeeping Operations*, ed. Aoi Chiyuki, Cedric de Coning, and Ramesh Thakur (New York: United Nations University Press, 2007), 34; ETAN Listserv, La'o Hamutuk, 2001 http://etan.org/lh/news06.html.

58. Csaky, *No One to Turn to*, 6.

59. Save the Children UK, *From Camp to Community: Liberia Study on Exploitation of Children* (London: Save the Children UK, 2006), 3.

60. Paul Higate and Marsha Henry, "Engendering (in) Security in Peace Support Operations," *Security Dialogue* 35, no. 4 (2004): 491; Paul Higate, "Peacekeepers, Masculinities, and Sexual Exploitation," *Men and Masculinities* 10, no. 1 (2007): 100.

61. Save the Children UK, *From Camp to Community*, 11.

62. See for instance the seminal study by Katharine Hyung-Sun Moon, *Sex among Allies: Military Prostitution in U.S.-Korea Relations* (New York: Columbia University Press, 1997).

63. United Nations Department of Peacekeeping Operations, "Ten Rules: Code of Personal Conduct for Blue Helmets," 1998, http://pseataskforce.org/uploads/tools/tenrulescode ofpersonalconductforbluehelmets_undpko_english.pdf.

64. Sarah W. Spencer, "Making Peace: Preventing and Responding to Sexual Exploitation by United Nations Peacekeepers," *Journal of Public and International Affairs* 16 (Spring 2005): 167; Higate, "Peacekeepers, Masculinities," 107.

65. Secretary-General, Investigation into Sexual Exploitation of Refugees.

66. Sieff, "The Growing U.N. Scandal."

67. Kate Holt and Sarah Hughes, "UN Staff Accused of Raping Children in Sudan," *Telegraph*, January 2, 2007, http://www.telegraph.co.uk/news/worldnews/1538476/UN-staff-accused-of-raping-children-in-Sudan.html.

68. Save the Children UK, *From Camp to Community*, 12–13.

69. Secretary-General, Special Measures 2003, 2.

70. Otto, "Making Sense"; Simić, *Regulation of Sexual Conduct*.

71. Interview with a senior official in the UN Conduct and Discipline Unit, New York, November 4, 2016.

72. "Fear over Haiti Child Abuse."

73. Higate, "Peacekeepers, Masculinities," 106.

74. Spencer, "Making Peace," 171.

75. Barbara Limanowska, *Trafficking in Human Beings in Southeastern Europe* (Sarajevo: UNICEF, 2002), 65, https://www.osce.org/odihr/18540; Sarah E. Mendelson, *Barracks and Brothels* (Washington DC: CSIS, 2005), 9, http://csis.org/files/media/csis/pubs/0502_bar racksbrothels.pdf.

76. Kathleen Jennings and Vesna Nikolić-Ristanović, "UN Peacekeeping Economies and Local Sex Industries: Connections and Implications," MICROCON Research Working Paper No. 17, 2009, 10–11, http://papers.ssrn.com/sol3/papers.cfm?abstract_id=1488842; Human Rights Watch, "Hopes Betrayed"; Simm, *Sex in Peace Operations*, 304; Kathryn Bolkovac and Cari Lynn, *The Whistleblower: Sex Trafficking, Military Contractors, and One Woman's Fight for Justice* (New York: Macmillan, 2011).

77. Peter Andreas, *Blue Helmets and Black Markets: The Business of Survival in the Siege of Sarajevo* (Ithaca: Cornell University Press, 2011), 47–48.

78. *The UN and the Sex Slave Trade in Bosnia: Isolated Case or Larger Problem in the UN System? Hearing before the Subcommittee on International Operations and Human Rights of the Committee on International Relations, House of Representatives*, 107th Cong. 85 (2002) (statement of David Lamb, former UN Human Rights Investigator in Bosnia), http://commdocs.house.gov/committees/intlrel/hfa78948.000/hfa78948_0.HTM#65.

79. Amnesty International, "'So Does It Mean That We Have the Rights? Protecting the Rights of Women and Girls Trafficked for Forced Prostitution in Kosovo," May 5, 2004, 7–8, https://www.amnesty.org/en/documents/eur70/010/2004/en/.

80. True, *Political Economy of Violence*, 141. See also Jennings and Nikolić-Ristanović, "UN Peacekeeping Economies and Local Sex Industries," 9.

81. Interview with a senior official in international missions in Bosnia-Herzegovina, location witheld, 2016.

82. Fanny Ruden and Mats Utas, *Sexual Exploitation and Abuse by Peacekeeping Operations in Contemporary Africa* (Uppsala: The Nordic Africa Institute, Policy Notes, 2009), 2; Amnesty International, "It's in Our Hands—Stop Violence against Women," December 31, 2004, 34, https://www.amnesty.ie/hands-stop-violence-women/.

83. Koyama and Myrttinen, "Unintended Consequences," 33.

84. See for examples of this: Sarah Martin, *Must Boys Be Boys? Ending Sexual Exploitation and Abuse in UN Peacekeeping Missions* (Washington DC: Refugees International, 2005), 5–8; Secretary-General, Special Measures for Protection from Sexual Exploitation and Sexual Abuse, A/70/729 (February 16, 2016), 729, https://undocs.org/A/70/729; United Nations Security Council, 7642nd Meeting of the UN Security Council (Transcript), S/PV.7642 (March 10, 2016); Keith J. Allred, "Peacekeepers and Prostitutes: How Deployment Forces Fuel the Demand for Trafficked Women and New Hope for Stopping It.," *Armed Forces & Society* 33, no. 1 (2006): 5–23. Similar suggestions about the importance of contextual factors were made during an interview with a senior staff member in the UN Conduct and Discipline Unit.

85. Secretary-General, Special Measures for Protection from Sexual Exploitation and Abuse: A New Approach, A/71/818 (February 28, 2017), https://undocs.org/A/71/818.

86. Nordås and Rustad, "Sexual Exploitation and Abuse by Peacekeepers," 526–30.

87. Stephen Moncrief, "Military Socialization, Disciplinary Culture, and Sexual Violence in UN Peacekeeping Operations," *Journal of Peace Research* 54, no. 5 (2017): 715–30.

88. Allred, "Peacekeepers and Prostitutes," 8–10.

89. Paul Kirby, "How Is Rape a Weapon of War? Feminist International Relations, Modes of Critical Explanation and the Study of Wartime Sexual Violence," *European Journal of International Relations* 19, no. 4 (2012): 799.

90. Razack, "From the 'Clean Snows of Petawawa,'" 138; Higate, "Peacekeepers, Masculinities," 106.

91. Helena Carreiras, "Gendered Culture in Peacekeeping Operations," *International Peacekeeping* 17, no. 4 (2010): 471–85; Whitworth, *Men, Militarism*.

92. Karim and Beardsley, *Equal Opportunity Peacekeeping*, 93–108.

93. Robert W. Connell and James W. Messerschmidt, "Hegemonic Masculinity: Rethinking the Concept," *Gender & Society* 19, no. 6 (2005): 829–59.

94. Paul Kirby, "Refusing to Be a Man? Men's Responsibility for War Rape and the Problem of Social Structures in Feminist and Gender Theory," *Men and Masculinities* 16, no. 1 (2013): 93–114.

95. Marsha Henry, "Sexual Exploitation and Abuse in UN Peacekeeping Missions: Problematising Current Responses," in *Gender, Agency, and Coercion*, ed. Sumi Madhok, Anne Phillips, and Kalpana Wilson (Houndmills: Palgrave Macmillan, 2013), 127. See also Enloe, *Maneuvers*.

96. Enloe, *Maneuvers*, 101.

97. Razack, "From the 'Clean Snows of Petawawa,'" 129; Sherene Razack, *Dark Threats and White Knights* (Toronto: University of Toronto Press, 2004).

98. M. Henry, "Sexual Exploitation and Abuse."

99. United Nations News Service, "UN Civilian Worker in DR of Congo Accused of Child Molestation," *UN News Service*, November 1, 2004; Muna Ndulo, "United Nations Responses to the Sexual Abuse and Exploitation of Women and Girls by Peacekeepers during Peacekeeping Missions," *Berkeley Journal of International Law* 27, no. 1 (2009): 144.

100. Secretary-General, Report of the Secretary-General on Conflict-Related Sexual Violence, S/2015/203 (March 23, 2015), 1, http://www.securitycouncilreport.org/atf/cf/%7B 65BFCF9B-6D27-4E9C-8CD3-CF6E4FF96FF9%7D/s_2015_203.pdf.

101. See for example Mervyn Christian et al., "Sexual and Gender Based Violence against Men in the Democratic Republic of Congo: Effects on Survivors, Their Families and the Community," *Medicine, Conflict and Survival* 27, no. 4 (October 1, 2011): 227–46, https://doi.org/10.1080/13623699.2011.645144; Sarah Chynoweth, *"We Keep It in Our Heart": Sexual Violence against Men and Boys in the Syria Crisis* (Geneva: UNHCR, 2017), https://data2.unhcr.org/en/documents/download/60864; Will Storr, "The Rape of Men: The Darkest Secret of War," *Guardian*, July 16, 2011, http://www.theguardian.com/society/2011/jul/17/the-rape-of-men; Megan Bastick, Karin Grimm, and Rahel Kunz, *Sexual Violence in Armed Conflict: Global Overview and Implications for the Security Sector* (Geneva: Geneva Centre for the Democratic Control of Armed Forces, 2007), https://www1.essex.ac.uk/armedcon/story_id/ sexualviolence_conflict_full%5B1%5D.pdf.

102. This was suggested to me by a number of high-level officials and other personnel working in response to CRSV in conflict. It also seems to be gaining ground in some policy research; for instance, this report deals with sexual exploitation and abuse as a type of conflict related sexual violence (Bastick, Grimm, and Kunz, *Sexual Violence in Armed Conflict*.)

103. Interview with a Timorese victims' advocate, Dili, July 23, 2016.

104. Bastick, Grimm, and Kunz, *Sexual Violence in Armed Conflict*, 10.

105. Bastick, Grimm, and Kunz, *Sexual Violence in Armed Conflict*, 15.

106. United Nations, "Sexual Exploitation and Abuse—Data," Conduct in UN Field Missions, January 23, 2017, https://conduct.unmissions.org/sea-data-introduction.

107. Humanitarian Women's Network, "Survey Data," 2016, www.humanitarianwom ensnetwork.org; Dyan Mazurana and Phoebe Donnelly, *STOP the Sexual Assault Against Humanitarian and Development Aid Workers* (Somerville: Feinstein International Center, Tufts University, 2017), http://fic.tufts.edu/publication-item/stop-the-sexual-assault-against-humanitarian-and-development-aid-workers/; Megan Nobert, *Humanitarian Experiences with Sexual Violence: Compilation of Two Years of Report the Abuse Data Collection* (Geneva: Report the Abuse, 2017), https://reliefweb.int/sites/reliefweb.int/files/resources/RTA%20Hu manitarian%20experiences%20with%20Sexual%20Violence%20-%20Compilation%20 of%20Two%20Years%20of%20Report%20the%20Abuse%20Data%20Collection.pdf; Juliet Bourke, *United Nations Safe Space Report: Survey on Sexual Harassment in Our Workplace* (Sydney: Deloitte, 2019; commissioned by the United Nations).

108. For data on this, see Mazurana and Donnelly, *STOP the Sexual Assault*, 12.

109. Megan Nobert, "Aid Worker: I Was Drugged and Raped by Another Humanitarian in South Sudan," *Guardian*, July 29, 2015, http://www.theguardian.com/global-devel opment-professionals-network/2015/jul/29/aid-worker-rape-humanitarian-south-sudan-sexual-violence.

110. Mazurana and Donnelly, *STOP the Sexual Assault*, 16, 34.

111. For an example of these stories, see "Forced to Have Oral Sex with a Colleague: Aid Workers Speak out on Assault | Secret Aid Worker," *Guardian*, November 13, 2017, http://www.theguardian.com/working-in-development/2017/nov/13/forced-to-have-oral-sex-with-a-colleague-aid-workers-speak-out-on-assault-harassment; Nicola Kelly, "Aid Workers and Sexual Violence: Survivors Speak Out," *Guardian*, February 17, 2017, http://www.theguardian.com/global-development-professionals-network/2017/feb/17/aid-workers-and-sexual-violence-survivors-speak-out; Anna Leach and Sandra Laville, "Raped by a Colleague Then Fired: The Aid Worker Who Refused to Keep Quiet," *Guardian*, October 19, 2015, http://www.theguardian.com/world/2015/oct/19/raped-by-a-colleague-then-fired-the-aid-worker-who-refused-to-keep-quiet; Nobert, "Humanitarian Experiences."

112. Kelly, "Aid Workers and Sexual Violence"; Nobert, "Humanitarian Experiences"; Humanitarian Women's Network, "Survey Data."

113. Humanitarian Women's Network, "Survey Data."

114. Humanitarian Women's Network, "Survey Data."

115. Humanitarian Women's Network, "Survey Data."

116. Nobert, "Humanitarian Experiences," 5–7.

117. Bourke, *Safe Space.*

118. Humanitarian Women's Network, "Survey Data"; Bourke, *Safe Space*, 28.

119. Humanitarian Women's Network, "Survey Data."

120. Mazurana and Donnelly, *STOP the Sexual Assault*, 44.

121. Megan Nobert, *Prevention, Policy and Procedure Checklist: Responding to Sexual Violence in Humanitarian and Development Settings* (Geneva: Report the Abuse, 2016), 13–19, https://www.eisf.eu/library/prevention-policy-and-procedure-checklist-responding-to-sexual-violence-in-humanitarian-and-development-settings/.

122. Humanitarian Women's Network, "Survey Data."

123. Mazurana and Donnelly, *STOP the Sexual Assault*, 21–23.

124. "Forced to Have Oral Sex with a Colleague."

125. Mazurana and Donnelly, *STOP the Sexual Assault*, 30–38.

2. Sexual Exploitation and Abuse in Bosnia and Timor-Leste

1. Secretary-General, Secretary-General's Bulletin: Observance by United Nations Forces of International Humanitarian Law, ST/SGB/1999/13 (August 6, 1999).

2. These are variously referred to as "protected areas," "safe areas," and "safe zones" in the literature and reporting on the UN presence in the former Yugoslavia.

3. "UNPROFOR," Department of Public Information, United Nations, last updated August 31, 1996, https://peacekeeping.un.org/mission/past/unprof_p.htm.

4. United Nations Security Council, UN Security Council Resolution 1031, S/RES/1031 (1995) (December 15, 1995).

5. United Nations Security Council, UN Security Council Resolution 1088, S/RES/1088 (1996) (December 21, 1996).

6. United Nations Security Council, UN Security Council Resolution 1035, S/RES/1035 (1995) (December 21, 1995), 10.

7. Peter Andreas, *Blue Helmets and Black Markets: The Business of Survival in the Siege of Sarajevo* (Ithaca, NY: Cornell University Press, 2011), 47–48, 128–35. See also Kathleen Jennings and Vesna Nikolić-Ristanović, "UN Peacekeeping Economies and Local Sex Industries: Connections and Implications," MICROCON Research Working Paper No. 17, 2009, http://papers.ssrn.com/sol3/papers.cfm?abstract_id=1488842.

8. Saliha Djuderija (assistant minister, Ministry of Human Rights and Refugees of Bosnia and Herzegovina), interview with the author, Sarajevo, September 14, 2016.

9. Djuderija, interview with the author; Andreas, *Blue Helmets and Black Markets*, 47–48; Nela Porobic (WILPF), interview with the author, Sarajevo, September 7, 2016; interview with Bosnian researchers and women's rights activists, Sarajevo, September 8, 2016.

10. Amra Pandzo (Bosnian peacebuilder), interview with the author, Sarajevo, September 7, 2016.

11. Interview with Bosnian researchers and women's rights activists.

12. Andreas, *Blue Helmets and Black Markets*, 46–58.

13. Sevima Sali Terzic (former director of Global Rights—Partners for Justice, current senior advisor to the Constitutional Court), interview with the author, Sarajevo, September 6, 2016; Pandzo, interview with the author.

14. Pandzo, interview with the author; Hasan Nuhanović (Bosnian translator for UN at Srebrenica), interview with the author, Sarajevo, September 8, 2016; interview with Bosnian gender advisor to intergovernmental organization, Sarajevo, September 7, 2016.

15. Pandzo, interview with the author.

16. Andreas, *Blue Helmets and Black Markets*, 128.

17. Kathryn Bolkovac and Cari Lynn, *The Whistleblower: Sex Trafficking, Military Contractors, and One Woman's Fight for Justice* (New York: Macmillan, 2011); Olivera Simić, *Regulation of Sexual Conduct in UN Peacekeeping Operations* (New York: Springer, 2012); Human Rights Watch, "Hopes Betrayed: Trafficking of Women and Girls to Post Conflict Bosnia and Herzegovina for Forced Prostitution" *Human Rights Watch* 14, no. 9 (D) (November, 2002), http://www.hrw.org/legacy/reports/2002/bosnia/; Djuderija, interview with the author; Interview with Bosnian NGO official and antitrafficking expert, Sarajevo, September 14, 2016.

18. Interview with Bosnian NGO official and antitrafficking expert; Djuderija, interview with the author; Andreas, *Blue Helmets and Black Markets*, 132.

19. Human Rights Watch, "Hopes Betrayed," 62.

20. Interview with independent expert on trafficking in Bosnia, Sarajevo, September 14, 2016.

21. Gabrielle Simm, *Sex in Peace Operations* (Cambridge: Cambridge University Press, 2015), 3; Human Rights Watch, "Hopes Betrayed," 65–66.

22. Human Rights Watch, "Hopes Betrayed," 19, 52–54, 62–66.

23. Human Rights Watch, "Hopes Betrayed," 51.

24. Simić, *Regulation of Sexual Conduct*.

25. Adisa Fišić Barukčija (TRIAL International), interview with the author, Sarajevo, September 6, 2016; interview with Bosnian legal advisor to intergovernmental organization, Sarajevo, September 7, 2016.

26. Interview with Bosnian staff member at international NGO providing legal aid to victims of wartime sexual violence, Sarajevo, September 6, 2016.

27. Nela Porobic (WILPF), interview with the author, Sarajevo, September 7, 2016.

28. Terzic, interview with the author; interview with Bosnian gender advisor to intergovernmental organization; interview with independent expert on trafficking in Bosnia, Sarajevo, September 14, 2016.

29. Interview with Bosnian NGO official and antitrafficking expert.

30. Interview with Bosnian researchers and women's rights activists.

31. Human Rights Watch, "Hopes Betrayed."

32. Human Rights Watch, "Hopes Betrayed," 51; Elisabeth Prugl and Hayley Thompson, "The Whistleblower: An Interview with Kathryn Bolkovac and Madeleine Rees,"

International Feminist Journal of Politics 15, no. 1 (2013): 103–4; Andreas, *Blue Helmets and Black Markets*, 128–32.

33. This is a reflection based on the extensive interviews I conducted in Timor-Leste, but other researchers have made similar findings; see e.g. Sofi Ospina, *A Review and Evaluation of Gender-Related Activities of UN Peacekeeping Operations and Their Impact on Gender Relations in Timor-Leste* (New York: UN Department of Peacekeeping Operations, 2006), 42–44.

34. UN Security Council, UN Security Council Resolution 1264, S/RES/1264 (1999) (September 15, 1999), http://unscr.com/en/resolutions/1264.

35. UN Security Council, UN Security Council Resolution 1272, S/RES/1272 (1999) (October 22, 1999).

36. UN Department of Public Information, "UNTAET," May 2002, https://peacekeeping. un.org/mission/past/etimor/UntaetB.htm.

37. UN Security Council, UN Security Council Resolution 1704, S/RES/1704 (2006) (August 25, 2006).

38. Shukuko Koyama and Henri Myrttinen, "Unintended Consequences of Peace Operations in Timor Leste from a Gender Perspective," in *Unintended Consequences of Peacekeeping Operations*, ed. Aoi Chiyuki, Cedric de Coning, and Ramesh Thakur (New York: United Nations University Press, 2007), 36–37.

39. Interview with former ET-WAV staff member, Dili, July 28, 2016. ET-WAV was a local NGO supporting women who had experienced sexual violence and sexual exploitation and abuse by interveners, including through ensuring medical evidence is collected at the hospital. This case was repoted directly to my respondent. Sofi Ospina, "A Review and Evaluation," 44; Mark Dodd, "Diggers in Timor 'Sex' Clash," *The Australian*, March 21, 2005, http:// www.etan.org/et2005/march/20/21digers.htm; Mark Dodd, "Hushed Rape of Timor," *Weekend Australian*, March 26, 2005; Asenio Bano (Timorese politician), interview with the author, Oecusse, July 25, 2016. Asenio Bano was involved in the investigation of sexual exploitation and abuse by peacekeepers in Oecusse, and prepared the report that was submitted to the UN Mission about the cases, but not publicly released. He is also a former social welfare minister in Timor-Leste.

40. Lindsay Murdoch, "UN Acts to Stamp Out Sex Abuse by Staff in East Timor," *Age*, August 30, 2006, http://www.theage.com.au/news/world/un-acts-to-stamp-out-sex-abuse-by-staff-in-east-timor/2006/08/29/1156816899264.html.

41. Koyama and Myrttinen, "Unintended Consequences," 36–37.

42. Cathleen Caron, *Trafficking in East Timor—A Look into the Sex Industry of the Newest Nation* (Dili: The Alola Foundation, 2004), http://www.alolafoundation.org/images/programs/ publications/ALOLA_TRAFFICKING_REPORT.pdf; Koyama and Myrttinen, "Unintended Consequences," 33–36; Lindsay Murdoch, "UN Turns Blind Eye to Use of Timor Brothels," *Age*, May 7, 2007, http://www.theage.com.au/news/world/un-turns-blind-eye-to-use-of-timor-brothels/2007/05/06/1178390140808.html.

43. Lindsay Murdoch, "Criminal Syndicate in Timor," *Sydney Morning Herald*, February 28, 2008, http://www.smh.com.au/news/world/criminal-syndicate-in-timor/2008/02/27/ 1203788443860.html.

44. Caron, *Trafficking in East Timor*, 18–29.

45. Lindsay Murdoch, "UN under Fire for Turning a Blind Eye to Peacekeepers' Misconduct," *Sydney Morning Herald*, May 7, 2007, http://www.smh.com.au/news/world/un-under-fire-for-turning-a-blind-eye-to-peacekeepers-misconduct/2007/05/06/1178390145310.html; Koyama and Myrttinen, "Unintended Consequences," 34.

46. Dodd, "Diggers in Timor 'Sex' Clash."

47. Interview with former UN Timorese staff member and current senior government official, Dili, July 28, 2016; Angkis Lay Leonor (coordinator, Scarlett Timor), interview with

the author, Dili, July 22, 2016; Another interviewee also recounted that women who engaged in transactional sex were often not paid the agreed fee, receiving as little as twenty-five cents in some cases. Interview with Timorese staff member working with UN and NGOs, Oecusse, July 26, 2016.

48. John McFarlane and William Maley, "Civilian Police in United Nations Peace Operations: Some Lessons from Recent Australian Experience," in *United Nations Peacekeeping Operations: Ad Hoc Missions, Permanent Engagement*, ed. Ramesh Thakur and Albrecht Schnabel (Tokyo: United Nations University Press, 2001), 198.

49. Madre Guillermina (Timorese religious and civil society leader), interview with the author, Dili, July 23, 2016; Manuela Leong Pereira (executive director, ACBIT, former director, FOKUPERS), interview with the author, Dili, July 20, 2016; Nelson Belo (executive director, Fundasaun Mahein), interview with the author, Dili, July 22, 2016; Teresa Verdial (former director, Alola Foundation), interview with the author, Dili, July 18, 2016.

50. Caron, *Trafficking in East Timor*, 39; Pereira, interview with the author; Susan Kendall (PRADET East Timor), interview with the author, Dili, July 21, 2016.

51. Maria Domingas Fernandes Alves et al., *Baseline Study on Sexual and Gender-based Violence in Bobonaro and Covalima* (Dili: Asia Pacific Support Collective Timor-Leste, 2009), 54–58; Verdial, interview with the author. It is worth noting that similar practices have occurred in other peacekeeping contexts, such as the DRC, where it is customary for communities to offer girls to outsiders who come and help the community (interview with UNHCR expert in Accountability to Affected Populations and Prevention of Sexual Exploitation and Abuse, Geneva, September 23, 2016.)

52. Koyama and Myrttinen, "Unintended Consequences," 37. "Sexual Misconduct Being Investigated: UNMIT's Gyorgy KAKUK," *East Timor Law and Justice Bulletin*, October 12, 2010, http://www.easttimorlawandjusticebulletin.com/2010/10/sexual-misconduct-being-investigated.html.

53. Leonor, interview with the author.

54. F. Reis (Timorese civil society leader), interview with the author, Dili, July 21, 2016.

55. Pereira, interview with the author; Marilia Alves (executive director, FOKUPERS), interview with the author, Dili, July 20, 2016; interview with Timorese staff member working with UN and NGOs.

56. Interview with Timorese UN official, Dili, July 19, 2016; interview with former ET-WAV staff member; Pereira, interview with the author; Alves, interview with the author; interview with international staff member who worked in UN human rights unit and international NGOs, Dili, July 19, 2016.

57. Interview with Timorese UN official.

58. Koyama and Myrttinen, "Unintended Consequences," 38.

59. Anne Barker, "UN Takes Step to Prevent Sex Abuse in East Timor. ABC Radio PM," *ABC Radio*, August 30, 2006, http://www.abc.net.au/pm/content/2006/s1728448.htm; Murdoch, "UN Acts to Stamp out Sex Abuse"; Lindsay Murdoch, "UN Legacy of Shame in Timor," *Age*, July 22, 2006, http://www.theage.com.au/news/world/uns-legacy-of-shame-in-timor/2006/07/21/1153166587803.html; Ospina, *A Review and Evaluation*, 42–44.

60. Interview with Timorese UN official.

61. Pereira, interview with the author; Leonor, interview with the author.

62. Pereira, interview with the author.

63. Pereira, interview with the author; Ana Paula Sequeira (former UN PKO Timorese staff member), interview with the author, Dili, July 20, 2016; Kendall, interview with the author.

64. Abel Dos Santos (program coordinator, Fundasaun Mahein), interview with the author, Dili, July 22, 2016.

65. Sequeira, interview with the author; Bano, interview with the author; Reis, interview with the author; Guillermina, interview with the author; interview with international staff member who worked in UN human rights unit and international NGOs.

66. Interview with Timorese staff member working with UN and NGOs; interview with Timorese NGO Representative, Dili, July 27, 2016; The Asia Foundation, *Understanding Violence against Women and Children in Timor-Leste: Findings from the Nabilan Baseline Study— Main Report* (Dili: The Asia Foundation, 2016), https://asiafoundation.org/wp-content/up loads/2016/05/UnderstandingVAWTL_main.pdf.

3. Making Matters Worse

1. Thelma Awori, Catherine Lutz, and Paban Thapa, *Final Report: Expert Mission to Evaluate Risks to SEA Prevention Efforts in MINUSTAH, UNMIL, MONUSCO, and UNMISS* (November 3, 2013), unreleased United Nations report, 2, https://static1.square space.com/static/514a0127e4b04d7440e8045d/t/55afcfa1e4b07b89d11d35ae/1437585313 823/2013+Expert+Team+Report+FINAL.pdf.

2. Marie Deschamps, Hassan B. Jallow, and Yasmin Sooka, *Taking Action on Sexual Exploitation and Abuse by Peacekeepers: Report of an Independent Review on Sexual Exploitation and Abuse by International Peacekeeping Forces in the Central African Republic*, UN External Independent Panel, 2015, 5.

3. United Nations Department of Peacekeeping Operations, "What We Do," accessed April 5, 2018, https://peacekeeping.un.org/en/what-we-do.

4. United Nations, Charter of the United Nations, October 24, 1945, http://www.ref world.org/docid/3ae6b3930.html.

5. Sarah von Billerbeck, *Whose Peace? Local Ownership and United Nations Peacekeeping* (Oxford: Oxford University Press, 2016), 51.

6. See for instance von Billerbeck, *Whose Peace?*; Roland Paris, "Peacekeeping and the Constraints of Global Culture," *European Journal of International Relations* 9, no. 3 (2003): 441–473; Roland Paris, *At War's End: Building Peace After Civil Conflict* (Cambridge: Cambridge University Press, 2004); Timothy D. Sisk, "Peacebuilding as Democratization: Findings and Recommendations," in *From War to Democracy: Dilemmas of Peacebuilding*, ed. Anna K. Jarstad and Timothy D. Sisk (Cambridge: Cambridge University Press, 2008), 239–59.

7. United Nations General Assembly and United Nations Security Council, Report of the Panel on United Nations Peace Operations (Brahimi Report), A/55/305, S/2000/809 (August 21, 2000), https://undocs.org/A/55/305; Secretary General's High-Level Panel on Threats, Challenges and Change, *A More Secure World: Our Shared Responsibility* (New York: United Nations, 2004); High-Level Independent Panel on United Nations Peace Operations, *Uniting Our Strengths for Peace: Politics, Partnership and People* (HIPPO report) (New York: United Nations, 2015), https://peaceoperationsreview.org/wp-content/uploads/2015/08/HIPPO_Report_1_ June_2015.pdf.

8. See for instance the UN Security Council Resolution that authorized the first peacekeeping operation in Timor-Leste, which "express[ed] its concern at reports indicating that systematic, widespread and flagrant violations of international humanitarian and human rights law have been committed in East Timor, and stress[ed] that persons committing such violations bear individual responsibility." United Nations Security Council, UN Security Council Resolution 1264, S/RES/1264 (September 15, 1999), http://unscr.com/en/resolutions/1264.

9. Dina Francesca Haynes, "Lessons from Bosnia's Arizona Market: Harm to Women in a Neoliberalized Postconflict Reconstruction Process," *University of Pennsylvania Law Review* 158, no. 6 (2010): 1784–85.

10. Haynes, "Lessons from Bosnia's Arizona Market."

11. Nelson Belo (executive director, Fundasaun Mahein), interview with the author, Dili, July 22, 2016.

12. Angkis Lay Leonor (coordinator, Scarlett Timor), interview with the author, Dili, July 22, 2016.

13. See for instance Marsha Henry and Paul Higate, *Insecure Spaces: Peacekeeping, Power and Performance in Haiti, Kosovo and Liberia* (London: Zed Books, 2009), 146; Preeti Patel and Paolo Tripodi, "Peacekeepers, HIV and the Role of Masculinity in Military Behaviour," *International Peacekeeping* 14, no. 5 (2007): 584–98; Maria Jansson, "The Logic of Protection: Narratives of HIV/AIDS in the UN Security Council," *International Feminist Journal of Politics* 19, no. 1 (2017): 71–85.

14. Interview with international staff member who worked in UN human rights unit and international NGOs, Dili, July 19, 2016; Susan Kendall (PRADET East Timor), interview with the author, Dili, July 21, 2016.

15. Human Rights Watch, "Hopes Betrayed: Trafficking of Women and Girls to Post Conflict Bosnia and Herzegovina for Forced Prostitution," *Human Rights Watch* 14, no. 9 (D) (November 2002), http://www.hrw.org/legacy/reports/2002/bosnia/; interview with Bosnian gender advisor to intergovernmental organization, Sarajevo, September 7, 2016; interview with Bosnian NGO official and antitrafficking expert, Sarajevo, September 14, 2016; interview with independent expert on trafficking in Bosnia, Sarajevo, September 14, 2016.

16. Interview with Bosnian NGO official and antitrafficking expert.

17. Interview with Bosnian gender advisor to intergovernmental organization; Saliha Djuderija (assistant minister, Ministry of Human Rights and Refugees of Bosnia and Herzegovina), interview with the author, Sarajevo, September 14, 2016; interview with independent expert on trafficking in Bosnia.

18. F. Reis (Timorese civil society leader), interview with the author, Dili, July 21, 2016; Madre Guillermina (Timorese religious and civil society leader), interview with the author, Dili, July 23, 2016.

19. Leonor, interview with the author.

20. Interview with Timorese NGO representative, Dili, July 27, 2016; Manuela Leong Pereira (executive director, ACBIT, former director, FOKUPERS), interview with the author, Dili, July 20, 2016.

21. Meagan Smith-Hrle (Human rights and rule of law expert who worked with OSCE, UNHCR and Human Rights Chamber), interview with the author, Sarajevo, September 12, 2016.

22. Interview with Bosnian gender advisor to intergovernmental organization.

23. Reis, interview with the author; Pereira, interview with the author; Guillermina, interview with the author; Teresa Verdial (former director, Alola Foundation), interview with the author, Dili, July 18, 2016.

24. Jeremy Farrall, "The Future of UN Peacekeeping and the Rule of Law," in *Proceedings of the Annual Meeting (American Society of International Law)* 101 (2007): 160–61.

25. United Nations General Assembly and United Nations Security Council, Brahimi report.

26. High-Level Independent Panel on United Nations Peace Operations, HIPPO report, xi.

27. High-Level Independent Panel on United Nations Peace Operations, HIPPO report, 40.

28. Ana Paula Sequeira (former UN PKO Timorese staff member), interview with the author, Dili, July 20, 2016; Kendall, interview with the author; Asenio Bano (Timorese politician), interview with the author, Oecusse, July 25, 2016; interview with chief of mission of unnamed intergovernmental organization, Dili, June 27, 2016.

29. CAVR, *Chega! Report of the Commission for Reception, Truth and Reconciliation in Timor-Leste* (Dili: CAVR, 2005), http://www.cavr-timorleste.org/en/chegaReport.htm.

30. Sequeira, interview with the author.

31. Interview with Timorese UN official, Dili, July 19, 2016.

32. Interview with former UN Timorese staff member and current senior government official, Dili, July 28, 2016.

33. Interview with Timorese staff member working with UN and NGOs, Oecusse, July 26, 2016.

34. The Asia Foundation, *Understanding Violence against Women and Children in Timor-Leste: Findings from the Nabilan Baseline Study—Main Report* (Dili: The Asia Foundation, 2016), https://asiafoundation.org/wp-content/uploads/2016/05/Understanding VAWTL_main.pdf.

35. Elisabeth Rehn and Ellen Johnson Sirleaf, *Women, War and Peace: The Independent Experts' Assessment on the Impact of Armed Conflict on Women and Women's Role in Peace-Building* (New York: United Nations Development Fund for Women, 2002), 61–62.

36. Shukuko Koyama and Henri Myrttinen, "Unintended Consequences of Peace Operations in Timor Leste from a Gender Perspective," in *Unintended Consequences of Peacekeeping Operations*, ed. Aoi Chiyuki, Cedric de Coning, and Ramesh Thakur (New York: United Nations University Press, 2007), 33; Kathleen Jennings and Vesna Nikolić-Ristanović, "UN Peacekeeping Economies and Local Sex Industries: Connections and Implications," MICROCON Research Working Paper No. 17, 2009, http://papers.ssrn.com/sol3/papers.cfm?abstract_id=1488842.

37. Djuderija, interview with the author; interview with independent expert on trafficking in Bosnia; interview with Bosnian NGO official and antitrafficking expert; Sevima Sali Terzic (former director, Global Rights—Partners for Justice, current senior advisor to the Constitutional Court), interview with the author, Sarajevo, September 6, 2016; interview with Bosnian legal advisor to intergovernmental organization, Sarajevo, September 7, 2016.

38. Terzic, interview with the author.

39. Jennings and Nikolić-Ristanović, "UN Peacekeeping Economies and Local Sex Industries," 11.

40. Reis, interview with the author; interview with former UN Timorese staff member and current senior government official.

41. Kendall, interview with the author; Belo, interview with the author; correspondence with counter-trafficking expert based in Timor-Leste, July 2016.

42. Kendall, interview with the author.

43. Kai Schultz and Rajneesh Bhandari, "Noted Humanitarian Charged With Child Rape in Nepal, Stunning a Village," *New York Times*, May 11, 2018, https://www.nytimes.com/2018/05/11/world/asia/nepal-peter-dalglish-aid-pedophilia.html.

44. Interview with chief of mission of unnamed intergovernmental organization.

45. Sam R. Bell, Michael E. Flynn, and Carla Martinez Machain, "U.N. Peacekeeping Forces and the Demand for Sex Trafficking," *International Studies Quarterly* 62, no. 3 (2018): 643–55, https://doi.org/10.1093/isq/sqy017.

46. Kathleen M. Jennings, "Unintended Consequences of Intimacy: Political Economies of Peacekeeping and Sex Tourism," *International Peacekeeping* 17, no. 2 (2010): 229–43.

47. Leonor, interview with the author.

48. Kendall, interview with the author.

49. Human Rights Watch, "Hopes Betrayed," 26–34.

50. Kathryn Bolkovac and Cari Lynn, *The Whistleblower: Sex Trafficking, Military Contractors, and One Woman's Fight for Justice* (New York: Macmillan, 2011).

51. Interview with Bosnian NGO official and antitrafficking expert.

52. Belo, interview with the author.

53. Koyama and Myrttinen, "Unintended Consequences," 31.

54. Leonor, interview with the author; Cathleen Caron, *Trafficking in East Timor— A Look into the Sex Industry of the Newest Nation* (Dili: The Alola Foundation, 2004), 29–30, http://www.alolafoundation.org/images/programs/publications/ALOLA_TRAFFICKING_REPORT.pdf.

55. Bano, interview with the author.

56. Interview with senior TCC military official, July 18, 2016. I have not been able to verify the details of this so have not included the name of the state alleged to have done this.

57. Megan Nobert (founder and director, Report the Abuse), interview with the author, Geneva, September 19, 2016.

58. Kate Holt and Sarah Hughes, "Sex and Death in the Heart of Africa," *Independent*, May 25, 2004, http://www.independent.co.uk/news/world/africa/sex-and-death-in-the-heart-of-africa-564563.html.

59. Interview with UN police official, New York, October 31, 2016.

60. Terzic, interview with the author.

61. Interview with UNHCR expert in Accountability to Affected Populations and Prevention of Sexual Exploitation and Abuse, Geneva, September 23, 2016; Nobert, interview with the author.

62. Bolkovac and Lynn, *The Whistleblower*, 219–30; interview with Timorese staff member of Rede Feto, Dili, July 20, 2016.

63. High-Level Independent Panel on United Nations Peace Operations, HIPPO report, 23.

64. Leonor, interview with the author; interview with Timorese staff member working with UN and NGOs.

65. Interview with Timorese staff member working with UN and NGOs; Marilia Alves (executive director, FOKUPERS), interview with the author, Dili, July 20, 2016; Sequeira, interview with the author.

66. Sarah Martin, *Must Boys Be Boys? Ending Sexual Exploitation and Abuse in UN Peacekeeping Missions* (Washington DC: Refugees International, 2005), 5.

67. Interview with Bosnian NGO official and antitrafficking expert.

68. Interview with Bosnian NGO official and antitrafficking expert; interview with independent expert on trafficking in Bosnia.

69. Interview with Bosnian researchers and women's rights activists, Sarajevo, September 8, 2016.

70. Smith-Hrle, interview with the author.

71. Hasan Nuhanović (Bosnian translator for UN at Srebrenica), interview with the author, Sarajevo, September 8, 2016.

72. Henry and Higate, *Insecure Spaces*, 149.

73. Belo, interview with the author; interview with former UN Timorese staff member and current senior government official; interview with former ET-WAV staff member, Dili, July 28, 2016.

74. Séverine Autesserre, *Peaceland: Conflict Resolution and the Everyday Politics of International Intervention* (Cambridge: Cambridge University Press, 2014), 194–215.

75. Sarah B. K. von Billerbeck, "Local Ownership and UN Peacebuilding: Discourse Versus Operationalization," *Global Governance* 21, no. 2 (2015): 37–38; United Nations Department of Peacekeeping Operations/Department of Field Support, *A New Partnership Agenda, Charting a New Horizon for UN Peacekeeping* (New York: United Nations, 2009), https://www.un.org/ruleoflaw/files/newhorizon.pdf.

76. Richard Caplan, *A New Trusteeship? The International Administration of War-Torn Territories* (London: Routledge, 2014).

77. Andrew Goldsmith and Vandra Harris, "Trust, Trustworthiness and Trust-Building in International Policing Missions," *Australian & New Zealand Journal of Criminology* 45, no. 2 (2012): 238.

78. Autesserre, *Peaceland*.

79. Interview with chief of mission of unnamed intergovernmental organization.

80. Henry and Higate, *Insecure Spaces*, 148.

81. Nuhanović, interview with the author.

82. Kate Grady, "Sexual Exploitation and Abuse by UN Peacekeepers: A Threat to Impartiality," *International Peacekeeping* 17, no. 2 (2010): 219–20.

83. Mark Dodd, "Diggers in Timor 'Sex' Clash," *Australian*, March 21, 2005, http://www.etan.org/et2005/march/20/21digers.htm.

84. Interview with senior TCC military official.

85. The importance of coordination and cooperation between contingents and units within a peace operation has been repeatedly emphasized in UN peacekeeping doctrine. See for example United Nations General Assembly and United Nations Security Council, Bramini report; High-Level Independent Panel on United Nations Peace Operations, HIPPO report; United Nations Department of Peacekeeping Operations, *Handbook on United Nations Multidimensional Peacekeeping Operations* (New York: United Nations, 2003).

86. Elisabeth Prugl and Hayley Thompson, "The Whistleblower: An Interview with Kathryn Bolkovac and Madeleine Rees," *International Feminist Journal of Politics* 15, no. 1 (2013): 107–8.

87. Interview with Bosnian legal advisor to intergovernmental organization.

88. Interview with UN police official.

89. Jeni Whalan, *How Peace Operations Work: Power, Legitimacy, and Effectiveness* (Oxford: Oxford University Press, 2013), 200.

90. Michael Mersiades, "Peacekeeping and Legitimacy: Lessons from Cambodia and Somalia," *International Peacekeeping* 12, no. 2 (2005): 206.

4. Legitimacy in Crisis

1. Natasha Tassell and Ross Flett, "Motivation in Humanitarian Health Workers: A Self-Determination Theory Perspective," *Development in Practice* 21, no. 7 (2011): 959–73.

2. Katarína Komenská, "The Moral Motivation of Humanitarian Actors," in *Humanitarian Action and Ethics*, ed. Ayesha Ahmad and James Smith (London: Zed Books, 2018), 65–66, 69.

3. IFRC, Code of Conduct for the International Red Cross and Red Crescent Movement and NGOs in Disaster Relief (International Federation of the Red Cross and Red Crescent Societies and the International Committee of the Red Cross Geneva, 1994).

4. Interview with international staff member who worked in UN human rights unit and international NGOs, Dili, July 19, 2016.

5. Interview with senior UN staff member with experience in multiple peace operations, New York, October 31, 2016.

6. Interview with UN police official, New York, October 31, 2016.

7. Interview with former senior focal point for sexual exploitation and abuse for large international NGO, Geneva, September 19, 2016.

8. Interview with former senior focal point for sexual exploitation and abuse for large international NGO; Teresa Verdial (former director, Alola Foundation), interview with the author, Dili, July 18, 2016; Abel Dos Santos (program coordinator, Fundasaun Mahein), interview with the author, Dili, July 22, 2016; interview with gender based violence coordinator at a UN agency, Geneva, September 23, 2016; interview with Bosnian gender advisor to

intergovernmental organization, Sarajevo, September 7, 2016; interview with Bosnian NGO official and anti-trafficking expert, Sarajevo, September 14, 2016.

9. Interview with former senior focal point for sexual exploitation and abuse for large international NGO.

10. Interview with gender advisor at an international NGO, Geneva, September 22, 2016; interview with former senior focal point for SEA for large international NGO.

11. Sarah von Billerbeck, *Whose Peace? Local Ownership and United Nations Peacekeeping* (Oxford: Oxford University Press, 2016), 120.

12. Billerbeck, *Whose Peace?*, 121.

13. United Nations, "Trust Fund in Support of Victims of Sexual Exploitation and Abuse," Preventing Sexual Exploitation and Abuse/United Nations, accessed May 30, 2018, https://www.un.org/preventing-sexual-exploitation-and-abuse/content/trust-fund. The nineteen member states that have donated to the trust fund (as of July 2018) are (in alphabetical order): Albania, Australia, Bangladesh, Bhutan, Canada, Cyprus, Finland, India, Italy, Japan, Luxembourg, Nigeria, Norway, Pakistan, Portugal, Slovakia, Sri Lanka, Switzerland, and Uganda.

14. Interview with UN Women official, New York, November 2, 2016; interview with senior official at NGO focusing on Women, Peace and Security issues, New York, November 3, 2016.

15. REDRESS, *Sexual Exploitation and Abuse in Peacekeeping Operations: Improving Victims' Access to Reparation, Support and Assistance* (London: REDRESS, 2017), 34–36, https://redress.org/wp-content/uploads/2017/08/REDRESS-peacekeeping-report-English.pdf.

16. Jeni Whalan, *How Peace Operations Work: Power, Legitimacy, and Effectiveness* (Oxford: Oxford University Press, 2013), 205; Jeni Whalan, "The Local Legitimacy of Peacekeepers," *Journal of Intervention and Statebuilding* 11, no. 3 (2017): 308, https://doi.org/10.1080/17502977.2017.1353756; Billerbeck, *Whose Peace?*, 121–24.

17. Billerbeck, *Whose Peace?*, 115.

18. For examples of these discursive strategies in practice, see the discussions in United Nations General Assembly and United Nations Security Council, Report of the Independent High-Level Panel on Peace Operations, A/70/95, S/2015/446 (June 17, 2015), http://www.un.org/en/ga/search/view_doc.asp?symbol=S/2015/446; United Nations Department of Peacekeeping Operations, "What We Do," accessed April 5, 2018, https://peacekeeping.un.org/en/what-we-do; United Nations Department of Peacekeeping Operations, "News from Our Missions," accessed July 13, 2018, https://peacekeeping.un.org/en/news-our-missions.

19. United Nations, Charter of the United Nations, October 24, 1945, http://www.refworld.org/docid/3ae6b3930.html.

20. See for example the articles and short films produced to celebrate seventy years of UN peacekeeping at United Nations Department of Peacekeeping Operations, "UN Peacekeeping: 70 Years of Service & Sacrifice," accessed July 13, 2018, https://peacekeeping.un.org/en/un-peacekeeping-70-years-of-service-sacrifice.

21. Whalan, "The Local Legitimacy of Peacekeepers," 308.

22. Sean O'Neill, "Top Oxfam Staff Paid Haiti Survivors for Sex," *Times*, February 9, 2018. Oxfam Great Britain is one of nineteen national member organizations (or "affiliates") of the Oxfam International confederation. Each member organization has responsibility for managing specific programs in partner countries, employs staff specifically to those ends, and has its own management, finance, and human resources processes. Thus, Oxfam GB is responsible for managing allegations against Oxfam GB staff, and these processes are independent of any other member organizations.

23. James Landale, "Oxfam Deputy Quits over Haiti Sex Claims," *BBC News*, February 12, 2018, https://www.bbc.com/news/uk-43027631; May Bulman, "Government Threatens to

Cut Aid Funding to Charities after Sex Abuse Scandal," *Independent*, February 10, 2018, http://www.independent.co.uk/news/uk/home-news/oxfam-sexual-exploitation-charity-aid-funding-government-penny-mordaunt-international-development-a8204896.html.

24. Caroline Thomson, "Press Release by Oxfam GB Chair of Trustees: Oxfam Commits to Improvements in Aftermath of Haiti Reports," Oxfam GB, February 11, 2018, https://www.oxfam.org.uk/media-centre/press-releases/2018/02/oxfam-commits-to-improvements-in-aftermath-of-haiti-reports.

25. Landale, "Oxfam Deputy Quits over Haiti Sex Claims."

26. Penny Mordaunt, "Statement from the International Development Secretary on Oxfam" (Department for International Development, UK Government, February 16, 2018), https://www.gov.uk/government/news/statement-from-the-international-development-sec retary-on-oxfam.

27. Laura Kuenssberg, "Oxfam Agrees to Withdraw Government Funding Bids," *BBC News*, February 16, 2018, https://www.bbc.com/news/uk-politics-43091489.

28. "Oxfam Haiti Scandal: Thousands Cancel Donations," *BBC News*, February 20, 2018, https://www.bbc.com/news/uk-43121833.

29. "Oxfam Sex Scandal: Haiti Suspends Charity's Operations," *BBC News*, February 22, 2018, https://www.bbc.com/news/uk-43163620.

30. Peter Beaumont, "'Lies and Exaggerations' Says Oxfam Official Accused of Hosting Sex Parties," *Guardian*, February 15, 2018, http://www.theguardian.com/global-develop ment/2018/feb/15/oxfam-official-accused-hosting-sex-parties-haiti-lies-exaggerations.

31. Vince Chadwick, "Exclusive: EU Ready to Tighten NGO Funding Rules after Sex Scandals," *Devex*, March 1, 2018, https://www.devex.com/news/sponsored/exclusive-eu-ready-to-tighten-ngo-funding-rules-after-sex-scandals-92205.

32. Bulman, "Government Threatens to Cut Aid Funding."

33. Michael Igoe, "USAID Chief Orders Review of All Current Oxfam Agreements," *Devex*, February 16, 2018, https://www.devex.com/news/sponsored/usaid-chief-orders-review-of-all-current-oxfam-agreements-92150.

34. Ean Higgins, "Bishop Stops Funds to Oxfam," *Australian*, February 27, 2018, https://www.theaustralian.com.au/national-affairs/foreign-affairs/julie-bishop-stops-funds-to-oxfam/news-story/71ec521a443f07b36a09d03a319fa42a.

35. Vince Chadwick, "Sweden Is the First Donor to Resume Oxfam Funding," *Devex*, March 14, 2018, https://www.devex.com/news/sponsored/sweden-is-the-first-donor-to-resume-oxfam-funding-92332; Shehab Khan, "Oxfam to Lay Off 100 People as Funding Falls Following Aid Worker Sex Scandal," *Independent*, May 18, 2018, https://www.independent.co.uk/news/uk/home-news/oxfam-charity-lay-off-100-people-haiti-sex-scandal-funding-cut-a8357476.html.

36. "Oxfam GB Banned from Haiti after Sex Scandal," *BBC News*, June 13, 2018, https://www.bbc.com/news/uk-44474211.

37. Hamish Mackay, "How Will the Haiti Scandal Affect Oxfam?," *BBC News*, February 12, 2018, https://www.bbc.com/news/uk-43030705; Alice Ross, "Fears Oxfam Scandal Could Hit All Major Charity Donations," *Financial Times*, February 18, 2018, https://www.ft.com/content/d93f95bc-14a5-11e8-9376-4a6390addb44.

38. For an example of this, see Andrew MacLeod, "When It Comes to Child Sex Abuse in Aid Work, the Oxfam Revelations Are Just the Tip of the Iceberg," *Independent*, February 10, 2018, http://www.independent.co.uk/voices/oxfam-aid-work-prostitutes-un-workers-child-sex-abuse-harassment-dfid-a8204526.html; For an assessment of the veracity of these claims and available evidence, see Amanda Taub, "Lies, Damned Lies, and One Very Misleading Statistic," *New York Times*, March 1, 2018, https://www.nytimes.com/2018/02/28/world/americas/un-sexual-assaults.html.

39. Oxfam International, "Our Purpose and Beliefs," Oxfam International, accessed May 24, 2019, https://oxf.am/2FOuLlO.

40. Sandra Laville, "UN Aid Worker Suspended for Leaking Report on Child Abuse by French Troops," *Guardian*, April 29, 2015, http://www.theguardian.com/world/2015/apr/29/un-aid-worker-suspended-leaking-report-child-abuse-french-troops-car.

41. Sandra Laville, "UN Whistleblower Who Exposed Sexual Abuse by Peacekeepers Is Exonerated," *Guardian*, January 18, 2016, http://www.theguardian.com/world/2016/jan/18/un-whistleblower-who-exposed-sexual-abuse-by-peacekeepers-is-exonerated.

42. Marie Deschamps, Hassan B. Jallow, and Yasmin Sooka, *Taking Action on Sexual Exploitation and Abuse by Peacekeepers: Report of an Independent Review on Sexual Exploitation and Abuse by International Peacekeeping Forces in the Central African Republic* (UN External Independent Panel, 2015), viii.

43. See AIDS-Free World, "Timeline of Events in the Central African Republic," accessed May 24, 2019, https://www.codebluecampaign.com/spotlight-car/#timeline, and Child Rights International Network, "Timeline of Events from the UN Sexual Abuse Revelations in Central African Republic," accessed July 27, 2019, https://archive.crin.org/en/home/campaigns/transparency/uncover.html, for timelines of these reactions.

44. Angelique Chrisafis and Sandra Laville, "Hollande: No Mercy over Claims French Soldiers Abused Children in CAR," *Guardian*, April 30, 2015, http://www.theguardian.com/world/2015/apr/30/hollande-no-mercy-over-allegations-of-child-abuse-in-car-by-french-soldiers.

45. Kim Willsher and Sandra Laville, "France Launches Criminal Inquiry into Alleged Sex Abuse by Peacekeepers," *Guardian*, May 8, 2015, http://www.theguardian.com/world/2015/may/07/france-criminal-inquiry-alleged-sex-abuse-french-soldiers-un-central-african-republic.

46. Secretary-General, Secretary-General's Remarks to Security Council Consultations on the Situation in the Central African Republic, August 13, 2015, http://www.un.org/sg/statements/index.asp?nid=8903.

47. Secretary-General, Statement Attributable to the Secretary-General on Allegations of Sexual Abuse in the Central African Republic, June 3, 2015, https://www.un.org/sg/en/content/sg/statement/2015-06-03/statement-attributable-secretary-general-allegations-sexual-abuse; Sandra Laville and Ben Quinn, "UN Chief Orders Review of Handling of Claims of Child Abuse by French Soldiers," *Guardian*, June 3, 2015, http://www.theguardian.com/world/2015/jun/03/united-nations-child-abuse-french-soldiers.

48. Laville and Quinn, "UN Chief Orders Review of Handling of Claims of Child Abuse by French Soldiers."

49. United Nations General Assembly and United Nations Security Council, Report of the Independent High-Level Panel on Peace Operations, 74.

50. Secretary-General, Secretary-General's Remarks to Security Council Consultations on the Situation in the Central African Republic.

51. United Nations Security Council, Security Council Resolution 2242, S/RES/2242 (2015) (October 13, 2015).

52. United Nations Security Council, Statement by the President of the Security Council, S/PRST/2015/22 (2015) (November 25, 2015), http://undocs.org/S/PRST/2015/22.

53. United Nations Security Council, Statement by the President of the Security Council, S/PRST/2015/26 (2015) (December 31, 2015), http://undocs.org/S/PRST/2015/26.

54. United Nations Security Council, Statement by the President of the Security Council, S/PRST/2005/21 (2015) (May 31, 2005), https://www.un.org/press/en/2005/sc8400.doc.htm.

55. United Nations Security Council, 7642nd Meeting of the UN Security Council (Transcript), S/PV.7642 (March 10, 2016). The following quotes are also drawn from this transcript.

56. Somini Sengupta, "U.S. Senators Threaten U.N. Over Sex Abuse by Peacekeepers," *New York Times*, December 21, 2017, https://www.nytimes.com/2016/04/14/world/africa/

us-senators-threaten-un-over-sex-abuse-by-peacekeepers.html; Louis Charbonneau, "U.N. Chief 'Inept' on Peacekeeper Sex Abuse: Key U.S. Senator," *Reuters*, April 14, 2016, https://www. reuters.com/article/us-un-peacekeepers-usa/u-n-chief-was-inept-on-peacekeeper-sex-abuse-key-u-s-senator-idUSKCN0XA2MK.

57. United States Senate Committee on Foreign Relations, "Corker Disgusted by Sexual Abuse by UN Peacekeepers, Demands Consequences for Countries That Fail to Punish Troops for Misconduct," April 13, 2016, https://www.foreign.senate.gov/press/chair/release/corker-disgusted-by-sexual-abuse-by-un-peacekeepers.

58. United States Senate Committee on Foreign Relations, "Corker Disgusted by Sexual Abuse by UN Peacekeepers."

59. Brett D Schaefer, Peacekeepers: Allegations of Abuse and Absence of Accountability at the United Nations, Testimony before the Subcommittee on Africa, Global Health, Global Human Rights, and International Organizations Committee on Foreign Affairs United States House of Representatives, April 13, 2016, 16, https://docs.house.gov/meetings/FA/FA16/20160413/104766/HHRG-114-FA16-Wstate-SchaeferB-20160413.pdf.

60. To Urge the President to Direct the United States Representative to the United Nations to Use the Voice and Vote of the United States to Hold the United Nations and Its Member States Accountable for Allegations of Sexual Abuse and Exploitation by United Nations Peacekeepers, H.Con.Res.62, 115th Congress (2017), https://www.congress.gov/bill/115th-congress/house-concurrent-resolution/62/text.

61. Jaïr van der Lijn and Stefanie Ros, "Peacekeeping Contributor Profile: The Netherlands," Providing for Peacekeeping, January 2014, http://www.providingforpeacekeeping.org/2014/04/08/contributor-profile-the-netherlands/; Niels van Willigen, "A Dutch Return to UN Peacekeeping?," *International Peacekeeping* 23, no. 5 (2016): 702–720.

62. Van der Lijn and Ros, "Peacekeeping Contributor Profile."

63. Van Willigen, "A Dutch Return to UN Peacekeeping?," 710.

64. Van Willigen, "A Dutch Return to UN Peacekeeping?," 714.

65. Evan Cinq-Mars, "Peacekeeping Contributor Profile: Canada," Providing for Peacekeeping, October 2017, http://www.providingforpeacekeeping.org/2014/04/03/contributor-profile-canada-2/; Bill Robinson and Peter Ibbott, *Canadian Military Spending: How Does the Current Level Compare to Historical Levels? To Allied Spending? To Potential Threats?* (Waterloo, Ontario: Project Ploughshares, 2003), http://ploughshares.ca/wp-content/uploads/2012/08/WP3.1.pdf.

66. Howard G. Coombs, "25 Years after Somalia: How It Changed Canadian Armed Forces Preparations for Operations," *Canadian Military Journal* 17, no. 4 (2017): 35–46; Ainius Lašas, "Legacies of Srebrenica: The Dutch Factor in EU-Serbian Relations," *Political Psychology* 34, no. 6 (2013): 899–915; Joyce van de Bildt, "Srebrenica: A Dutch National Trauma," *Journal of Peace, Conflict and Development*, no. 21 (2015): 115–45.

67. Details of pledges made annually are compiled at "United Nations Peacekeeping Pledges," Providing for Peacekeeping, http://www.providingforpeacekeeping.org/capabilities-summits/united-nations-peacekeeping-pledge-counter/.

68. Manuela Leong Pereira (executive director, ACBIT, former director, FOKUPERS), interview with the author, Dili, July 20, 2016; Marilia Alves (executive director, FOKUPERS), interview with the author, Dili, July 20, 2016; interview with Bosnian legal advisor to intergovernmental organization, Sarajevo, September 7, 2016.

69. Interview with senior staff from a major humanitarian organization, Geneva, September 20, 2016.

70. Amra Pandzo (Bosnian peacebuilder), interview with the author, Sarajevo, September 7, 2016; Hasan Nuhanović (Bosnian translator for UN at Srebrenica), interview with the

author, Sarajevo, September 8, 2016; Sevima Sali Terzic (former director, Global Rights—Partners for Justice, current senior advisor to the Constitutional Court), interview with the author, Sarajevo, September 6, 2016.

71. Interview with senior diplomat to the UN, New York, November 4, 2016.

72. Chris McGreal, "Stop Protecting Peacekeepers Who Rape, Ban Ki-Moon Tells UN Member States," *Guardian*, September 17, 2015, http://www.theguardian.com/world/2015/sep/17/stop-protecting-peacekeepers-who-rape-ban-ki-moon-tells-un-member-states.

73. "UN Peacekeepers Accused of Sexually Abusing Street Children in Central African Republic," *Guardian*, June 23, 2015, http://www.theguardian.com/world/2015/jun/23/un-peacekeepers-accused-sexually-abusing-street-children-central-african-republic; "UN Receives New Allegations of Rape by Minusca Peacekeepers in CAR," *Guardian*, August 19, 2015, http://www.theguardian.com/world/2015/aug/19/un-receives-new-allegations-of-by-minusca-peacekeepers-in-car; Secretary-General, Statement of the Secretary-General: Receiving Report on Mali Violence, Secretary-General Condemns "Excessive Use of Force" by Formed Police Unit, SG/SM/16640-AFR/3102-PKO/476 (April 2, 2015), https://www.un.org/press/en/2015/sgsm16640.doc.htm.

74. McGreal, "Stop Protecting Peacekeepers Who Rape."

75. United Nations Security Council, 7642nd Meeting of the UN Security Council.

76. Angelique Chrisafis, "French Minister Calls on Soldiers Who Sexually Abused Children to Come Clean," *Guardian*, May 3, 2015, http://www.theguardian.com/world/2015/may/03/french-minister-jean-yves-le-drian-peacekeepers-abuse-children-come-forward.

77. For a comprehensive treatment of the challenges to implementing Resolution 2272, see Jeni Whalan, *Dealing with Disgrace: Implementing Resolution 2272 on the Challenges of Sexual Exploitation and Abuse in UN Peacekeeping* (International Peace Institute, 2017).

78. AIDS-Free World, "Leaked Files Reveal Hidden Scope of UN Sex Abuse," September 13, 2017, http://www.codebluecampaign.com/press-releases/2017/9/13.

79. McGreal, "Stop Protecting Peacekeepers Who Rape."

80. Justine Brabant and Leila MiÑano, "The DNA of Sangaris," *Mediapart*, March 1, 2017, https://zeroimpunity.com/sangaris/?lang=en; Benoît Morenne, "No Charges in Sexual Abuse Case Involving French Peacekeepers," *New York Times*, December 22, 2017, https://www.nytimes.com/2017/01/06/world/africa/french-peacekeepers-un-sexual-abuse-case-central-african-republic.html; Tony Cross, "No Charges over CAR Sex Abuse Allegations against French Soldiers," *RFI*, April 1, 2017, http://en.rfi.fr/africa/20170104-no-charges-over-car-sex-abuse-allegations-against-french-soldiers; Owen Bowcott, "UN Accused of 'Gross Failure' over Alleged Sexual Abuse by French Troops," *Guardian*, December 17, 2015, http://www.theguardian.com/world/2015/dec/17/un-gross-failure-sexual-abuse-french-troops-central-african-republic; "Case against French Troops Accused of Child Rape Dismissed," *National*, January 16, 2016, https://www.thenational.ae/world/africa/case-against-french-troops-accused-of-child-rape-dismissed-1.695712; AIDS-Free World, "The UN's Dirty Secret: The Untold Story of Child Sexual Abuse in the Central African Republic and Anders Kompass," May 29, 2015, http://www.codebluecampaign.com/carstatement/.

81. Kathryn Bolkovac and Cari Lynn, *The Whistleblower: Sex Trafficking, Military Contractors, and One Woman's Fight for Justice* (New York: Macmillan, 2011).

82. Brabant and MiÑano, "The DNA of Sangaris."

83. UN Security Council, 7642nd Meeting of the UN Security Council.

84. Keith J. Allred, "Peacekeepers and Prostitutes: How Deployment Forces Fuel the Demand for Trafficked Women and New Hope for Stopping It," *Armed Forces & Society* 33, no. 1 (2006): 5–23.

85. Interview with UN Women official; interview with UN police official; interview with UNICEF sexual exploitation and abuse expert, New York, October 31, 2016.

86. Interview with senior diplomat to the UN; interview with Department of Peacekeeping Operations staff, New York, November 2, 2016.

87. Jose Ramos Horta (former president of Timor-Leste, senior official in UN peace operations, chair of the UN High-Level Independent Panel on Peace Operations), interview with the author, Dili, July 21, 2016.

Conclusion

1. Human Rights Watch, "The Fall of Srebrenica and the Failure of UN Peacekeeping in Bosnia and Herzegovina," *Human Rights Watch* 7, no. 13 (1995): 11.

2. Human Rights Watch, "The Fall of Srebenica," 11–12.

3. For photographs of this graffiti, see Dado Ruvic, "Drawings on the Wall," *Reuters: The Wider Image*, July 7, 2015, https://widerimage.reuters.com/story/drawings-on-the-wall; "Dutch Graffiti in Srebrenica," *Srebrenica Genocide Blog* (blog), June 27, 2008, http://srebrenica-genocide.blogspot.com/2008/06/dutch-graffiti-in-srebrenica-sickening.html.

4. Hasan Nuhanović (Bosnian translator for UN at Srebrenica), interview with the author, Sarajevo, September 8, 2016.

5. Hasan Nuhanović, *Under the UN Flag: The International Community and the Srebrenica Genocide* (Sarajevo: DES, 2007), 545.

6. Nuhanović, *Under the UN Flag*; Nuhanović, interview with the author.

7. Séverine Autesserre, *Peaceland: Conflict Resolution and the Everyday Politics of International Intervention* (Cambridge: Cambridge University Press, 2014), 9.

8. Autesserre, *Peaceland*, 9.

9. Jeni Whalan, *How Peace Operations Work: Power, Legitimacy, and Effectiveness* (Oxford: Oxford University Press, 2013).

10. Jasmine-Kim Westendorf and Louise Searle, "Sexual Exploitation and Abuse in Peace Operations: Trends, Policy Responses and Future Directions," *International Affairs* 93, no. 2 (2017): 381–82.

11. Nicola Dahrendorf, *Sexual Exploitation and Abuse: Lessons Learned Study, Addressing Sexual Exploitation and Abuse in MONUC* (New York: UNDPKO, 2006).

12. For a timeline of major sexual misconduct scandals and policy development that illustrates this reactive cycle, see Jasmine Westendorf, "Discussion Paper: Mapping the Impact of Sexual Exploitation and Abuse by Interveners in Peace Operations," pilot project findings, December 2016, 5, https://www.latrobe.edu.au/__data/assets/pdf_file/0003/769800/Mapping-the-impact-of-sexual-abuse-by-interveners-in-peace-operations.pdf.

13. Westendorf and Searle, "Sexual Exploitation and Abuse in Peace Operations."

14. Paul Kirby, "Ending Sexual Violence in Conflict: The Preventing Sexual Violence Initiative and Its Critics," *International Affairs* 91, no. 3 (2015): 464.

15. For the full set of leaked documents, see Code Blue, "UN Documents," http://www.codebluecampaign.com/un-docs. Marie Deschamps, Hassan B. Jallow, and Yasmin Sooka, *Taking Action on Sexual Exploitation and Abuse by Peacekeepers: Report of an Independent Review on Sexual Exploitation and Abuse by International Peacekeeping Forces in the Central African Republic* (UN External Independent Panel, 2015), viii.

16. Angelique Chrisafis and Sandra Laville, "Hollande: No Mercy over Claims French Soldiers Abused Children in CAR," *Guardian*, April 30, 2015, http://www.theguardian.com/world/2015/apr/30/hollande-no-mercy-over-allegations-of-child-abuse-in-car-by-french-soldiers; Benoît Morenne, "No Charges in Sexual Abuse Case Involving French Peacekeepers," *New York Times*, December 22, 2017, https://www.nytimes.com/2017/01/06/world/africa/french-peacekeepers-un-sexual-abuse-case-central-african-republic.html?nytmobile=0.

17. United Nations News Service, "New Allegations of Sexual Abuse Emerge against UN Peacekeepers in Central African Republic," *UN News Service Section*, February 4, 2016, https://www.un.org/apps/news/story.asp?NewsID=53163.

18. Interview with UN Women official, New York, November 2, 2016.

19. Secretary-General, Note to Correspondents: The Secretary-General's Report on Special Measures for Protection from Sexual Exploitation and Abuse: A New Approach | United Nations Secretary-General, March 9, 2017, https://www.un.org/sg/en/content/sg/note-corre spondents/2017-03-09/note-correspondents-secretary-general%E2%80%99s-report-special.

20. These leaked documents are also available at Code Blue, "Open Letter: Leaked Documents Reveal Scandalous Inaction by UN to Prevent Sexual Abuse," June 6, 2017, http://www.codebluecampaign.com/press-releases/2017/6/6.

21. Interview with senior TCC military official, Dili, July 18, 2016.

22. UN Security Council Resolution 2272, S/RES/2272 (2016) (March 11, 2016), 13.

23. Radhika Coomaraswamy et al., *Preventing Conflict, Transforming Justice, Securing the Peace: A Global Study on the Implementation of United Nations Security Council Resolution 1325* (New York: UNWomen, 2015).

24. Sabrina Karim and Kyle Beardsley, *Equal Opportunity Peacekeeping: Women, Peace, and Security in Post-Conflict States* (Oxford: Oxford University Press, 2017).

25. Dianne Otto, "Making Sense of Zero Tolerance Policies in Peacekeeping Sexual Economies," in *Sexuality and the Law*, ed. by Vanessa Munro and Carl Stychin (Abingdon: Routledge, 2007), 260–61.

26. Paul Higate, "Peacekeepers, Masculinities, and Sexual Exploitation," *Men and Masculinities* 10, no. 1 (2007): 100–107.

27. Save the Children UK, *From Camp to Community: Liberia Study on Exploitation of Children* (London: Save the Children UK, 2006), 13.

28. Secretary-General, Secretary-General's Bulletin: Special Measures for Protection from Sexual Exploitation and Sexual Abuse, ST/SGB/2003/13 (October 9, 2003), http://oios.un.org/resources/2015/01/ST-SGB-2003-13.pdf, para. 3(d).

29. For a more detailed discussion of this, see Jasmine-Kim Westendorf, "Sexual Exploitation and Abuse in Peace Operations: Viewing from the Perspective of WPS," in *Oxford Handbook on Women, Peace and Security*, ed. Jacqui True and Sara Davies (Oxford: Oxford University Press, 2018).

30. This was borne out in many of the interviews conducted during this project in East Timor, Bosnia-Herzegovina, Geneva, and New York.

31. These comments were made exclusively about relationships between male personnel and local women, even though it is possible that relationships between female personnel and local men are equally relevant, particularly given the increasing numbers of women deployed as a result of WPS commitments to improve women's representation. Interview with senior TCC military official.

32. Elisabeth Jean Wood, "Armed Groups and Sexual Violence: When Is Wartime Rape Rare?," *Politics & Society* 37, no. 1 (2009): 140.

33. Amelia Hoover Green, *The Commander's Dilemma: Violence and Restraint in Wartime* (Ithaca, NY: Cornell University Press, 2018).

34. Deschamps, Jallow, and Sooka, *Taking Action*, x.

35. Details of this work and its progress are available at United Nations, Preventing Sexual Exploitation and Abuse, https://www.un.org/preventing-sexual-exploitation-and-abuse/.

BIBLIOGRAPHY

List of Interviews

This list includes the names and organizations of interviewees whom I have been permitted to acknowledge and gives a general description of the organization or position of interviewees who did not want to be directly identified. In most cases I include interviewees' current roles or positions, as directed by them, although in the text I also refer to past positions or roles when relevant to the information shared at that point. Some interviews have not been included in this list at the request of the interviewees, and some interviews have not been directly referenced in the text, also at the request of interviewees.

Abel Dos Santos (program coordinator, Fundasaun Mahein), Dili, July 22, 2016

Adisa Fišić Barukčija (TRIAL International), Sarajevo, September 6, 2016

Amra Pandžo (Bosnian peacebuilder), Sarajevo, September 7, 2016

Ana Paula Sequeira (former UN peacekeeping operations Timorese staff member), Dili, July 20, 2016

Angkis Leonora (coordinator, Scarlet Timor Collective), Dili, July 22, 2016

Asenio Bano (Timorese politician), Oecusse, July 25, 2016

Australian government staff member, Dili, July 22, 2016

Bosnian gender adviser to intergovernmental organization, Sarajevo, September 7, 2016

Bosnian legal adviser to intergovernmental organization, Sarajevo, September 7, 2016

Bosnian NGO official and antitrafficking expert, Sarajevo, September 14, 2016

Bosnian researchers and women's rights activists, Sarajevo, September 8, 2016

Bosnian staff member at international NGO providing legal aid to victims of wartime sexual violence, Sarajevo, September 6, 2016

Chief of mission of intergovernmental organization, Dili, June 27, 2016

Diplomat in a mission to the UN, New York, November 1, 2016

Diplomatic staff member in a mission to the UN, New York, November 2, 2016

Dulcie Leimbach (editor, PassBlue), New York, November 5, 2016

Expatriate NGO official, Sarajevo, September 8, 2016

F. Reis (Timorese civil society leader), Dili, July 21, 2016

Former staff member at ET-WAV (East Timorese Women Against Violence), Dili, July 28, 2016

Former senior focal point for sexual exploitation and abuse for large international NGO, Geneva, September 19, 2016

Senior government official; former UN Timorese staff member, Dili, July 28, 2016

Gender and SEA experts at international humanitarian organization, Geneva, September 20, 2016

Gender adviser at an international NGO, Geneva, September 22, 2016

Gender-based violence coordinator at a UN agency, Geneva, September 23, 2016

Geneva Call staff member, Geneva, September 22, 2016

Geneviève Cycot (accountability manager, CHS Alliance [Core Humanitarian Standard on Quality and Accountability]), Geneva, September 19, 2016

Hasan Nuhanović (Bosnian translator for UN at Srebrenica), Sarajevo, September 8, 2016

Horacio de Almeida (former UN national staff member), Dili, July 28, 2016

Independent expert on trafficking in Bosnia, Sarajevo, September 14, 2016

International staff member who worked in UN human rights unit and international NGOs, Dili, July 19, 2016

Jasminka Džumhur (human rights ombudsperson of Bosnia and Herzegovina), Sarajevo, September 15, 2016

Kaila Mintz (coordinator of Code Blue Campaign at AIDS-Free World), phone interview, October 27, 2016

Kerry Brogan (former director of the Nabilan Program at the Asia Foundation; former staff member in UN Human Rights Monitoring and Reporting Unit 2007–10), Dili, July 19, 2016

Knut Ostby (UN resident coordinator in Timor-Leste), Dili, July 19, 2016

Madre Guillermina (Timorese religious and civil society leader), Dili, July 23, 2016

Manuela Leong Pereira (executive director, ACbit [Asosiasaun Chega! Ba Ita]; former executive director, FOKUPERS [Communication forum for Timorese women]), Dili, July 20, 2016

Marilia da Silva Alves (executive director, FOKUPERS [Communication forum for Timorese women]), Dili, July 20, 2016

Meagan Smith-Hrle (Human-rights and rule-of-law expert who worked with Organization for Security and Cooperation in Europe, UN High Commissioner for Refugees [UNHCR], and Human Rights Chamber), Sarajevo, September 12, 2016

Megan Nobert (founder and director, Report the Abuse), Geneva, September 19, 2016

Nela Porobić Isaković (Women's International League for Peace and Freedom), Sarajevo, September 15, 2016

Nelson Belo (executive director, Fundasaun Mahein), Dili, July 22, 2016

New Zealand Defence Force peacekeeping representative, Dili, July 27, 2016

Office of Military Affairs officer, UN Department of Peacekeeping Operations, November 1, 2016

Paula Donovan (CEO, AIDS-Free World), phone interview, November 10, 2016

Saliha Djuderija (assistant minister, Ministry of Human Rights and Refugees of Bosnia and Herzegovina), Sarajevo, September 14, 2016

Security Council Report staff member, New York, November 4, 2016

Senior diplomat to the UN, New York, November 4, 2016

Senior official at NGO focusing on women, peace, and security issues, New York, November 3, 2016

Senior official in international missions in Bosnia-Herzegovina, location and date withheld, 2016

Senior official, UN Office of Internal Oversight Services, New York, November 4, 2016

Senior staff from a major humanitarian organization, Geneva, September 20, 2016

Senior staff member, UN Conduct and Discipline Unit, New York, November 4, 2016

Senior staff member, UN Office of the Special Coordinator on Sexual Exploitation and Abuse, New York, October 31, 2016

Senior-troop contributing country military official, Dili, July 18, 2016

Senior UN staff member with experience in multiple peace operations, New York, October 31, 2016

Sevima Sali Terzic (senior adviser to the Constitutional Court; former director, Global Rights: Partners for Justice), Sarajevo, September 6, 2016

Susan Kendall (PRADET [Psychosocial Recovery and Development in East Timor]), Dili, July 21, 2016

Teresa Verdial (former director, Alola Foundation), Dili, July 18, 2016

Timorese NGO representative, Dili, July 27, 2016

Timorese staff member, REDE FETO, Dili, July 20, 2016

Timorese staff member working with UN and NGOs, Oecusse, July 26, 2016

Timorese UN official, Dili, July 19, 2016

Timorese victims' advocate, Dili, July 23, 2016

UN Department of Field Support staff member, New York, November 2, 2016

UN Department of Peacekeeping Operations staff member, New York, November 2, 2016

UN police official, New York, October 31, 2016

UN Women representative, Sarajevo, September 14, 2016

UN Women official, New York, November 2, 2016

UNHCR expert in accountability to affected populations and prevention of sexual exploitation and abuse, Geneva, September 23, 2016
UNICEF expert on sexual exploitation and abuse, New York, October 31, 2016

Published Sources

AIDS-Free World. "Another 41 Allegations of Peacekeeper Sex Abuse Undisclosed by
the UN." April 13, 2016. http://www.codebluecampaign.com/press-releases/2016/
4/13.
——. "Leaked Files Reveal Hidden Scope of UN Sex Abuse." September 13, 2017.
http://www.codebluecampaign.com/press-releases/2017/9/13.
——. "Shocking New Reports of Peacekeeper Sexual Abuse in the Central African Repub-
lic." March 30, 2016. http://www.codebluecampaign.com/press-releases/2016/3/30.
——. "Timeline of Events in the Central African Republic." Accessed May 24, 2019,
https://www.codebluecampaign.com/spotlight-car/#timeline.
——. "The UN's Dirty Secret: The Untold Story of Child Sexual Abuse in the Central
African Republic and Anders Kompass." May 29, 2015. http://www.codebluecam
paign.com/carstatement/.
Allred, Keith J. "Peacekeepers and Prostitutes: How Deployment Forces Fuel the
Demand for Trafficked Women and New Hope for Stopping It." *Armed Forces &
Society* 33, no. 1 (2006): 5–23.
Amnesty International. "It's in Our Hands—Stop Violence against Women." Decem-
ber 31, 2004. https://www.amnesty.ie/hands-stop-violence-women/.
——. "'So Does It Mean That We Have the Rights?' Protecting the Rights of Women
and Girls Trafficked for Forced Prostitution in Kosovo." May 5, 2004. https://www.
amnesty.org/en/documents/eur70/010/2004/en/.
Andreas, Peter. *Blue Helmets and Black Markets: The Business of Survival in the Siege
of Sarajevo.* Ithaca, NY: Cornell University Press, 2011.
The Asia Foundation. *Understanding Violence against Women and Children in Timor-
Leste: Findings from the Nabilan Baseline Study—Main Report.* Dili: The Asia
Foundation, 2016. https://asiafoundation.org/wp-content/uploads/2016/05/Under
standingVAWTL_main.pdf.
Autesserre, Séverine. *Peaceland: Conflict Resolution and the Everyday Politics of Inter-
national Intervention.* Cambridge: Cambridge University Press, 2014.
——. *The Trouble with the Congo.* Cambridge: Cambridge University Press, 2010.
Awori, Thelma, Catherine Lutz, and Paban Thapa. *Final Report: Expert Mission to
Evaluate Risks to SEA Prevention Efforts in MINUSTAH, UNMIL, MONUSCO,
and UNMISS.* November 3, 2013. Unreleased United Nations report. Accessed May 6,
2019. https://static1.squarespace.com/static/514a0127e4b04d7440e8045d/t/55afcfa
1e4b07b89d11d35ae/1437585313823/2013+Expert+Team+Report+FINAL.pdf.
Barker, Anne. "UN Takes Step to Prevent Sex Abuse in East Timor. ABC Radio PM."
ABC Radio, August 30, 2006. http://www.abc.net.au/pm/content/2006/s1728448.htm.

Bastick, Megan, Karin Grimm, and Rahel Kunz. *Sexual Violence in Armed Conflict: Global Overview and Implications for the Security Sector*. Geneva: Geneva Centre for the Democratic Control of Armed Forces, 2007. https://www1.essex.ac.uk/armedcon/story_id/sexualviolence_conflict_full%5B1%5D.pdf.

Beaumont, Peter. "'Lies and Exaggerations' Says Oxfam Official Accused of Hosting Sex Parties." *Guardian*, February 15, 2018. http://www.theguardian.com/global-developm ent/2018/feb/15/oxfam-official-accused-hosting-sex-parties-haiti-lies-exaggerations.

Beber, Bernd, Michael Gilligan, Jenny Guardado, and Sabrina Karim. "Peacekeeping, Compliance with International Norms, and Transactional Sex in Monrovia, Liberia." *International Organization* 71, no.1 (2017): 1–30.

Bell, Sam R., Michael E. Flynn, and Carla Martinez Machain. "U.N. Peacekeeping Forces and the Demand for Sex Trafficking." *International Studies Quarterly* 62, no. 3 (2018): 643–55. https://doi.org/10.1093/isq/sqy017.

Berdal, Mats. *Building Peace After War*. London: International Institute for Strategic Studies, 2009.

Billerbeck, Sarah B. K. von. "Local Ownership and UN Peacebuilding: Discourse Versus Operationalization." *Global Governance* 21, no. 2 (2015): 299–315.

——. *Whose Peace? Local Ownership and United Nations Peacekeeping*. Oxford: Oxford University Press, 2016.

Bolkovac, Kathryn, and Cari Lynn. *The Whistleblower: Sex Trafficking, Military Contractors, and One Woman's Fight for Justice*. New York: Macmillan, 2011.

Bourke, Juliet. *United Nations Safe Space Report: Survey on Sexual Harassment in Our Workplace*. Sydney: Deloitte, 2019. Commissioned by the United Nations.

Bowcott, Owen. "UN Accused of 'Gross Failure' over Alleged Sexual Abuse by French Troops." *Guardian*, December 17, 2015. http://www.theguardian.com/world/2015/ dec/17/un-gross-failure-sexual-abuse-french-troops-central-african-republic.

Brabant, Justine, and Leila MiÑano. "The DNA of Sangaris." *Mediapart*, March 1, 2017. https://zeroimpunity.com/sangaris/?lang=en.

Bulman, May. "Government Threatens to Cut Aid Funding to Charities after Sex Abuse Scandal." *Independent*, February 10, 2018. http://www.independent.co.uk/news/ uk/home-news/oxfam-sexual-exploitation-charity-aid-funding-government-penny-mordaunt-international-development-a8204896.html.

Burke, Róisín. "Attribution of Responsibility: Sexual Abuse and Exploitation, and Effective Control of Blue Helmets." *Journal of International Peacekeeping* 16, no. 1 (2012): 1–46.

Caplan, Richard. *A New Trusteeship? The International Administration of War-Torn Territories*. London: Routledge, 2014.

Caron, Cathleen. *Trafficking in East Timor—A Look into the Sex Industry of the Newest Nation*. Dili: The Alola Foundation, 2004. http://www.alolafoundation.org/ images/programs/publications/ALOLA_TRAFFICKING_REPORT.pdf.

Carreiras, Helena. "Gendered Culture in Peacekeeping Operations." *International Peacekeeping* 17, no. 4 (2010): 471–85.

Carson, Lisa. "Pre-Deployment 'Gender 'Training and the Lack Thereof for Australian Peacekeepers." *Australian Journal of International Affairs* 70, no. 3 (2016): 275–92.

"Case against French Troops Accused of Child Rape Dismissed." *National*, January 16, 2016. https://www.thenational.ae/world/africa/case-against-french-troops-accused-of-child-rape-dismissed-1.695712.

CAVR. *Chega! Report of the Commission for Reception, Truth and Reconciliation in Timor-Leste*. Dili: CAVR, 2005. http://www.cavr-timorleste.org/en/chegaReport.htm.

Chadwick, Vince. "Exclusive: EU Ready to Tighten NGO Funding Rules after Sex Scandals." *Devex*, March 1, 2018. https://www.devex.com/news/sponsored/exclusive-eu-ready-to-tighten-ngo-funding-rules-after-sex-scandals-92205.

——. "Sweden Is the First Donor to Resume Oxfam Funding." *Devex*, March 14, 2018. https://www.devex.com/news/sponsored/sweden-is-the-first-donor-to-resume-oxfam-funding-92332.

Charbonneau, Louis. "U.N. Chief 'Inept' on Peacekeeper Sex Abuse: Key U.S. Senator." *Reuters*, April 14, 2016. https://www.reuters.com/article/us-un-peacekeepers-usa/u-n-chief-was-inept-on-peacekeeper-sex-abuse-key-u-s-senator-idUSKCN0XA2MK.

Child Rights International Network. "Timeline of Events from the UN Sexual Abuse Revelations in Central African Republic." Accessed July 27, 2019. https://archive.crin.org/en/home/campaigns/transparency/uncover.html, for timelines of these reactions.

Chrisafis, Angelique. "French Minister Calls on Soldiers Who Sexually Abused Children to Come Clean." *Guardian*, May 3, 2015. http://www.theguardian.com/world/2015/may/03/french-minister-jean-yves-le-drian-peacekeepers-abuse-children-come-for ward.

Chrisafis, Angelique, and Sandra Laville. "Hollande: No Mercy over Claims French Soldiers Abused Children in CAR." *Guardian*, April 30, 2015. http://www.theguardian.com/world/2015/apr/30/hollande-no-mercy-over-allegations-of-child-abuse-in-car-by-french-soldiers.

Christian, Mervyn, Octave Safari, Paul Ramazani, Gilbert Burnham, and Nancy Glass. "Sexual and Gender Based Violence against Men in the Democratic Republic of Congo: Effects on Survivors, Their Families and the Community." *Medicine, Conflict and Survival* 27, no. 4 (2011): 227–46. https://doi.org/10.1080/13623699.201 1.645144.

Chynoweth, Sarah. *"We Keep It in Our Heart": Sexual Violence against Men and Boys in the Syria Crisis*. Geneva: UNHCR, 2017. https://data2.unhcr.org/en/documents/download/60864.

Cinq-Mars, Evan. "Peacekeeping Contributor Profile: Canada." Providing for Peacekeeping, October 2017. http://www.providingforpeacekeeping.org/2014/04/03/contributor-profile-canada-2/.

Cohen, Dara Kay. *Rape during Civil War*. Ithaca, NY: Cornell University Press, 2016.

Connell, Robert W., and James W. Messerschmidt. "Hegemonic Masculinity: Rethinking the Concept." *Gender & Society* 19, no. 6 (2005): 829–59.

Connors, Jane. "UNMISS ASG VRA Media Briefing (Transcript)." UNMISS, December 8, 2017. https://unmiss.unmissions.org/unmiss-asg-vra-media-briefing-near-verbatim-transcript.

Coomaraswamy, Radhika, et al. *Preventing Conflict, Transforming Justice, Securing the Peace: A Global Study on the Implementation of United Nations Security Council Resolution 1325*. New York: UNWomen, 2015.

Coombs, Howard G. "25 Years after Somalia: How It Changed Canadian Armed Forces Preparations for Operations." *Canadian Military Journal* 17, no. 4 (2017): 35–46.

Cross, Tony. "No Charges over CAR Sex Abuse Allegations against French Soldiers." *RFI*, April 1, 2017. http://en.rfi.fr/africa/20170104-no-charges-over-car-sex-abuse-all egations-against-french-soldiers.

Csaky, Corinna. *No One to Turn to—The Under-Reporting of Child Sexual Exploitation and Abuse by Aid Workers and Peacekeepers*. London: Save the Children UK, 2008.

Dahrendorf, Nicola. *Sexual Exploitation and Abuse: Lessons Learned Study, Addressing Sexual Exploitation and Abuse in MONUC*. New York: UNDPKO, 2006.

Deschamps, Marie, Hassan B. Jallow, and Yasmin Sooka. *Taking Action on Sexual Exploitation and Abuse by Peacekeepers: Report of an Independent Review on Sexual Exploitation and Abuse by International Peacekeeping Forces in the Central African Republic*. UN External Independent Panel, 2015. https://www.un.org/News/dh/ infocus/centafricrepub/Independent-Review-Report.pdf.

Dodd, Mark. "Diggers in Timor 'Sex' Clash." *Australian*, March 21, 2005. http://www. etan.org/et2005/march/20/21digers.htm.

——. "Hushed Rape of Timor." *Weekend Australian*, March 26, 2005.

Dodds, Craig. "SA Soldiers' Shame in the DRC." *IOL News*, June 13, 2013. http:// www.iol.co.za/dailynews/news/sa-soldiers-shame-in-the-drc-1531660.

Domingas Fernandes Alves, Maria, Isabel M. M. Sequeira, Laura S. Abrantesm, and Filomena Reis. *Baseline Study on Sexual and Genderbased Violence in Bobonaro and Covalima*. Dili: Asia Pacific Support Collective Timor-Leste, 2009.

"Dutch Graffiti in Srebrenica." *Srebrenica Genocide Blog* (blog), June 27, 2008. http:// srebrenica-genocide.blogspot.com/2008/06/dutch-graffiti-in-srebrenica-sickening. html.

Enloe, Cynthia. *Maneuvers: The International Politics of Militarizing Women's Lives*. Berkeley: University of California Press, 2000.

——. "Wielding Masculinity inside Abu Ghraib: Making Feminist Sense of an American Military Scandal." *Asian Journal of Women's Studies* 10, no. 3 (2004): 89–102.

Farrall, Jeremy. "The Future of UN Peacekeeping and the Rule of Law." In *Proceedings of the Annual Meeting (American Society of International Law)* 101 (2007): 160–63.

"Fear over Haiti Child Abuse." *BBC News*, November 30, 2006. http://news.bbc.co.uk/ 2/hi/6159923.stm.

"Forced to Have Oral Sex with a Colleague: Aid Workers Speak out on Assault | Secret Aid Worker." *Guardian*, November 13, 2017. http://www.theguardian.com/work ing-in-development/2017/nov/13/forced-to-have-oral-sex-with-a-colleague-aid-workers-speak-out-on-assault-harassment.

Goldsmith, Andrew, and Vandra Harris. "Trust, Trustworthiness and Trust-Building in International Policing Missions." *Australian & New Zealand Journal of Criminology* 45, no. 2 (2012): 231–54.

Grady, Kate. "Sex, Statistics, Peacekeepers and Power: UN Data on Sexual Exploitation and Abuse and the Quest for Legal Reform." *Modern Law Review* 79, no. 6 (2016): 931–60.

———. "Sexual Exploitation and Abuse by UN Peacekeepers: A Threat to Impartiality." *International Peacekeeping* 17, no. 2 (2010): 215–28.

Haynes, Dina Francesca. "Lessons from Bosnia's Arizona Market: Harm to Women in a Neoliberalized Postconflict Reconstruction Process." *University of Pennsylvania Law Review* 158, no. 6 (2010): 1779–1829.

Henry, Marsha. "Sexual Exploitation and Abuse in UN Peacekeeping Missions: Problematising Current Responses." In *Gender, Agency, and Coercion*, edited by Sumi Madhok, Anne Phillips, and Kalpana Wilson, 122–42. Houndmills: Palgrave Macmillan, 2013.

Henry, Marsha, and Paul Higate. *Insecure Spaces: Peacekeeping, Power and Performance in Haiti, Kosovo and Liberia*. London: Zed Books, 2009.

Henry, Nicola. "Theorizing Wartime Rape." *Gender and Society* 30, no. 1 (2016): 44–56.

Higate, Paul. "Peacekeepers, Masculinities, and Sexual Exploitation." *Men and Masculinities* 10, no. 1 (2007): 99–119.

Higate, Paul, and Marsha Henry. "Engendering (in) Security in Peace Support Operations." *Security Dialogue* 35, no. 4 (2004): 481–98.

Higgins, Ean. "Bishop Stops Funds to Oxfam." *Australian*, February 27, 2018. https://www.theaustralian.com.au/national-affairs/foreign-affairs/julie-bishop-stops-funds-to-oxfam/news-story/71ec521a443f07b36a09d03a319fa42a.

High-Level Independent Panel on United Nations Peace Operations. *Uniting Our Strengths for Peace: Politics, Partnership and People* (HIPPO report). New York: United Nations, 2015. https://peaceoperationsreview.org/wp-content/uploads/2015/08/HIPPO_Report_1_June_2015.pdf.

Holt, Kate, and Sarah Hughes. "Sex and Death in the Heart of Africa." *Independent*, May 25, 2004. http://www.independent.co.uk/news/world/africa/sex-and-death-in-the-heart-of-africa-564563.html.

———. "UN Staff Accused of Raping Children in Sudan." *Telegraph*, January 2, 2007. http://www.telegraph.co.uk/news/worldnews/1538476/UN-staff-accused-of-raping-children-in-Sudan.html.

Hoover Green, Amelia. *The Commander's Dilemma: Violence and Restraint in Wartime*. Ithaca, NY: Cornell University Press, 2018.

Human Rights Watch. "Central African Republic: Murder by Peacekeepers." June 7, 2016. https://www.hrw.org/news/2016/06/07/central-african-republic-murder-peacekeepers.

———. "Central African Republic: Rape by Peacekeepers." February 4, 2016. https://www.hrw.org/news/2016/02/04/central-african-republic-rape-peacekeepers.

———. "The Fall of Srebrenica and the Failure of UN Peacekeeping in Bosnia and Herzegovina." *Human Rights Watch* 7, no. 13 (1995): 1–80.

———. "Hopes Betrayed: Trafficking of Women and Girls to Post Conflict Bosnia and Herzegovina for Forced Prostitution." *Human Rights Watch* 14, no. 9 (D) (November 2002). http://www.hrw.org/legacy/reports/2002/bosnia/.

———. "We'll Kill You If You Cry: Sexual Violence in the Sierra Leone Conflict." January 16, 2003. http://www.hrw.org/en/reports/2003/01/15/well-kill-you-if-you-cry.

Humanitarian Women's Network. "Survey Data," 2016. www.humanitarianwomensnetwork.org.

IFRC. Code of Conduct for the International Red Cross and Red Crescent Movement and NGOs in Disaster Relief. International Federation of the Red Cross and Red Crescent Societies and the International Committee of the Red Cross Geneva, 1994.

Igoe, Michael. "USAID Chief Orders Review of All Current Oxfam Agreements." *Devex*, February 16, 2018. https://www.devex.com/news/sponsored/usaid-chief-orders-review-of-all-current-oxfam-agreements-92150.

Inter-Agency Standing Committee. "Six Core Principles Relating to Sexual Exploitation and Abuse." IASC, June 13, 2002. http://www.pseataskforce.org/en/tools.

Jansson, Maria. "The Logic of Protection: Narratives of HIV/AIDS in the UN Security Council." *International Feminist Journal of Politics* 19, no. 1 (2017): 71–85.

Jennings, Kathleen M. *Protecting Whom? Approaches to Sexual Exploitation and Abuse in UN Peacekeeping Operations*. Oslo: Fafo, 2008. http://lastradainterna tional.org/lsidocs/fafo_approaches_abuse_0309.pdf.

——. "Service, Sex, and Security: Gendered Peacekeeping Economies in Liberia and the Democratic Republic of the Congo." *Security Dialogue* 45, no. 4 (2014): 313–30.

——. "Unintended Consequences of Intimacy: Political Economies of Peacekeeping and Sex Tourism." *International Peacekeeping* 17, no. 2 (2010): 229–43.

Jennings, Kathleen M., and Morten Bøås. "Transactions and Interactions: Everyday Life in the Peacekeeping Economy." *Journal of Intervention and Statebuilding* 9, no. 3 (2015): 281–95.

Jennings, Kathleen, and Vesna Nikolić-Ristanović. "UN Peacekeeping Economies and Local Sex Industries: Connections and Implications." MICROCON Research Working Paper No. 17, 2009. http://papers.ssrn.com/sol3/papers.cfm?abstract_id=1488842.

Karim, Sabrina, and Kyle Beardsley. *Equal Opportunity Peacekeeping: Women, Peace, and Security in Post-Conflict States*. Oxford: Oxford University Press, 2017.

——. "Explaining Sexual Exploitation and Abuse in Peacekeeping Missions: The Role of Female Peacekeepers and Gender Equality in Contributing Countries." *Journal of Peace Research* 53, no. 1 (2016): 100–115.

Kelly, Nicola. "Aid Workers and Sexual Violence: Survivors Speak Out." *Guardian*, February 17, 2017. http://www.theguardian.com/global-development-professionals-network/2017/feb/17/aid-workers-and-sexual-violence-survivors-speak-out.

Khan, Shehab. "Oxfam to Lay Off 100 People as Funding Falls Following Aid Worker Sex Scandal." *Independent*, May 18, 2018. https://www.independent.co.uk/news/uk/home-news/oxfam-charity-lay-off-100-people-haiti-sex-scandal-funding-cut-a8357476.html.

Kirby, Paul. "Ending Sexual Violence in Conflict: The Preventing Sexual Violence Initiative and Its Critics." *International Affairs* 91, no. 3 (2015): 457–72.

——. "How Is Rape a Weapon of War? Feminist International Relations, Modes of Critical Explanation and the Study of Wartime Sexual Violence." *European Journal of International Relations* 19, no. 4 (2012): 797–821. http://doi.org/10.1177/1354066 111427614.

——. "Refusing to Be a Man? Men's Responsibility for War Rape and the Problem of Social Structures in Feminist and Gender Theory." *Men and Masculinities* 16, no. 1 (2013): 93–114. http://doi.org/10.1177/1097184X12468100.

Komenská, Katarína. "The Moral Motivation of Humanitarian Actors." In *Humanitarian Action and Ethics*, edited by Ayesha Ahmad and James Smith, 62–78. London: Zed Books, 2018.

Koyama, Shukuko, and Henri Myrttinen. "Unintended Consequences of Peace Operations in Timor Leste from a Gender Perspective." In *Unintended Consequences of Peacekeeping Operations*, edited by Aoi Chiyuki, Cedric de Coning, and Ramesh Thakur, 23–43. New York: United Nations University Press, 2007.

Kreutz, Joakim, and Magda Cardenas. "Women, Peace and Intervention: How the International Community Responds to Sexual Violence in Civil Conflict." *Canadian Foreign Policy Journal* 23, no. 3 (2017): 260–76.

Kuenssberg, Laura. "Oxfam Agrees to Withdraw Government Funding Bids." *BBC News*, February 16, 2018. https://www.bbc.com/news/uk-politics-43091489.

Landale, James. "Oxfam Deputy Quits over Haiti Sex Claims." *BBC News*, February 12, 2018. https://www.bbc.com/news/uk-43027631.

Lašas, Ainius. "Legacies of Srebrenica: The Dutch Factor in EU-Serbian Relations." *Political Psychology* 34, no. 6 (2013): 899–915.

Laville, Sandra. "UN Aid Worker Suspended for Leaking Report on Child Abuse by French Troops." *Guardian*, April 29, 2015. http://www.theguardian.com/world/2015/apr/29/un-aid-worker-suspended-leaking-report-child-abuse-french-troops-car.

——. "UN Whistleblower Who Exposed Sexual Abuse by Peacekeepers Is Exonerated." *Guardian*, January 18, 2016. http://www.theguardian.com/world/2016/jan/18/un-whistleblower-who-exposed-sexual-abuse-by-peacekeepers-is-exonerated.

Laville, Sandra, and Ben Quinn. "UN Chief Orders Review of Handling of Claims of Child Abuse by French Soldiers." *Guardian*, June 3, 2015. http://www.theguardian.com/world/2015/jun/03/united-nations-child-abuse-french-soldiers.

Leach, Anna, and Sandra Laville. "Raped by a Colleague Then Fired: The Aid Worker Who Refused to Keep Quiet." *Guardian*, October 19, 2015. http://www.theguardian.com/world/2015/oct/19/raped-by-a-colleague-then-fired-the-aid-worker-who-refused-to-keep-quiet.

Ledgerwood, Judy L. "UN Peacekeeping Missions." Analysis from the East-West Center. Asia Pacific Issues. Honolulu: East-West Center, March 1994. http://www.seasite.niu.edu/khmer/ledgerwood/PDFAsiaPacific.htm.

Limanowska, Barbara. *Trafficking in Human Beings in Southeastern Europe*. Sarajevo: UNICEF, 2002. https://www.osce.org/odihr/18540.

Mackay, Hamish. "How Will the Haiti Scandal Affect Oxfam?" *BBC News*, February 12, 2018. https://www.bbc.com/news/uk-43030705.

MacLeod, Andrew. "When It Comes to Child Sex Abuse in Aid Work, the Oxfam Revelations Are Just the Tip of the Iceberg." *Independent*, February 10, 2018. http://www.independent.co.uk/voices/oxfam-aid-work-prostitutes-un-workers-child-sex-abuse-harassment-dfid-a8204526.html.

Martin, Sarah. *Must Boys Be Boys? Ending Sexual Exploitation and Abuse in UN Peacekeeping Missions*. Washington DC: Refugees International, 2005.

Mazurana, Dyan, and Phoebe Donnelly. *STOP the Sexual Assault Against Humanitarian and Development Aid Workers*. Somerville: Feinstein International Center, Tufts

University, 2017. http://fic.tufts.edu/publication-item/stop-the-sexual-assault-against-humanitarian-and-development-aid-workers/.

McFarlane, John, and William Maley. "Civilian Police in United Nations Peace Operations: Some Lessons from Recent Australian Experience." In *United Nations Peacekeeping Operations: Ad Hoc Missions, Permanent Engagement*, edited by Ramesh Thakur and Albrecht Schnabel, 182–212. Tokyo: United Nations University Press, 2001.

McGill, Jena. "Survival Sex in Peacekeeping Economies: Re-Reading the Zero Tolerance Approach to Sexual Exploitation and Sexual Abuse in United Nations Peace Support Operations." *Journal of International Peacekeeping* 18 (2014): 1–44.

McGreal, Chris. "Stop Protecting Peacekeepers Who Rape, Ban Ki-Moon Tells UN Member States." *Guardian*, September 17, 2015. http://www.theguardian.com/world/2015/sep/17/stop-protecting-peacekeepers-who-rape-ban-ki-moon-tells-un-member-states.

Meger, Sara. "Rape of the Congo: Understanding Sexual Violence in the Conflict in the Democratic Republic of Congo." *Journal of Contemporary African Studies* 28, no. 2 (2010): 119–35. https://doi.org/10.1080/02589001003736728.

Mendelson, Sarah E. *Barracks and Brothels*. Washington, DC: CSIS, 2005. http://csis.org/files/media/csis/pubs/0502_barracksbrothels.pdf.

Mersiades, Michael. "Peacekeeping and Legitimacy: Lessons from Cambodia and Somalia." *International Peacekeeping* 12, no. 2 (2005): 205–21.

Moncrief, Stephen. "Military Socialization, Disciplinary Culture, and Sexual Violence in UN Peacekeeping Operations." *Journal of Peace Research* 54, no. 5 (2017): 715–30.

Moon, Katharine Hyung-Sun. *Sex among Allies: Military Prostitution in U.S.-Korea Relations*. New York: Columbia University Press, 1997.

Mordaunt, Penny. "Statement from the International Development Secretary on Oxfam." Department for International Development, UK Government, February 16, 2018. https://www.gov.uk/government/news/statement-from-the-international-development-secretary-on-oxfam.

Morenne, Benoît. "No Charges in Sexual Abuse Case Involving French Peacekeepers." *New York Times*, December 22, 2017. https://www.nytimes.com/2017/01/06/world/africa/french-peacekeepers-un-sexual-abuse-case-central-african-republic.html.

Mudgway, Cassandra. "Sexual Exploitation by UN Peacekeepers: The 'Survival Sex' Gap in International Human Rights Law." *International Journal of Human Rights* 21, no. 9 (2017): 1453–1476.

Murdoch, Lindsay. "Criminal Syndicate in Timor." *Sydney Morning Herald*, February 28, 2008. http://www.smh.com.au/news/world/criminal-syndicate-in-timor/2008/02/27/1203788443860.html.

——. "UN Acts to Stamp Out Sex Abuse by Staff in East Timor." *Age*, August 30, 2006. http://www.theage.com.au/news/world/un-acts-to-stamp-out-sex-abuse-by-staff-in-east-timor/2006/08/29/1156816899264.html.

——. "UN Legacy of Shame in Timor." *Age*, July 22, 2006. http://www.theage.com.au/news/world/uns-legacy-of-shame-in-timor/2006/07/21/1153166587803.html.

——. "UN Turns Blind Eye to Use of Timor Brothels." *Age*, May 7, 2007. http://www.theage.com.au/news/world/un-turns-blind-eye-to-use-of-timor-brothels/2007/05/06/1178390140808.html.

——. "UN under Fire for Turning a Blind Eye to Peacekeepers' Misconduct." *Sydney Morning Herald*, May 7, 2007. http://www.smh.com.au/news/world/un-under-fire-for-turning-a-blind-eye-to-peacekeepers-misconduct/2007/05/06/1178390145310.html.

Myrttinen, Henri. "Disarming Masculinities." *Disarmament Forum* 4 (2003): 37–46.

Ndulo, Muna. "United Nations Responses to the Sexual Abuse and Exploitation of Women and Girls by Peacekeepers during Peacekeeping Missions." *Berkeley Journal of International Law* 27, no. 1 (2009): 127–61.

Neudorfer, Kelly. "Reducing Sexual Exploitation and Abuse: Does Deterrence Work to Prevent SEAs in UN Peacekeeping Missions?" *International Peacekeeping* 21, no. 5 (2014): 623–41.

——. *Sexual Exploitation and Abuse in UN Peacekeeping: An Analysis of Risk and Prevention Factors*. Lanham, MD: Lexington Books, 2014.

Nobert, Megan. "Aid Worker: I Was Drugged and Raped by Another Humanitarian in South Sudan." *Guardian*, July 29, 2015. http://www.theguardian.com/global-development-professionals-network/2015/jul/29/aid-worker-rape-humanitarian-south-sudan-sexual-violence.

——. *Humanitarian Experiences with Sexual Violence: Compilation of Two Years of Report the Abuse Data Collection*. Geneva: Report the Abuse, 2017. https://reliefweb.int/sites/reliefweb.int/files/resources/RTA%20Humanitarian%20experiences%20with%20Sexual%20Violence%20-%20Compilation%20of%20Two%20Years%20of%20Report%20the%20Abuse%20Data%20Collection.pdf.

——. *Prevention, Policy and Procedure Checklist: Responding to Sexual Violence in Humanitarian and Development Settings*. Geneva: Report the Abuse, 2016. https://www.eisf.eu/library/prevention-policy-and-procedure-checklist-responding-to-sexual-violence-in-humanitarian-and-development-settings/.

Nordås, Ragnhild, and Siri Rustad. "Sexual Exploitation and Abuse by Peacekeepers: Understanding Variation." *International Interactions* 39, no. 4 (2013): 511–34.

Nuhanović, Hasan. *Under the UN Flag: The International Community and the Srebrenica Genocide*. Sarajevo: DES, 2007.

Odello, Marco, and Róisín Burke. "Between Immunity and Impunity: Peacekeeping and Sexual Abuses and Violence." *International Journal of Human Rights* 20, no. 6 (2016): 839–53.

"One in Four Men Rape." *IRIN*, June 18, 2009. http://www.irinnews.org/report/84909/south-africa-one-four-men-rape.

O'Neill, Sean. "Top Oxfam Staff Paid Haiti Survivors for Sex." *Times*, February 9, 2018.

O'Neill, Sean, and Leila Haddou. "Oxfam Sex Scandal: Sacked Staff Found New Aid Jobs." *Times*, February 10, 2018. https://www.thetimes.co.uk/article/new-shame-for-oxfam-h5nq8lmfn.

Ospina, Sofi. *A Review and Evaluation of Gender-Related Activities of UN Peacekeeping Operations and Their Impact on Gender Relations in Timor-Leste*. New York: UN Department of Peacekeeping Operations, 2006.

Otto, Dianne. "Making Sense of Zero Tolerance Policies in Peacekeeping Sexual Economies." In *Sexuality and the Law*, edited by Vanessa Munro and Carl Stychin, 259–82. Abingdon: Routledge, 2007.

"Oxfam GB Banned from Haiti after Sex Scandal." *BBC News*, June 13, 2018. https://www.bbc.com/news/uk-44474211.

Oxfam Great Britain. *Haiti Investigation Final Report FRN5 (Confidential)*. London: Oxfam Great Britain, 2011.

"Oxfam Haiti Scandal: Thousands Cancel Donations to Charity." *BBC News*, February 20, 2018. https://www.bbc.com/news/uk-43121833.

Oxfam International. "Our Purpose and Beliefs." Oxfam International. Accessed May 24, 2019 https://oxf.am/2FOuLlO.

"Oxfam Sex Scandal: Haiti Suspends Charity's Operations." *BBC News*, February 22, 2018. https://www.bbc.com/news/uk-43163620.

Paris, Roland. *At War's End: Building Peace After Civil Conflict*. Cambridge: Cambridge University Press, 2004.

——. "Peacekeeping and the Constraints of Global Culture." *European Journal of International Relations* 9, no. 3 (2003): 441–73.

Patel, Preeti, and Paolo Tripodi. "Peacekeepers, HIV and the Role of Masculinity in Military Behaviour." *International Peacekeeping* 14, no. 5 (2007): 584–98.

Prugl, Elisabeth, and Hayley Thompson. "The Whistleblower: An Interview with Kathryn Bolkovac and Madeleine Rees." *International Feminist Journal of Politics* 15, no. 1 (2013): 102–9.

Razack, Sherene. *Dark Threats and White Knights*. Toronto: University of Toronto Press, 2004.

——. "From the 'Clean Snows of Petawawa': The Violence of Canadian Peacekeepers in Somalia." *Cultural Anthropology* 15, no. 1 (2000): 127–63.

REDRESS. *Sexual Exploitation and Abuse in Peacekeeping Operations: Improving Victims' Access to Reparation, Support and Assistance*. London: REDRESS, 2017. https://redress.org/wp-content/uploads/2017/08/REDRESS-peacekeeping-report-English.pdf.

Rehn, Elisabeth, and Ellen Johnson Sirleaf. *Women, War and Peace: The Independent Experts' Assessment on the Impact of Armed Conflict on Women and Women's Role in Peace-Building*. New York: United Nations Development Fund for Women, 2002.

Robinson, Bill, and Peter Ibbott. *Canadian Military Spending: How Does the Current Level Compare to Historical Levels? To Allied Spending? To Potential Threats?* Waterloo, Ontario: Project Ploughshares, 2003. http://ploughshares.ca/wp-content/uploads/2012/08/WP3.1.pdf.

Ross, Alice. "Fears Oxfam Scandal Could Hit All Major Charity Donations." *Financial Times*, February 18, 2018. https://www.ft.com/content/d93f95bc-14a5-11e8-9376-4a6390addb44.

Ruden, Fanny, and Mats Utas. *Sexual Exploitation and Abuse by Peacekeeping Operations in Contemporary Africa*. Uppsala: The Nordic Africa Institute, Policy Notes, 2009.

Ruvic, Dado. "Drawings on the Wall." *Reuters: The Wider Image*, July 7, 2015. https://widerimage.reuters.com/story/drawings-on-the-wall.

Save the Children UK. *From Camp to Community: Liberia Study on Exploitation of Children*. London: Save the Children UK, 2006.

Schaefer, Brett D. Peacekeepers: Allegations of Abuse and Absence of Accountability at the United Nations. Testimony before the Subcommittee on Africa, Global Health, Global Human Rights, and International Organizations Committee on Foreign Affairs United States House of Representatives, April 13, 2016. https://docs.house.gov/meetings/FA/FA16/20160413/104766/HHRG-114-FA16-Wstate-SchaeferB-20160413.pdf.

Schultz, Kai, and Rajneesh Bhandari. "Noted Humanitarian Charged With Child Rape in Nepal, Stunning a Village." *New York Times*, May 11, 2018. https://www.nytimes.com/2018/05/11/world/asia/nepal-peter-dalglish-aid-pedophilia.html.

Secretary General's High-Level Panel on Threats, Challenges and Change. *A More Secure World: Our Shared Responsibility.* New York: United Nations, 2004.

Secretary-General. Investigation into Sexual Exploitation of Refugees by Aid Workers in West Africa. A/57/465 (October 11, 2002).

——. Note to Correspondents: The Secretary-General's Report on Special Measures for Protection from Sexual Exploitation and Abuse: A New Approach | United Nations Secretary-General. March 9, 2017. https://www.un.org/sg/en/content/sg/note-correspondents/2017-03-09/note-correspondents-secretary-general%E2%80%99s-report-special.

——. Remarks of the Secretary-General at the Informal Meeting of the General Assembly. presented at the General Assembly Meeting, New York, January 16, 2018. https://www.un.org/sg/en/content/sg/speeches/2018-01-16/remarks-informal-meeting-general-assembly.

——. Report of the Secretary-General on Conflict-Related Sexual Violence. S/2015/203 (March 23, 2015). http://www.securitycouncilreport.org/atf/cf/%7B65BFCF9B-6D27-4E9C-8CD3-CF6E4FF96FF9%7D/s_2015_203.pdf.

——. Report of the Secretary-General on Special Measures for Protection from Sexual Exploitation and Sexual Abuse. A/69/779 (February 13, 2015). http://reliefweb.int/report/world/special-measures-protection-sexual-exploitation-and-sexual-abuse-report-secretary.

——. Secretary-General's Bulletin: Observance by United Nations Forces of International Humanitarian Law. ST/SGB/1999/13 (August 6, 1999).

——. Secretary-General's Bulletin: Special Measures for Protection from Sexual Exploitation and Sexual Abuse. ST/SGB/2003/13 (October 9, 2003). http://oios.un.org/resources/2015/01/ST-SGB-2003-13.pdf.

——. Secretary-General's Remarks to Security Council Consultations on the Situation in the Central African Republic. August 13, 2015. https://www.un.org/sg/statements/index.asp?nid=8903.

——. Special Measures for Protection from Sexual Exploitation and Sexual Abuse. A/61/957 (June 15, 2007). https://undocs.org/A/61/957.

——. Special Measures for Protection from Sexual Exploitation and Sexual Abuse. A/70/729 (February 16, 2016). https://undocs.org/A/70/729.

——. Special Measures for Protection from Sexual Exploitation and Abuse. A/72/751 (February 15, 2018). https://conduct.unmissions.org/sites/default/files/a_72_751_0.pdf.

——. Special Measures for Protection from Sexual Exploitation and Abuse: A New Approach. A/71/818 (February 28, 2017). https://undocs.org/A/71/818.

———. Statement Attributable to the Secretary-General on Allegations of Sexual Abuse in the Central African Republic. June 3, 2015. https://www.un.org/sg/en/content/sg/statement/2015-06-03/statement-attributable-secretary-general-allegations-sexual-abuse.

———. Statement of the Secretary-General: Receiving Report on Mali Violence, Secretary-General Condemns "Excessive Use of Force" by Formed Police Unit. SG/SM/16640-AFR/3102-PKO/476 (April 2, 2015). https://www.un.org/press/en/2015/sgsm16640.doc.htm.

Selk, Avi, and Eli Rosenberg. "Oxfam Prostitution Scandal Widens to at Least Three Countries." *Washington Post*, February 13, 2018. https://www.washingtonpost.com/news/worldviews/wp/2018/02/13/oxfam-prostitution-scandal-widens-to-at-least-three-countries/.

Sengupta, Somini. "U.S. Senators Threaten U.N. Over Sex Abuse by Peacekeepers." *New York Times*, December 21, 2017. https://www.nytimes.com/2016/04/14/world/africa/us-senators-threaten-un-over-sex-abuse-by-peacekeepers.html.

"Sexual Misconduct Being Investigated: UNMIT's Gyorgy KAKUK." *East Timor Law and Justice Bulletin*. October 12, 2010. http://www.easttimorlawandjusticebulletin.com/2010/10/sexual-misconduct-being-investigated.html.

Sieff, Kevin. "The Growing U.N. Scandal over Sex Abuse and 'Peacekeeper Babies.'" *Washington Post*, February 27, 2016. http://www.washingtonpost.com/sf/world/2016/02/27/peacekeepers/.

Simić, Olivera. "Does the Presence of Women Really Matter? Towards Combating Male Sexual Violence in Peacekeeping Operations." *International Peacekeeping* 17, no. 2 (2010): 188–99.

———. *Regulation of Sexual Conduct in UN Peacekeeping Operations*. New York: Springer, 2012.

Simm, Gabrielle. *Sex in Peace Operations*. Cambridge: Cambridge University Press, 2015.

Sisk, Timothy D. "Peacebuilding as Democratization: Findings and Recommendations." In *From War to Democracy: Dilemmas of Peacebuilding*, edited by Anna K. Jarstad and Timothy D. Sisk, 239–59. Cambridge: Cambridge University Press, 2008.

Smith, Sarah. "Accountability and Sexual Exploitation and Abuse in Peace Operations." *Australian Journal of International Affairs* 71, no. 4 (2017): 405–22.

Spencer, Sarah W. "Making Peace: Preventing and Responding to Sexual Exploitation by United Nations Peacekeepers." *Journal of Public and International Affairs* 16 (Spring 2005): 167–81.

Storr, Will. "The Rape of Men: The Darkest Secret of War." *Guardian*, July 16, 2011. http://www.theguardian.com/society/2011/jul/17/the-rape-of-men.

Tassell, Natasha, and Ross Flett. "Motivation in Humanitarian Health Workers: A Self-Determination Theory Perspective." *Development in Practice* 21, no. 7 (2011): 959–73.

Taub, Amanda. "Lies, Damned Lies, and One Very Misleading Statistic." *New York Times*, March 1, 2018. https://www.nytimes.com/2018/02/28/world/americas/un-sexual-assaults.html.

Thomson, Caroline. "Press Release by Oxfam GB Chair of Trustees: Oxfam Commits to Improvements in Aftermath of Haiti Reports." Oxfam GB, February 11, 2018.

https://www.oxfam.org.uk/media-centre/press-releases/2018/02/oxfam-commits-to-improvements-in-aftermath-of-haiti-reports.

To Urge the President to Direct the United States Representative to the United Nations to Use the Voice and Vote of the United States to Hold the United Nations and Its Member States Accountable for Allegations of Sexual Abuse and Exploitation by United Nations Peacekeepers. H.Con.Res.62, 115th Congress (2017). https://www.congress.gov/bill/115th-congress/house-concurrent-resolution/62/text.

True, Jacqui. *The Political Economy of Violence against Women*. Oxford: Oxford University Press, 2012.

The UN and the Sex Slave Trade in Bosnia: Isolated Case or Larger Problem in the UN System? Hearing before the Subcommittee on International Operations and Human Rights of the Committee on International Relations, House of Representatives. 107th Cong. 85 (2002) (statement of David Lamb, former UN Human Rights Investigator in Bosnia). http://commdocs.house.gov/committees/intlrel/hfa78948.000/hfa78948_0.HTM#65.

"UN Peacekeepers Accused of Sexually Abusing Street Children in Central African Republic." *Guardian*, June 23, 2015. http://www.theguardian.com/world/2015/jun/23/un-peacekeepers-accused-sexually-abusing-street-children-central-african-republic.

"UN Receives New Allegations of Rape by Minusca Peacekeepers in CAR." *Guardian*, August 19, 2015. http://www.theguardian.com/world/2015/aug/19/un-receives-new-allegations-of-by-minusca-peacekeepers-in-car.

UNAIDS. "AIDS and the Military." UNAIDS Best Practices Collection. Geneva: UNAIDS, 1998.

UNHCR, and Save the Children UK. Sexual Violence & Exploitation: The Experience of Refugee Children in Guinea, Liberia and Sierra Leone. February 2002. https://www.savethechildren.org.uk/content/dam/global/reports/health-and-nutrition/sexual_violence_and_exploitation_1.pdf.

United Nations. Charter of the United Nations, October 24, 1945. http://www.refworld.org/docid/3ae6b3930.html.

——. A Comprehensive Strategy to Eliminate Future Sexual Exploitation and Abuse in United Nations Peacekeeping Operations. A/59/710 (March 24, 2005).

——. "Sexual Exploitation and Abuse—Data." Conduct in UN Field Missions, January 23, 2017. https://conduct.unmissions.org/sea-data-introduction.

——. "Trust Fund in Support of Victims of Sexual Exploitation and Abuse." Preventing Sexual Exploitation and Abuse/United Nations. Accessed May 30, 2018. https://www.un.org/preventing-sexual-exploitation-and-abuse/content/trust-fund.

United Nations Conduct in UN Field Missions. "Sexual Exploitation and Abuse: Table of Allegations." Conduct in UN Field Missions, April 5, 2017. https://conduct.unmissions.org/table-of-allegations.

——. "Sexual Exploitation and Abuse Data," June 23, 2016, https://conduct.unmissions.org/table-of-allegations.

United Nations Department of Peacekeeping Operations. *Handbook on United Nations Multidimensional Peacekeeping Operations*. New York: United Nations, 2003.

——. "News from Our Missions." Accessed July 13, 2018. https://peacekeeping.un.org/en/news-our-missions.

—— "Ten Rules: Code of Personal Conduct for Blue Helmets," 1998. http://pseatask force.org/uploads/tools/tenrulescodeofpersonalconductforbluehelmets_undpko_eng lish.pdf.

——. "UN Peacekeeping: 70 Years of Service & Sacrifice." Accessed July 13, 2018. https://peacekeeping.un.org/en/un-peacekeeping-70-years-of-service-sacrifice.

——. "What We Do." Accessed April 5, 2018. https://peacekeeping.un.org/en/what-we-do.

United Nations Department of Peacekeeping Operations/Department of Field Support. *A New Partnership Agenda, Charting a New Horizon for UN Peacekeeping.* New York: United Nations, 2009. https://www.un.org/ruleoflaw/files/newhorizon.pdf.

United Nations Department of Public Information. "UNTAET," May 2002. https://peacekeeping.un.org/mission/past/etimor/UntaetB.htm.

United Nations General Assembly. Resolution Adopted by the General Assembly: Investigation into Sexual Exploitation of Refugees by Aid Workers in West Africa. A/RES/ 57/306 (May 22, 2003). http://www.un.org/en/ga/search/view_doc.asp?symbol=A/RES/ 57/306.

United Nations General Assembly and United Nations Security Council. Report of the Independent High-Level Panel on Peace Operations, A/70/95, S/2015/446 (June 17, 2015). http://www.un.org/en/ga/search/view_doc.asp?symbol=S/2015/446.

——. Report of the Panel on United Nations Peace Operations (Brahimi Report). A/55/305, S/2000/809 (August 21, 2000). https://undocs.org/A/55/305.

United Nations News Service. "New Allegations of Sexual Abuse Emerge against UN Peacekeepers in Central African Republic." *UN News Service Section*, February 4, 2016. https://www.un.org/apps/news/story.asp?NewsID=53163.

——. "UN Civilian Worker in DR of Congo Accused of Child Molestation." *UN News Service*, November 1, 2004.

United Nations Security Council. 7642nd Meeting of the UN Security Council (Transcript). S/PV.7642 (March 10, 2016).

——. Statement by the President of the Security Council. S/PRST/2005/21 (2005) (May 31, 2005). https://www.un.org/press/en/2005/sc8400.doc.htm.

——. Statement by the President of the Security Council. S/PRST/2015/22 (2015) (November 25, 2015). http://undocs.org/S/PRST/2015/22.

——. Statement by the President of the Security Council. S/PRST/2015/26 (2015) (December 31, 2015). http://undocs.org/S/PRST/2015/26.

——. UN Security Council Resolution 1031. S/RES/1031 (1995) (December 15, 1995).

——. UN Security Council Resolution 1035. S/RES/1035 (1995) (December 21, 1995).

——. UN Security Council Resolution 1088. S/RES/1088 (1996) (December 12, 1996).

——. UN Security Council Resolution 1264. S/RES/1264 (1999) (September 15, 1999), http://unscr.com/en/resolutions/1264.

——. UN Security Council Resolution 1272. S/RES/1272 (1999) (October 22, 1999).

——. UN Security Council Resolution 1542. S/RES/1542 (2004) (April 30, 2004).

——. UN Security Council Resolution 1704. S/RES/1704 (2006) (August 24, 2006).

——. UN Security Council Resolution 2242. S/RES/2242 (2015) (October 13, 2015).

——. UN Security Council Resolution 2272. S/RES/2272 (2016) (March 11, 2016).

United States Senate Committee on Foreign Relations. "Corker Disgusted by Sexual Abuse by UN Peacekeepers, Demands Consequences for Countries That Fail to

Punish Troops for Misconduct." April 13, 2016. https://www.foreign.senate.gov/press/chair/release/corker-disgusted-by-sexual-abuse-by-un-peacekeepers.

"UNPROFOR." Department of Public Information, United Nations. Last updated August 31, 1996. http://peacekeeping.un.org/mission/past/unprof_p.htm.

Van de Bildt, Joyce. "Srebrenica: A Dutch National Trauma." *Journal of Peace, Conflict and Development*, no. 21 (2015): 115–45.

Van der Lijn, Jaïr, and Stefanie Ros. "Peacekeeping Contributor Profile: The Netherlands." Providing for Peacekeeping, January 2014. http://www.providingforpeacekeeping.org/2014/04/08/contributor-profile-the-netherlands/.

Van Willigen, Niels. "A Dutch Return to UN Peacekeeping?" *International Peacekeeping* 23, no. 5 (2016): 702–20.

Wax, Emily. "Congo's Desperate 'One-Dollar U.N. Girls.'" *Washington Post*, March 21, 2005. https://www.washingtonpost.com/wp-dyn/articles/A52333-2005Mar20.html.

Westendorf, Jasmine-Kim. "Discussion Paper: Mapping the Impact of Sexual Exploitation and Abuse by Interveners in Peace Operations," pilot project findings, December 2016, 5, https://www.latrobe.edu.au/__data/assets/pdf_file/0003/769800/Mapping-the-impact-of-sexual-abuse-by-interveners-in-peace-operations.pdf.

——. *Why Peace Processes Fail: Negotiating Insecurity After Civil War*. Boulder: Lynne Rienner, 2015.

Westendorf, Jasmine-Kim, and Louise Searle. "Sexual Exploitation and Abuse in Peace Operations: Trends, Policy Responses and Future Directions." *International Affairs* 93, no. 2 (2017): 365–87.

Whalan, Jeni. *Dealing with Disgrace: Implementing Resolution 2272 on the Challenges of Sexual Exploitation and Abuse in UN Peacekeeping*. International Peace Institute, 2017.

——. *How Peace Operations Work: Power, Legitimacy, and Effectiveness*. Oxford: Oxford University Press, 2013.

——. "The Local Legitimacy of Peacekeepers." *Journal of Intervention and Statebuilding* 11, no. 3 (2017): 306–20. https://doi.org/10.1080/17502977.2017.1353756.

Whitworth, Sandra. "Gender, Race and the Politics of Peacekeeping." In *A Future for Peacekeeping?*, edited by Edward Moxon-Browne, 176–91. Houndmills: Macmillan, 1998.

——. *Men, Militarism, and UN Peacekeeping: A Gendered Analysis*. Boulder: Lynne Rienner Publishers, 2004.

Willsher, Kim, and Sandra Laville. "France Launches Criminal Inquiry into Alleged Sex Abuse by Peacekeepers." *Guardian*. May 8, 2015. http://www.theguardian.com/world/2015/may/07/france-criminal-inquiry-alleged-sex-abuse-french-soldiers-un-central-african-republic.

Wood, Elisabeth Jean. "Armed Groups and Sexual Violence: When Is Wartime Rape Rare?" *Politics & Society* 37, no. 1 (2009): 131–61.

——. "Conflict-Related Sexual Violence and the Policy Implications of Recent Research." *International Review of the Red Cross* 96, no. 894 (2014): 457–78.

INDEX